W9-DAQ-958

DA   Read, Donald.
690
.M4   Peterloo: the
R26   "massacre" and its
1973   background

DATE			

PETERLOO

The 'Massacre' and its Background

A VIEW OF ST PETER'S PLACE

Frontispiece

A CONTEMPORARY PICTURE SHOWING THE MANCHESTER YEOMANRY
RIDING FOR THE HUSTINGS

PETERLOO

The 'Massacre' and its Background

BY

DONALD READ

MANCHESTER UNIVERSITY PRESS
AUGUSTUS M. KELLEY PUBLISHERS

TO
MY PARENTS

© 1958 Manchester University Press
Published by the University of Manchester at
THE UNIVERSITY PRESS
316-324 Oxford Road, Manchester M13 9NR

First published, 1958
Reprinted with additional note, 1973

ISBN 0 7190 0526 4

U.S.A.

AUGUSTUS M. KELLEY PUBLISHERS
305 Allwood Road, Clifton, N.J. 07012

Library of Congress Cataloging in Publication Data

Read, Donald.
    Peterloo: the "massacre" and its background.

    Bibliography: p.
    1. Manchester, Eng.—Peterloo Massacre, 1819.
I. Title.
DA690.M4R26 1973   942.7′2   72-7212
ISBN 0-678-06791-0

Printed in Great Britain by Butler & Tanner Ltd
Frome and London

CONTENTS

ILLUSTRATIONS

*(Reproduced from F. A. Bruton's article in the Bulletin of the John Rylands
Library, 1919, by kind permission)*

PREFACE

THE purpose of this study is to fill in the background to an event which, as a name, is one of the best known in nineteenth-century history. No textbooks dealing with English history during the post-Napoleonic period are without a paragraph describing the 'Peterloo Massacre' of August 16, 1819. Yet it is surprising how superficial our knowledge of the massacre really is. Virtually no study has been made of the background to Peterloo. All enquiry has been concentrated on the events of August 16th itself, on the crowds and the casualties and the rest. No writer has asked why it was that these crowds came together or how they were brought together. Yet here are two questions of the first importance for an understanding of the massacre. The question of why the crowds came together is fundamentally an economic question: the Lancashire operatives were spurred to attend the great meeting by the pressure of overwhelming economic distress. The question of how the crowds assembled is one of political organization: it centres round the working-class Radical Reformers and their extensive network of agitation. The first part of the present study attempts to deal with the economic background to Peterloo, and the second with its political background; part three describes the actual course of events up to and including the massacre, and part four discusses the aftermath of Peterloo.

'Peterloo' is a name so well-established in English history that it is perhaps easy to forget that it is in fact a soubriquet, angrily fabricated in bitter mockery of the feat of British arms at Waterloo four years before. It first appeared in print in the *Manchester Observer* newspaper on August 21, 1819. The successful designation of Peterloo as a 'massacre' represents another piece of successful propaganda. Perhaps only in peace-loving England could a death-roll of only eleven persons have been so described.

While this study was in the press Mr. R. J. White's readable volume *Waterloo to Peterloo* was published. Perhaps I may be allowed here to express a difference of opinion with him as to the significance of Peterloo in subsequent English working-class history. He writes that 'Peterloo marked the final conversion of provincial England to the doctrine of "first things first",' i.e. to the doctrine that political reform must precede social and economic improvement. I would not myself make such a decided claim for the influence of the massacre. The masses were not much more systematic in their agitations after Peterloo than in those before. In 1826 in Lancashire they reverted to simple rioting and Luddism in the face of economic distress; similarly in 1842 they deserted Chartist political action for the direct action of the Plug Riots. Certainly, Peterloo was never forgotten in the industrial districts as a symbol of working-class suffering and oppression; but I doubt if its 'lesson', as taught by Mr. White, was ever really learnt by the operative classes of the early nineteenth century.

It remains now only for me to acknowledge the generous help which I have received in the preparation of this book. I owe a great debt to the librarian and staff of the Manchester Reference Library, to Dr. W. H. Chaloner of Manchester University, to Professor G. P. Jones of Sheffield University, and to the Reverend J. T. Wilkinson, Principal of the Hartley Victoria Methodist College, Manchester. I must thank also the trustees of the Knoop Research Fund in the University of Sheffield for two generous grants towards my travelling expenses, my colleague Mr. G. C. F. Forster for help with the proofs, and my wife for assistance and patience at every stage. Finally, I am indebted for the help I have received from the late Mr. A. P. Wadsworth, editor of the *Manchester Guardian* 1944–56, and from Professor Asa Briggs of Leeds University: without their kindness and encouragement the book could never have appeared.

University of Leeds

May 1957

NOTE TO 1973 REPRINT

This book, first published in 1958, is now reprinted without alteration. Discussion of the character of the Peterloo massacre, and of responsibility for it, has continued vigorously and at length during the ensuing decade and a half, notably in E. P. Thompson's *Making of the English Working Class* (2nd ed., Penguin, 1968) and in R. Walmsley's *Peterloo: the Case Re-Opened* (Manchester University Press, 1969). I have given my reasons for disagreeing with Walmsley's 'right wing' defence of the magistrates in *History*, vol. 55 (1970), 138–40. For a penetrating dissection of Thompson's 'left-wing' view see J. D. Chambers' review article in *History*, vol. LI (1966), 183–8. My own middle position, blaming the magistrates but clearing the Home Secretary of direct responsibility, has been accepted in P. Ziegler's readable and authoritative life of the latter, *Addington* (Collins, 1965), 374–5. H. J. Perkin has argued in his *Origins of Modern English Society 1780–1880* (Routledge, 1969), ch. VI, that the years 1815–20 witnessed 'the birth of a new class society': in *Northern History*, V (1970) I have briefly suggested that this period witnessed not the *birth* of class consciousness in industrial Britain, but its coming of age. In my book *The English Provinces 1760–1960* (Arnold, 1964) I have set Peterloo within its context of emerging provincial opinion. And I have expanded upon the newspaper background and aftermath in *Press and People 1790–1850* (Arnold, 1961), and in my introduction to A. Prentice's *Historical Sketches and Personal Recollections of Manchester* (3rd ed. Cass, 1970).

University of Kent   DONALD READ
May 1972

ABBREVIATIONS USED IN THE FOOTNOTES

Add. Mss. . . Additional Manuscripts (British Museum).

Aspinall . . Aspinall, Arthur, *The Early English Trade Unions* (1949).

Bamford . . Bamford, Samuel, *Passages in the Life of a Radical* (1844).

H.O. . . . Home Office Papers (Public Record Office).

Kinsey . . Kinsey, W. W., 'Some Aspects of Lancashire Radicalism 1816–21' (M.A. Thesis, Manchester University, 1927).

Marshall . . Marshall, L. S., *The Development of Public Opinion in Manchester, 1790–1820* (1946).

Philips . . Philips, Francis, *An Exposure of the Calumnies Circulated by the Enemies of Social Order, and Reiterated by their Abettors against the Magistrates and the Yeomanry Cavalry of Manchester and Salford* (2nd ed., 1819).

Prentice . . Prentice, Archibald, *Historical Sketches and Personal Recollections of Manchester, intended to illustrate the Progress of Public Opinion from 1792 to 1832* (2nd ed., 1851).

Taylor . . [Taylor, J. E.], *Notes and Observations, Critical and Explanatory, on the Papers Relative to the Internal State of the Country recently presented to Parliament: to which is appended a Reply to Mr. Francis Philips's 'Exposure . . .'*, by A Member of the Manchester Committee for Relieving the Sufferers of the 16th of August 1819 (1820).

Part One

THE ECONOMIC AND SOCIAL BACKGROUND

CHAPTER ONE

MANCHESTER IN 1819[1]

'A PLACE more destitute of all interesting objects than Manchester it is not easy to conceive.' So wrote Robert Southey in 1807. The town merely consisted of a

> multitude crowded together in narrow streets, the houses all built of brick and blackened with smoke; frequent buildings among them as large as convents, without their antiquity, without their beauty, without their holiness; where you hear from within . . . the everlasting din of machinery; and where when the bell rings it is to call wretches to their work instead of their prayers.[2]

The poet was clearly not impressed. He sought a town with 'antiquity' and buildings of stone, a town with roots in the past: he found instead something of a new kind. Manchester in the early nineteenth century had few links with (and less time for) the past. The Industrial Revolution in cotton had transformed it within two generations from a country town into the second largest

---

[1] In an administrative sense 'Manchester' in 1819 meant different things for different purposes. There were several administrative units. There was the great Hundred of Salford, the unit for Quarter Sessions, which included 'Manchester' in all its various forms; there was the large parish of Manchester, the ecclesiastical unit; there was the township of Manchester, the old administrative unit under the Court Leet; there were the separate townships surrounding Manchester; and finally there was the area administered by the Manchester Police Commissioners. This study when it refers to 'Manchester' will, except where reference is specially made to one of the above units, be considering as a whole the great townships of Manchester and Salford and the inner townships of Cheetham, Hulme, Chorlton Row, and Ardwick, which by 1819 had become in effect suburbs of the township of Manchester.

[2] R. Southey, *Letters from England*, ed. J. Simmons (1951), 213.

urban unit in the country. In 1773 the population of the township
of Manchester was only some 24,000: by 1821 it was 108,000, and
by 1831, 142,000, nearly six times that of sixty years before.[1]

Progress in local government had not kept pace with this pro-
digious population increase, and it was shortcomings in local
government which were in large measure responsible for the loss
of life at Peterloo. In 1819 the medieval Manchester Court Leet
still survived. Every Michaelmas a jury of the Court Leet was still
summoned by the Lord of the Manor of Manchester to choose the
manorial officers. A Boroughreeve was selected who became the
first citizen of the township and two Constables who were
responsible for the maintenance of law and order. To assist them
these Constables had a permanent Deputy Constable and a handful of beadles. This was all that Manchester had for normal day
police during the disturbances of 1819. And the night police was
even less impressive—only fifty-five night-watchmen, mostly 'old
men past all other work'.[2] In an emergency these meagre forces
could be supplemented by calling out the special constables;
Manchester had some two hundred of these in 1819. And as a
last resort the peace might be maintained by compelling all
citizens to take their turns at Watch and Ward. This was enforced,
for example, during the Peterloo period. Not surprisingly, the
under-policed state of the town made outbreaks of violence
regular and expected occurrences:[3] to the country at large in the
early nineteenth century Manchester was a byword for civil
disturbance.[4]

Most active of all the local government bodies in Manchester
was the Police Commission, set up under an Act of 1792. The
Police Commissioners were responsible for scavenging and street
cleaning, for general street improvement and lighting, and for the

[1] A. P. Wadsworth and J. de L. Mann, *The Cotton Trade and Industrial
Lancashire 1600-1780* (1931), Appendix A; E. Baines, *The History of the County
Palatine and Duchy of Lancaster* (1836), II, 111.
   The population of Lancashire as a whole doubled between 1801 and 1831,
growing from 672,565 to 1,335,600.
[2] *Manchester Guardian*, Feb. 18, 1882.
[3] During the strikes of 1818 the spinners on one occasion stoned the
beadles. Norris, the Manchester stipendiary magistrate, was not at all put
out by this: 'the beadles of so large a town [were]', he wrote, 'necessarily
obnoxious to the lower orders' (Norris to Sidmouth, July 29, 1818. Aspinall,
no. 234).
[4] 'Manchester has . . . obtained at a distance, an unenviable notoriety on
account of its rioting propensities' [B. Love], *Manchester as It Is* (1839), 26).

supervision of the night-watch and fire-engine establishments.[1] The administration of justice in the town rested with the county magistrates resident in the division. Some eighteen magistrates acted, including a stipendiary magistrate who had the chief responsibility for the day to day administration of justice. The administration of local poor relief and the payment of the Constables' accounts was in the hands of the churchwardens and overseers of the poor.

Local administration was thus diverse and involved, and in consequence far from efficient. A passably coherent state of affairs was only maintained because the several branches of government were in practice controlled by the same set of people; 'the magistrates, the principal officers of the Court Leet, the principal officers of the parish, and the leaders of the Police Commissioners, were all, or almost all, members of a close knit oligarchy'. Most of them were Tory in politics and Anglican in religion.[2]

Like its administration the intellectual life of Manchester was left in the hands of a very few. In things of the mind and spirit the town was very backward. It had grown too quickly and had concentrated too much on business to have acquired the social graces and cultural tone properly appropriate to its new importance in the world. It had its small coteries of intellectuals, meeting together in clubs and societies, and its Literary and Philosophical Society had an international reputation. But the vast majority of Manchester businessmen took no part in its learned discussions. A few of them subscribed to the local newsrooms and read there the six Manchester weekly newspapers being published in 1819:[3] but this was generally the limit of their literary interests. Business and the making of money was the all-absorbing occupation of the typical Manchester man of the period.

A thorough Manchester man, [admitted a contemporary] sees more

---

[1] The qualification in 1819 for membership of the Police Commission was ownership or occupation of any building of the yearly rental or value of £30 or more.

[2] A. Redford, *The History of Local Government in Manchester* (1939–40), I, 258 and *passim*, for details of the state of local government in Manchester in the early nineteenth century.

[3] The *Manchester Mercury*, the *Manchester Chronicle*, the *Exchange Herald*, the *British Volunteer*, the *Manchester Gazette*, and the *Manchester Observer*. The first four generally supported the local oligarchy and the Tory government, the *Gazette* reflected the opinions of the local middle-class reformers, and the *Observer* was the working-class Radical organ.

beauty in rows of red brick than he would in groves and 'alleys green'; he hears more music in the everlasting motion of the loom than he would in the songs of the lark or the nightingale. For him philosophy has no attraction, poetry no enchantment . . .

> 'The only news he asks, or wants to know,
> Has but one aim, to learn how markets go!'[1]

A grimy town, archaic local government, lack of culture—all were of no importance. Business was the sole occupation, profit the great goal. And as almost the entire business of Manchester in 1819 was its cotton trade, it is to the condition of that great industry that we must first turn in our survey of the economic and social background to Peterloo.

[1] [J. S. Gregson], *Gimcrackiana, or Fugitive Pieces on Manchester Men and Manners Ten Years Ago* (1833), 159-60.

CHAPTER TWO

THE COTTON TRADE IN THE MANCHESTER AREA IN 1819

THE COTTON MASTERS

THE buying, making up, and selling of cotton was far and away the principal occupation of the inhabitants of the Manchester area in 1819. The processes involved represented an extensive division of labour, made possible only by the invention and application of many new techniques in the previous fifty years and by the development of highly organized distributing channels. The manufacturing process was a long one. The raw cotton arrived at Liverpool, chiefly from America; the dealers there sold it to the Manchester merchants and dealers, who in turn sold it to the master spinners. Arriving at the mills, it was first cleansed and carded, then spun into yarn; next it was woven into cloth and bleached, and finally dyed, printed, or otherwise finished.[1] The two basic processes were the spinning into yarn and the weaving into cloth. By 1819 the former was already largely done in factories by machinery, but the weaving process was still chiefly the work of handloom weavers working at home.

In many respects the difference between the humble handloom weavers and their masters was not great. Most manufacturers had risen by their own efforts from similar circumstances. Indeed, such origins were almost an essential for success: 'the only men who have made their fortunes', declared John Kennedy, a leading Manchester master spinner, in 1828, 'have been those who started with nothing'. Few outsiders with large capital made much progress in the face of local men with local knowledge and great ruthlessness. Ruthlessness and complete concentration on business were the all-important qualifications: successful manufacturers, admitted Kennedy, were all 'entirely given up to business'.[2]

[1] E. Baines, *History of the Cotton Manufacture in Great Britain* (1835), *passim;* T. Ellison, *The Cotton Trade of Great Britain* (1886), 175–76; C. R. Fay, *Great Britain from Adam Smith to the Present Day* (5th ed., 1950), 291–92; S. J. Chapman, *The Lancashire Cotton Industry* (1904), 113.
[2] G. D'Eichtal, 'Condition de la Classe Ouvriére en Angleterre (1828)' (*Revue Historique*, LXXIX (1902), 94).

But though similar in character and in origins masters and men had different economic interests and were in different social classes. And in the cotton-dominated society of Manchester in 1819 masters and men faced each other almost alone: social cleavage was pronounced. It was not as in the agricultural counties where society was linked together through a series of gradations. The operative weaver saw no gradation: 'There was only himself toiling, and his employer apparently enjoying all the luxuries of life.'[1]

Such occupations as did apparently exist outside the cotton trade were often in fact completely dependent on it. Builders, machine-makers, carriers, bankers, lawyers, the many trades ancillary to calico printing, these and many more were all dependent almost entirely on the cotton trade for their prosperity.[2]

Within the master class some shades of status did exist. Large manufacturers like the Peels and the Kennedys naturally had a standing higher than that of their many lesser rivals. The Manchester cotton merchants, too, still regarded themselves as superior to the cotton manufacturers. Late eighteenth-century society in Manchester had been dominated by a handful of merchants with some pretensions to luxury and culture. When the *nouveaux riches* manufacturers began to spring up in great numbers in the generation before Peterloo,[3] the merchants had exhibited considerable hostility towards them and had attempted to exclude them from the Manchester clubs.[4] These attempts had failed, but their successors in 1819 were still a little superior to the majority of manufacturers. The manufacturers were 'without education or address, except what they have acquired by their intercourse with the little world of merchants in the exchange', remarked a correspondent to the *Manchester Observer* in 1818, the implication clearly being that the merchants were more educated and less

[1] *Parliamentary Debates*, XLI (1819–20), 895–96 (Bennet), 916–17 (Stuart Wortley); Bootle Wilbraham to Liverpool, Sept. 25, 1819 (Add. Mss. 38280 f. 20); L. Faucher, *Manchester in 1844* (1844), 21.

[2] Baines, *op. cit.*, 423–25.

[3] Even the largest manufacturing firms were comparatively new in 1819. M'Connel and Kennedy, for instance, did not begin until 1791 (G. W. Daniels, 'The Early Records of a Great Manchester Cotton-spinning Firm', *Economic Journal*, XXV (1915), 175).

[4] J. M. Main, 'The Parliamentary Reform Movement in Manchester 1825–1832' (B.Litt. Thesis, Oxford University, 1951), 15–17.

uncouth than many of the master spinners.[1] Compared with the number of manufacturers, however, the number of merchants was relatively small.[2]

This difference between merchants and manufacturers was also reflected in their political beliefs. Most of the cotton merchants were 'Tory', declared one Radical writer in 1818, whereas most of the cotton manufacturers were 'Whig', greater conservatism coming presumably with longer standing.[3] This political difference was particularly brought out by the reaction of the merchants and manufacturers to Peterloo. Immediately after the massacre a Declaration and Protest was circulated by the local middle-class Radicals, and in reply a petition sponsored by the local 'loyalists' appeared in October. Analysis of the signatures to these two documents is revealing. Seventy-one cotton manufacturers can be identified as signing the Declaration and Protest attacking the Tory government and local authorities, but only sixteen merchants and fourteen dealers. By contrast, forty-three merchants and twenty-five dealers signed the 'loyal' petition, and also sixty-five manufacturers.[4]

Too much must not be made of this political separation, however, or of the labels 'Whig' and 'Tory'. In normal circumstances

[1] *Manchester Observer*, Oct. 3, 1818.

[2] *The Number of Cotton Merchants and Manufacturers*
(Some firms are listed under more than one heading)

	1815 Directory	1819–20 Directory
Cotton merchants	131	150
Cotton dealers	—	79
Cotton spinners	110	143
Manufacturers of and dealers in cotton goods	299	326
Calico printers and print warehouses .	128	168
Manufacturers of fustians . . .	98	122
Dyers	64	70
Calenderers and makers-up . .	39	38
Bleachers	16	18
Manufacturers of silk and cotton .	30	41

(The figures for 1815 are taken from Harland's analysis of Pigot and Dean's Manchester and Salford Directory for 1815 (J. Harland, *Collectanea Relating to Manchester and its Neighbourhood at Various Periods*, Chetham Soc. (1866), LXVIII, pt. I, 165); those for 1819 are taken from Pigot and Dean's Directory for 1819–20).

[3] *Manchester Spectator*, Nov. 7, 1818.

[4] See below, p. 174 ff.

2

the Manchester cotton masters were not really much interested in
politics. Before the Radical agitations of the Peterloo period
disturbed the local scene their political leanings had been very ill-
defined, perhaps best described as a type of vague conservative
apathy:

[During the war they] had a long course of comparative or at least
average, prosperity; they were busily occupied with their own private
affairs; they read the details of the foreign news in the columns of the
public journals, but they did not interest themselves about the internal
policy of their own country, or if they meddled at all, saved themselves
the trouble of inquiry, by a general determination to 'support the
government', meaning thereby the ministry of the day.[1]

In other words, the Manchester cotton masters had given a vague
general support to the established institutions of the country so
long as they were left free to concentrate their energies on
business. This had meant in practice the acceptance of the Tory
government at Westminster and of the Tory ruling oligarchy in
Manchester.[2]

This reluctance to engage in politics and in political speculation
had been the outcome of prudence as well as of inclination. Many
masters feared that to encourage political feeling in the town
would encourage the lower orders to unrest and disturbance;
and this was something they feared above all else, 'the fearful
strength (as a contemporary put it) . . . of that multitude of the
labouring population, which lies like a slumbering giant at their
feet'.[3] This fear did much in the 1790's and during the first years
of the nineteenth century to check any desire among the cotton
masters for parliamentary representation for Manchester. Election
turmoil, they believed, would produce unforeseeable disturbance
to the great detriment of trade.[4]

[1] Taylor, 202.
[2] 'Many had sunk into a hopeless and selfish indifference. The management
of town's affairs was allowed to remain in the hands of the self-styled
"friends of social order", who swore by "Church and King" ' (Prentice, 34).
[3] J. P. Kay, *The Moral and Physical Condition of the Working Classes employed
in the Cotton Manufacture in Manchester* (2nd ed., 1832), 77.
[4] A. Briggs, 'The Background to the Parliamentary Reform Movement in
Three English Cities (1830-2)', *Cambridge Historical Journal*, X (1952), 295-96;
G. Whale, 'The Influence of the Industrial Revolution (1760-1790) on the
Demand for Parliamentary Reform', *Trans. Royal Hist. Soc.*, 4th series, V
(1922), 112-14.

That so many masters should sign such a decidedly political document as the Declaration and Protest was thus a very novel development, but the long-term significance of this gesture must not be exaggerated. Much of the new-found interest in politics expressed in the Declaration and Protest died away with the Radical agitations which were its prime cause. There were other and much more important influences at work in Manchester about 1819 making for an increased and more liberal interest by the cotton masters in political questions, influences in the field of business and trade. In the long term, these more particular and personal factors carried much more weight than did Peterloo and its attendant agitations. It was business grievances rather than the Radical disturbances, which eventually led the Manchester cotton masters seriously to consider the wisdom of political reform.

The thinking of the cotton masters on economic affairs was controlled by a rigid attachment to the *laissez-faire* principle expressed in its most simple and unqualified form. In this they believed that they were following the teaching of Adam Smith. In all spheres of commercial activity, they contended, economic forces were best left to find their own level. They were opposed to any interference whatsoever in matters of trade and industry: 'Every interference, either in the way of help or of hostility', ought to be removed. Complete freedom for commerce both at home and abroad was their ideal.[1]

About the time of Peterloo the masters were very busy engaged in defending this *laissez-faire* principle in industry. The elder Sir Robert Peel's Cotton Factories Regulation Act of 1819 caused his fellow manufacturers in Manchester great alarm. Most of the manufacturers regarded the measure as an entirely unjustifiable interference with the liberty both of the operatives to sell their labour and of masters to buy it. 'The Bill is founded upon an unprecedented and dangerous principle', wrote a typical opponent of the bill to the *Exchange Herald*, 'as it restricts free labour, supersedes parental authority, and establishes an inquisitorial inspection over Manufacturers.'[2] He alone among all the local master spinners, claimed Joseph Brotherton (the Radical M.P. for

[1] *Manchester Gazette*, June 13, 1818.
[2] *Exchange Herald*, March 31, 1818.

Salford) in 1836, had supported Peel in his agitation for the measure.[1]

Another proposed contravention of the *laissez-faire* principle which was being much canvassed in the area about the time of Peterloo, was the fixing by legislation of a minimum wage for the cotton operatives and especially for the distressed handloom weavers. Though this agitation came to nothing, it does appear to have had slightly more support locally than Peel's bill. A minimum wage, it was argued, would help to keep the distressed operatives from turning to Radical Reform, 'Shall we not exert ourselves then', asked one advocate of the scheme in the *Manchester Gazette* two days before Peterloo, 'to see that they and their families have the common necessaries of life . . . rather than let them get into the hand of *demagogue orators*?'[2]

Some steps towards positive action were taken. A few master hatters in Stockport, Oldham, and Manchester agreed to a minimum wage, though at a rate one-third lower than previous average wages; and on June 16, 1819, fourteen Lancashire calico manufacturers issued a declaration, approved by twenty-seven firms in a further declaration, regretting the low rates of pay given to operatives. A meeting of masters to discuss a minimum was called by thirty-five firms to meet in Manchester on August 24, 1819, but was postponed indefinitely because of Peterloo.[3] Even after the massacre, however, the idea was still being discussed in the local press. A letter appeared in the *Exchange Herald* on August 31st calling for a meeting of 'Magistrates, Manufacturers, Merchants, and Tradesmen of Lancashire' to petition parliament '*not for a reform*—not by the exhibition of Caps of Liberty', but for a minimum wage. A correspondent wrote to the *Manchester Gazette* in January 1820 contending that if trade were interfered with by measures such as the Corn Law, this made it correspondingly necessary to interfere to regulate wages.[4] The attitude of this writer was revealing, conveniently illustrating the assumptions of economic thought general among the Manchester

[1] *Parliamentary Debates*, 3rd ser. XXXIII (1836), 756.

[2] Letter from 'A Manchester Manufacturer' in the *Manchester Gazette*, Aug. 14, 1819.

[3] P. M. Giles, 'The Economic and Social Development of Stockport, 1815–36' (M.A. Thesis, Manchester University, 1950), 213; J. L. and B. Hammond, *The Skilled Labourer 1760–1832* (1919), 121–22.

[4] *Manchester Gazette*, Jan. 15, 1820.

cotton masters of the period. Even some supporters of the minimum wage did not support it as a good principle in itself: it was an interference with the free play of economic forces. But as such interference already existed in the shape of the Corn Laws, the raw cotton duty, and other restrictive imposts which indirectly influenced the rate of wages, the only solution, they contended, was to interfere directly with wages by way of compensation.[1] The *Gazette* correspondent in January, hoped, however, for another solution: 'I trust rather that we shall retrace our steps.' He wanted less, not more interference with trade. And this was the feeling of the great majority of the Manchester merchants and manufacturers irrespective of politics. If only trade were allowed to run freely, they believed, there would be no need for minimum wage legislation: labour would soon happily find its own level.

So much for Peel's cotton factory agitation and the campaign for a minimum wage. The attitude of the Manchester cotton masters towards these two important questions throws interesting light on their general principles of economic *laissez faire*. The two agitations were, however, comparatively short-lived. It is necessary now to turn to issues which, because they were prominent for much longer periods, were much more influential in their long-term effects.

Those advocates of a minimum wage who supported it only as an unfortunate but necessary compensatory interference with trade, did so solely because they believed that the other interfering regulations and imposts—the Corn Law, the raw cotton duty, and the rest—were not likely to be removed. But about the time of Peterloo agitations had in fact begun locally which were eventually to succeed in removing or reducing many of them.

The Corn Law of 1815, for instance, met with a critical reception in Manchester, and a Town's Meeting of protest was held on February 27, 1815. The chair was taken by the Boroughreeve, H. H. Birley, who (it is important to notice) was a prominent local Pittite manufacturer and who four years later commanded the troop of Manchester Yeomanry which charged into the crowd at Peterloo.[2] The Manchester opponents of the Corn Law in 1815 did not think in the terms of social justice later used by the Anti-Corn Law League: their arguments were undisguised cheap

[1] Letter from 'A Manufacturer' in *Manchester Gazette*, Oct. 16, 1819.
[2] See below, p. 80.

labour ones. High food prices, they argued, would force masters to pay high wages, and in consequence their products would become uncompetitive in world markets. The landowning aristocracy was denounced in strong terms for promoting the measure, and fifty-four thousand signatures were obtained in support of a Manchester protest petition.[1]

The Corn Law was, however, by no means the chief of the trade grievances of the Manchester merchants and manufacturers in the years about Peterloo. Their opposition to the bill was faint compared with their reaction to some other measures. 'Of eight petitions on the subject of taxation and of thirty-two on all subjects received from Manchester and Salford and printed by the House of Commons between 1816 and 1820, not one was for repeal of the Corn Laws.' [2] These petitions dealt with grievances which seemed even more pressing to the Manchester cotton masters of the period. Most prominent of these were the imposts levied on the cotton trade, and in particular the duty on the importation of raw cotton. On February 2, 1815, some three weeks before the Corn Law meeting, a meeting was held in Manchester to press for the repeal of this duty; Birley, the Boroughreeve, was again in the chair. Reductions were secured in that year and again in 1819, but the Manchester Chamber of Commerce when founded in 1820 still pressed for complete repeal. The arguments of the masters against the duty were closely related to the economic distress prevailing in the area. A freer trade petition sponsored by the Chamber in May 1820 argued that 'the imposition of heavy duties on those raw materials which form the basis of our manufactures is in the highest degree impolitic, evidently tending to diminish the labour and reduce the wages of our industrious population'.[3] Naturally, the cotton masters had their own interests in mind as well as those of their operatives: raw cotton imports which for 1791–95 had averaged 26 million lb. per annum, averaged 139 million lb. for the period 1816–20. The

---

[1] *Manchester Gazette*, March 4, 1815; *Exchange Herald*, March 7, 1815; Prentice, 68–72. Opposition was to the increase in the import price of corn from 63*s*. to 80*s*. per quarter, rather than to the Corn Law in general. Until Cobden's day movements for complete repeal were regarded as outside the scope of practical politics (A. Redford, *Manchester Merchants and Foreign Trade 1794–1858* (1934), 134–35).

[2] Marshall, 196; Prentice, 69.

[3] Redford, *op. cit.*, 139–40; Baines, *op. cit.*, 327.

burden of the duties must therefore have made itself increasingly apparent.[1] They survived until 1845.

Another vexatious impost was the duty on printed cottons. In April 1818, after a meeting at the Manchester Police Office, Birley and T. S. Withington, another prominent local Pittite and a cotton merchant, took a memorial against this duty up to the Chancellor of the Exchequer.[2] In the following year two protest meetings were held just before Peterloo, and resolutions were passed stressing the harmful effects of the duty on the distressed operatives: the 'lamentable and greatly increasing calamities' proved that the continuance of the duty would be 'a general evil of the greatest magnitude'.[3] Despite frequent pressure from the Chamber of Commerce during the 1820's, it was not abolished until 1831.

The Irish Union duties protecting the Irish cotton industry were further burdens. Following their usual principle the Manchester manufacturers pressed for complete freedom of trade between the two countries, and in 1824 they secured the complete abolition of the duties.[4]

All these were actual burdens. Manchester was equally active in resisting *proposed* restraints of a similar kind. When a tax on cotton goods exported was proposed in 1818 a meeting of protest was held at the Police Office, and Birley and Francis Philips (another leading Pittite manufacturer and author of the principal pamphlet written in defence of the magistrates at Peterloo) took a memorial up to the Chancellor of the Exechequer.[5] Another suggestion firmly resisted was a proposed duty on inland coal which threatened to raise manufacturing costs. With the Boroughreeve in the chair a Town's Meeting of protest was held on March 3, 1819, and a petition prepared.[6]

These were some of the chief problems and grievances of the Lancashire cotton trade in the years following 1815. Despite them, and despite periodic depressions like those of 1817 and 1819, the overall picture in the cotton trade was one of expansion. Through-

[1] Chapman, *op. cit.*, 144.
[2] Baines, *op. cit.*, 328; Redford, *op. cit.*, 140–41; *Exchange Herald*, April 28, 1819.
[3] *Manchester Chronicle*, July 10, 1819.
[4] Redford, *op. cit.*, 141–43.
[5] *Manchester Gazette*, April 18, 1818.
[6] *Ibid.*, March 6, 1819.

out the post-war years the official value of cotton manufactures and yarns exported showed a steady overall rise, as also did cotton-wool imports.[1] Several new and promising markets were being opened up by 1820. Exports to the Far East, in particular, were growing with remarkable speed, and one of the very first concerns of the new Chamber of Commerce in 1820 was the preparation of a free trade petition on the subject of Far Eastern trade: 'every practicable effort', declared the petition, 'should be made to extend the Foreign Commerce of the Country, so that by an increased demand for the products of labour, the wages of labour may be augmented'.[2]

Clearly the cotton masters were implying in this argument that the economic distress of the Peterloo period was in part the consequence of the illiberal trade policy of the Tory government. The petition of the same year urging a repeal of the raw cotton duty and the calico printers' petition of 1819 (both already quoted) likewise emphasized this same point. Opponents contended that in using these arguments the cotton masters were really seeking only their own advantage, not that of their employees, and that it was mere coincidence that their two sets of interests happened to agree. But to the masters this was the whole point. Given complete freedom for trade, given unimpeded room for their own search for profits, they firmly believed that both their own interests and those of their workpeople would always coincide. Only let nature's economic laws operate freely, unimpeded on the one side by restrictive or injurious action by the workers and on the other by legislative interference by the government, and their own and their operatives' economic prosperity would be equally assured. Such was the simple *laissez-faire* economic creed of the Manchester cotton masters about the time of Peterloo.

[1]

				Cotton Manufacture and Yarn Exports in £m.	Cotton Wool Imports in lbs. million.
1816	.	.	.	17½	94
1817	.	.	.	21⅓	125
1818	.	.	.	22½	177½
1819	.	.	.	18½	149½
1820	.	.	.	22½	151½
1821	.	.	.	23½	132½
1822	.	.	.	27	143
1823	.	.	.	26½	191½

Exports to nearest £½m., imports to nearest ½m. lb. (Baines, *op. cit.*, 347, 350).

[2] *Manchester Mercury*, June 27, 1820; Redford, *op. cit.*, 112–14.

THE COTTON OPERATIVES

The two main groups of cotton operatives in Lancashire in 1819 were the factory spinning workers and the domestic handloom weavers.[1] Over twenty thousand spinning operatives were employed in some sixty-six spinning mills in the Manchester area alone.[2] The number of spinners proper, men operating the mules, was relatively small: only a little over two thousand in 1819.[3] These men spinners, especially if they produced the fine yarns, were the really prosperous aristocrats among the local cotton operatives.[4] Much more numerous were the women and children employed in processes ancillary to spinning. Women spun on the spindle and fly-frames, or worked as reelers or throstle spinners, or in the card room.[5] The smallest children worked as scavengers, the older boys and girls as piecers. Infants began work in the mills at about the age of seven or eight, sometimes younger. They worked the same long hours as adults, from thirteen to fifteen hours a day for six days a week. The elder Peel's Cotton Factories Act of 1819 attempted to reduce these hours for juveniles, but it was never very effective.[6]

Still in 1819 outside the factory system were the cotton weavers. Some forty thousand handloom weavers lived in Manchester itself and many more in the surrounding districts; power-loom weaving in factories was not yet widespread.[7] Fancy weaving and the

---

[1] The calico printers and their dependents were also quite a large group. A petition against the duty on printed cotton in 1819 claimed that calico printing gave employment to one-quarter of the local cotton operatives; but this was perhaps an interested exaggeration (*Manchester Chronicle*, July 10, 1819).

[2] The elder Peel said that 20,000 spinning operatives were employed in Manchester, George Philips (a leading Manchester master spinner) said 24,000 (*Parliamentary Debates*, XXXVII (1818 55),9, 584; Redford, *op. cit.*, 238).

[3] Hammond, *Skilled Labourer*, 97.

[4] Baines, *op. cit.*, 446, D'Eichtal, *loc. cit.*, 72.

[5] Redford, *op. cit.*, Appendix A; J. L. and B. Hammond, *The Town Labourer 1760–1832* (*Guild Books* ed., 1949), I, 159; *D'Eichtal*, *loc. cit.*, 82.

[6] Hammond, *Town Labourer*, I, 158, 163, 168–69.

[7] G. H. Wood (*The History of Wages in the Cotton Trade during the Past Hundred Years* (1910), 127) estimated the total number of cotton factory operatives in Great Britain in 1819 at about 125,000, as against 236,000 hand-loom weavers. Just how many handloom weavers there were in Manchester in particular at this time is not apparent; but if Wood's general two to one proportion between weavers and spinners can be applied to Manchester taken by itself, then as there were some 20,000 spinners in the town in 1819

weaving of quilting was usually done by men, the common grades of weaving by women and children also.[1]

In the spring of 1819 all types of operatives were feeling the effects of a trade depression. 'The distresses of the labouring classes are great beyond all expression', wrote Norris, the Manchester stipendiary magistrate, in June. 'At this season of the year', exclaimed the *Manchester Observer* in April, 'when all used to be bustle and activity—when our tradesmen had scarcely time to bid you good morning—we are now a mass of worse than still life—all is now doubt and despondency.'[2]

Especially, it was the handloom weavers who were suffering. A return of wages and prices in the Manchester area prepared for the prosecution at the trials following Peterloo estimated that the lowest grade weavers in 1819 were receiving no more than 6s. per week for a twelve-hour day and the highest only 11s. 3d.[3] *The Times* correspondent reported that 10s.–12s. was the maximum

so there would also be some 40,000 handloom weavers. Wood estimated (125) that there were only some 11,000 power-loom weavers in the whole country in 1820.

[1] Redford, *op. cit.*, Appendix A; Baines, *op. cit.*, 485.

[2] Norris to Sidmouth, June 30, 1819 (Aspinall, no. 328); *Manchester Observer*, April, 24, 1819.

[3] This return is most easily accessible in *Reports of State Trials*, new series (1888), I, Appendix G. It was published locally in the *Manchester Mercury*, Jan. 18, 1820, and in the *Manchester Gazette*, Jan. 22, 1820. It gave the prices of the various grades of weaving as follows:

	1810		1812		1814		1816		1817		1818		1819	
	s.	d.	s.	d.	s.	d.	s.	d.	s.	d.	s.	d.	s.	d.
Nankeens	16	3	13	0	15	7	13	2	9	6	9	6	9	6
Best 74–7/8 calicoes .	—		11	4	13	8	9	2	8	4	9	8	8	3
Third ditto . . .	—		6	8	15	3	8	1	6	4½	8	1	6	0
Strong 9/8 calicoes .	13	0	9	7	11	4	7	4	6	1½	7	0	7	0
Velveteens. . . .	12	0	9	0	10	10	7	8	5	7	6	1	8	9
Bolton camb 60 reed 6/4 . . .	16	10½	9	5	15	4	8	4	6	4	8	0	7	8
Manchester 80 reed 6/4	14	0	10	3	16	9	8	3	6	9	8	10	7	9
Quiltings, 36 reed .	16	5½	9	6	15	0	11	11	9	8	9	8	9	8
Quiltings, fine. . .	17	2	14	0	18	0	15	6	11	1	11	0	11	3
Fancy articles . . .	21	0	14	2	20	0	12	2	9	5	11	9	10	3

The *Gazette* commentary on these figures rightly pointed out that, being averages, low as they were, some weavers must have been earning even less.

possible reward even for sixteen hours work per day.[1] A
few years previously earnings had been double this. In 1810,
according to the return, the rate for weaving fancy articles had
been 21s. per week, in 1819 it was only 10s. 3d., in 1810 the rate
for velveteens had been 12s., by the year of Peterloo it was down
to 8s. 9d., and so on through all the grades of weaving. Nor was
this merely a money decline: it was real wages which fell so
catastrophically, for prices according to the return fell little if at
all.[2] The spinning operatives, by contrast, were decidedly better

[1] *The Times*, Aug. 10, 1819; *Parliamentary Debates*, XLI (1819–20), 897
(Bennet).

[2]   *Index of the Cost of Diet in Manchester and other*
              Textile Towns, 1810–1819

(From T. S. Ashton, 'The Standard of Life of the Workers in England,
1790–1830', in F. A. Hayek (ed.), *Capitalism and the Historians* (1954), 155.
This table is based on the figures given in *State Trials*, Appendix G, as
reprinted in the *Manchester Mercury*, Jan. 18, 1820. Professor Ashton does
not state why the price list was prepared)

		Oatmeal	Flour	Potatoes	Best Beef	Coarse Beef
1810	. .	100	100	100	100	100
1811	. .	100	91	100	100	100
1812	. .	150	127	165	100	100
1813	. .	130	111	120	106	108
1814	. .	93	76	110	112	117
1815	. .	87	69	110	100	108
1816	. .	83	80	110	94	92
1817	. .	127	120	130	94	92
1818	. .	107	91	135	100	100
1819	. .	90	73	130	100	100

				Bacon	Butter	Cheese	Index of Cost of Diet
1810	.	.	. .	100	100	100	100
1811	.	.	. .	82	112	100	97
1812	.	.	. .	91	108	100	129
1813	.	.	. .	100	119	106	116
1814	.	.	. .	100	119	100	96
1815	.	.	. .	95	112	100	91
1816	.	.	. .	73	85	79	86
1817	.	.	. .	64	85	79	111
1818	.	.	. .	91	108	94	97
1819	.	.	. .	91	92	94	86

(1810 = 100)

For the weavers in 1819 an index including flour, meat, bacon, butter,
and cheese is perhaps a little unrealistic. Potatoes or oatmeal mixed with

off. Fine spinners were earning upwards of thirty shillings a week, and even the lowest-paid adult workers were earning more than the highest-paid weavers.[1]

It is hardly surprising against this background of a catastrophic fall in their living standards to find that many of the weavers were living in conditions of great squalor and distress. One of the principal operative residential districts in Manchester in 1819 was the area around the New Cross. *The Times* correspondent reported:

It is occupied chiefly by spinners, weavers, and Irish of the lowest description . . . its present situation is truly heart-rending and over-powering. The streets are confined and dirty; the houses neglected, and the windows often without glass. Out of the windows the miserable rags of the family . . . hung up to dry; the household furniture, the bedding, the clothes of the children and the husband were seen at the pawnbroker's.[2]

And when all was pawned, reported another witness, the operatives made bedding out of sacks stuffed with wood shavings and lived in cellars.[3] For many there was no work at all. The unemployed, reported *The Times*, wandered about 'with emaciated faces and dejected and despairing looks', and they and their families lived almost entirely on potatoes or on oatmeal mixed with salt.[4]

salt were almost their sole subsistence (Prentice, 168; *Parliamentary Debates'* XXV (1817), 1010). Taking oatmeal and potatoes alone, therefore, and weighting them equally the weavers' index of cost of diet for 1819 stands at 110 as against 100 for 1810. Their wages between the same dates had almost halved. Whether the index for 1819 be taken as 110 or 86, the serious extent of the collapse of the weavers' standard of living is apparent.

[1] The wages of the spinning operatives were given in the return as follows:

	1810	1812	1814	1816	1817	1818	1819
Fine spinners . .	42s. 6d.	30s.	32s.	32s.	32s.	32s.	32s.
Coarse spinners .	20s.–28s. throughout						
Women spinners .	—	15s. 7d.	17s.	17s.	17s.	17s.	17s.
Reelers	12s.	9s. 11d.	10s.	10s.	10s.	10s.	10s.
Stretchers . . .	15s. 6d.	13s. 5d.	14s.	14s.	14s.	14s.	14s.
Pickers . . .	11s. 3d.	10s. 1d.	10s.	9s.	9s.	9s.	9s.

The *Manchester Gazette* (Jan. 22, 1820) justifiably criticized the evenness of some of these figures: the spinners' wages cannot really have been as steady as is here suggested. Furthermore, the spinners on strike in 1818 claimed that their highest rate of pay was only some 18s. (see below, p. 103). Even this rate, however, was appreciably above that paid to the handloom weavers.

[2] *The Times*, Aug. 24, 1819.
[3] *Parliamentary Debates*, XLI (1819–20), 897 (Bennet).
[4] *The Times*, Aug. 10, 1819.

Such was the condition of the weavers in Manchester. And things were as bad in Stockport[1] and in the other outlying towns, nearly all of which sent contingents to Peterloo. Yet despite all this suffering and squalor the surprising thing was that the numbers of the weavers were actually increasing. At the end of the Napoleonic Wars great hosts of disbanded soldiers and sailors had been thrown on to the labour market. Many of them had found that handloom weaving was very easily learnt; they had therefore adopted it as their trade and entered into competition with the older-established weavers. These old weavers were also teaching the trade to their numerous children, while many of the Irish immigrants who were pouring into the area throughout the period also took up weaving. In these several ways, therefore, the number of weavers was being augmented at the very time when government orders were being drastically reduced and a general post-war slump was setting in. Nor did depression automatically drive out most of the surplus labour from the trade. Handloom weaving could be carried on at home in an atmosphere of independence, and most of the weavers were reluctant to transfer to other branches of the cotton industry where they would have to submit themselves to factory discipline.[2]

The depressed economic condition of the handloom weavers in the Manchester area about 1819 had a direct connection with Peterloo. It was chiefly because of their wretched condition that the handloom weavers began to lend support to the Radical Reformers early in 1819. 'Their wretchedness', reported *The Times*, 'seems to madden them against the rich, who they dangerously imagine engross the fruits of their labour, without having any sympathy for their wants.'[3] It was in this spirit that the weavers turned to the attractively simple nostrums of the Radical reformers, and we must now trace this process as it developed in the ten years before Peterloo.

The weavers were not by inclination much interested in politics,[4] and for several years they had attempted to find economic

---

[1] *Ibid.*
[2] Baines, *op. cit.*, 493–96.
[3] *The Times*, Aug. 24, 1819.
[4] 'In good times the weavers hardly ever concern themselves with politics. But when distress sets in they begin to dabble in it, believing that the government is the cause of their suffering' (D'Eichtal, *loc. cit.*, 68).

remedies for their distresses without involving themselves in political arguments. In particular, they made several attempts to secure a minimum wage for their trade, fixed by act of parliament. In 1807 and 1808 they petitioned for such a scheme, and the government in response introduced a minimum wage bill into parliament. Ministers soon had second thoughts, however, and the bill was withdrawn. In consequence, feeling ran high all over Lancashire, and in Manchester a riot broke out followed by an abortive strike.[1] In 1811 the weavers tried again. A deputation of operatives from Stockport went to see the Home Secretary to seek alleviation for their distresses, but the minister could only recommend them to patience until the natural course of economic events brought better things.[2] In 1816 Prescott, the local rector and magistrate, forwarded a request from the Stockport weavers for the prohibition of the export of cotton yarn and for a minimum wage, and the weavers themselves sent a memorial to the Prince Regent; but once again nothing came of their requests.[3]

The regular failure of these attempts at a direct economic remedy for their distress now began gradually to drive the weavers to a consideration of political methods. In 1817, the year of the March of the Blanketeers, we find some of them dabbling in Radical Reform politics for the first time.[4] Many weavers took part in the march and the petitions which they intended to carry to the Prince Regent showed quite clearly how distress was the uppermost influence in their minds, how the failure of their various agitations for economic solutions rankled with them, and how they had at last been driven to politics in an effort to discover both the cause of their present distresses and the remedies for them.

The petitions began by recalling the failure of the economic agitations of the later war years:

your petitioners, before the last war, neither felt nor feared either difficulties or privations; but during its continuance have frequently experienced both, and have repeatedly applied to your Royal Father,
your Royal Highness, and the House of Commons, for redress, which
applications, we are sorry to say, have in our humble, but firm, belief,

[1] See below, p. 95.
[2] Giles, *op. cit.*, 126.
[3] *Ibid.*, 62–63, 171.
[4] The Radical background to the March of the Blanketeers is described below, p. 97 ff.

not received that attention which their importance merited; so that now, when the waste of war is over, our sufferings are become both more general and deeper than ever.

The petitioners next turned to a consideration of this sad state of affairs, and significantly they now found its cause to be political:

This state of things we . . . attribute to the rapid increase of taxation, which has been quadrupled, together with the increase of rent, which has probably been doubled during the war; which, together so nearly absorb the whole produce of the kingdom, as to leave a quantity very far short of sufficient to keep your Petitioners in existence, and therefore their lives are now become a burden and a plague to them.

This evil, the petitioners concluded, was the outcome of the unfortunate state of political affairs, and its remedy therefore lay in political reform:

your distressed Petitioners are . . . convinced, that if the House of Commons had really emanated from and been wholly and annually appointed by, the People at large, this war, and the taxation resulting therefrom, would long ago have received sufficient check . . . Your petitioners therefore, humbly but fervently pray, that your Royal High-ness will instantly dismiss from your Councils all those Ministers who have advised or devised such cruel, such unjust measures, and call to your Councils men who are declared or avowed friends to conciliatory measures—to Parliamentary Reform—and a general and very consider-able retrenchment in every part of national expenditure. Our lives are in your hands—our happiness, in great measure, depends on you. *If you procure the adoption of measures calculated to relieve us, you may then safely rely upon our support and gratitude*—WITHOUT THIS WE CAN NEITHER SUPPORT YOU NOR OURSELVES.[1]

It is amply clear that the Blanket meeting owed its extensive working-class support to the pressure of distress.

The attachment of the weavers to reform was not yet a very strong one, however. Many of those who supported reform at Peterloo certainly had no connection with the Blanket movement. Some 60,000 attended Peterloo, not more than 12,000 attended the Blanket meeting.[2] And furthermore, soon after the dispersal of the Blanketeers many of those operatives who *had* dabbled in

[1] *Manchester Mercury*, April 1, 1817.
[2] The sources differ considerably as to the numbers assembled at the meet-ing, but Hay, the Chairman of Quarter Sessions, said that 'about 12,000' were present (H. W. C. Davis, 'Lancashire Reformers 1816–17'. *Bulletin of the John Rylands Library*, vol. 10 (1926), doc. no. 28).

Radicalism now withdrew their support from it, frightened no
doubt by the arrest of many of the Radical leaders and by the
repressive measures passed by parliament.

The collapse of the reform campaign did not lead, however, to
any reduction in popular disturbance in Manchester. 1818, like
1817 and 1819, was a year of great civil commotion in the town.
Throughout the summer business was disturbed by a series of
strikes by the cotton operatives, culminating in turn-outs by the
spinners and weavers. Both sets of operatives wanted large wage-
increases, the weavers 7s. in the £.[1]

During the strikes the weavers, unlike the spinners, deliberately
dissociated themselves from the Radical leaders, who were trying
to make capital out of the unrest. At their first strike meeting in
Stockport, for example, they refused to give a hearing to Bagguley,
the spinners' hero and one of the Radical leaders; and on
September 1st they held a separate meeting from the spinners of
the town who were eagerly listening to inflammatory harangues
from the Radical leaders. Despite this spurning of the Radicals,
however, the weavers received little, if any, permanent relief from
their strikes. By mid-September the turn-outs had collapsed, and
their leaders in the end actually suffered far heavier punishment
than those of the spinners who had been openly dabbling in
politics.[2]

Not surprisingly, therefore, we find them slowly turning again
to the schemes of the Radical Reformers. When in January 1819,
Henry Hunt, the Radical leader and the chief speaker at Peterloo,
visited Manchester, Norris, the Manchester stipendiary, reported
significantly that the operatives 'seemed to hold a different tone
and feeling and appeared in *many townships* in the neighbourhood
ripe for any tumult or strife'.[3]

Some at least of the weavers had by now clearly gone over to
the Radicals, and tension grew throughout the spring and early
summer. But even yet there were many operatives still hoping for
some remedy from the Tory government. In Stockport especially
they had long been hopeful of securing such remedy, and there
the final change-over to Radical Reform showed itself very clearly.
When it became obvious that the government was prepared to do

---

[1] The strikes are described in greater detail below, p. 103 ff.
[2] G. D. H. Cole, *Attempts at General Union* (1953), 12.
[3] Norris to Sidmouth, Feb. 3, 1819 (H.O. 42/184).

nothing but continue to urge patience and recourse to the in-effectual Arbitration Law,[1] the local weavers' committee addressed a declaration to the 'Magistrates and other Gentlemen of the District'. This declaration traced the causes 'which over a period of more than twenty years have been operating to annihilate the means of subsistence to the Cotton Weavers'. It pointed out that their agitations for a minimum wage had met with no response: 'The fate of their subsequent petitions and memorials to Parlia-ment is so well known as not to require description. By those whom the weavers sought protection they have been rewarded with punishment.' The declaration concluded by indicating where the weavers were now looking for relief:

Their hopes appear to have died within them and their general opinion is that the only means by which their present most appalling difficulty can be removed and by which they will ever be enabled to extricate themselves from the gulph of misery and despair will be an effectual change of administration, and a radical reform in Parliament, the pressing necessity of which they believe is forcibly demonstrated by the state of the Country and of their own situation in particular.[2]

In Manchester the final transformation was even more striking. The distressed weavers of the town organized a meeting for June 21st to ask for relief or for assisted emigration to North America. Instead of pursuing these ends, however, the assembly was won over by two Radical leaders, Saxton and Walker, to declare for Radical Reform:

He should . . . take the liberty [declared Saxton] to recommend to those poor fellows, the language of whose petition breathed throughout every line a feeling of despondency and forlorn hope, to seek for a redress of their manifold grievances, through a channel completely opposite to that which they were then pursuing . . . He advised them to give up the language of despair, and to join hand and heart in the restoration of their rights . . . to give up all ideas of leaving the country, and to join with the great body of the people who . . . had embarked in a firm and constitutional way to reform the House of Commons, and never to vere either to the right or left till Annual Parliaments, Universal Suffrage, and Election by Ballot, were established in the land.[3]

[1] The Cotton Arbitration Act of 1804 gave the magistrates power to arrange impartial arbitration in cotton labour disputes. The magistrates, however, did not like using the act (Hammond, *Skilled Labourer*, 62–64, 67–69, 121).

[2] Lloyd to Hobhouse, June 28, 1819, enclosure (H.O. 42/188), quoted in Giles, *op. cit.*, 215–16.

[3] *Manchester Observer*, June 26, 1819.

Thus for a time in 1819 large numbers of weavers went over in desperation to the Radical side; and when the requisition calling the Peterloo meeting appeared in August the weavers were far and away the largest occupational group among its signatories. Of about 300 signatures in all 69 can be traced in the directory for 1819: of these no less than 46 were weavers.[1] Similarly the weavers were easily the largest occupational group among the killed and injured at Peterloo; over 150 of some 200 names listed with occupations in the report of the Metropolitan Relief Committee were those of weavers.[2]

Clearly the change-over in opinion had been very great. As the declaration of the Stockport weavers had said, the hopes of the handloom weavers of economic relief from the government 'had died within them', and by the summer of 1819 they had come to the conclusion that their only hope lay in extensive political change, in Radical Reform as advocated by the organizers of the Peterloo meeting.

[1] *Manchester Observer*, Aug. 14, 1819; Pigot and Dean, *op. cit.*
[2] *Report of the Metropolitan and Central Committee for the Relief of the Manchester Sufferers* (1820).

CHAPTER THREE

THE RELIGIOUS ASPECT

THE introduction of the factory system into cotton spinning revolutionized the cotton industry in Lancashire in the generation preceding Peterloo. Important new social groups of master and operative spinners sprang up, and this led to important changes in the religious condition of Manchester. Many of the new cotton manufacturers and many of their workpeople (especially the large numbers of immigrants from Ireland and Scotland) were Dissenters or Roman Catholics. As a result, in the thirty years before Peterloo Manchester was transformed from a predominantly Anglican into a predominantly Nonconformist town. 'In 1784 the Anglican places of worship outnumbered the Dissenters by almost three to one; by 1804 the Anglican churches were as three to four; by 1825 they were fewer than one to two; in 1836 fewer than one to three.' [1] At the time of Peterloo Nonconformists of all sorts in Manchester probably outnumbered Anglicans by about two to one. [2]

This new Nonconformity was of many varieties, and numerous shades of belief were represented in the town's churches and chapels. The great Anglican centre was the ancient Collegiate Church with its Warden and Four Fellows, and there were also eleven other places of worship under the Establishment. For the Dissenters chapels of all sorts abounded, Baptist chapels, In-

---

[1] A. P. Wadsworth, 'The First Manchester Sunday Schools', *Bulletin of the John Rylands Library*, vol. 33 (1950–51), 319; Prentice, 154.

[2] An article by John Shuttleworth, a middle-class Radical, in the *Manchester Guardian*, May 5, 1821 (see Shuttleworth Scrapbook for identification of authorship), estimated that 15,461 children in Manchester, Salford, and Ardwick were educated in the Dissenting and Roman Catholic Sunday schools as against 7,647 by the Establishment. Joseph Aston gave much the same figures in a list in verse of the number of Sunday school children taking part in the coronation procession of 1821 (J. Aston, *Metrical Records of Manchester* (1822), 92–93). Sunday school figures can, of course, only be taken as very rough guides to the proportionate relationship between the local Anglican and Nonconformist followings. But as nearly all the town's children appear to have been on the books of the schools (see below, p. 29, n 2.4), they do perhaps represent a fair cross-section of the Manchester community of the period.

dependent chapels, Wesleyan Methodist chapels, Unitarian chapels, and many more.[1] The steadily growing numbers of the Dissenting establishments were a cause of increasing disquiet to zealous Anglicans in Manchester, and in the years after 1800 they began to make strenuous efforts to make up the ground recently lost to Nonconformity. In consequence, rivalry between Church and Chapel was the dominating feature in the religious life of Manchester in the twenty years before Peterloo. In 1814, for example, the Reverend C. W. Ethelston, a Fellow of the Collegiate Church and a prominent magistrate at Peterloo, published a highly partisan pamphlet entitled *The Unity of the Church Inculcated and Enforced*. He denounced in forthright fashion the existence in Manchester of 'as many sects and ramifications of sects as there are vain imaginations in the prolific brain of man'. The only hope of salvation for the Dissenters was for them to re-join the Established Church: 'the lenient forbearance of our laws does not, in the high national court of conscience, acquit any man of the guilt of schism'.[2]

In the eyes of many staunch Anglicans dissent from the Established Church automatically implied dissent also from loyalty to the established constitution: Church and constitution were regarded as inextricably bound together. The Younger Pitt, for example, considered the Church of England to be an 'essential part of the constitution': whatever endangered the security of the Church would, he believed, 'necessarily affect the security of the whole'.[3] Such a view as this, virtually equating Dissent with sedition, was very popular among the Anglican clergy in Manchester during the years before Peterloo. In 1801, for example, the Reverend W. R. Hay, another local magistrate very prominent at Peterloo, reported his suspicions of the disaffected in Dukinfield who were holding district meetings. A person of the name of Ine Wild, he noted, always chose the delegates from one of the districts: 'Wild is a Methodist', he added as if to clinch his case, 'and has regular Methodist meetings at his house.' Clearly, to Hay Jacobinism and Methodism were almost synonymous terms.[4]

[1] Pigot and Dean, *op. cit.*, 171–72.
[2] Ethelston, *op. cit.*, 5, 8, and *passim*. For Ethelston see below, pp. 76–77.
[3] R. F. Wearmouth, *Methodism and the Working-Class Movements of England, 1800–1850* (1937), 56.
[4] *Ibid.*, 55. For Hay see below, pp. 75–76.

Towards Roman Catholicism and the question of Catholic Emancipation the Anglican attitude in Manchester was one of even more uncompromising hostility. Just after Peterloo the Reverend Melville Horne, curate of St. Stephen's, Salford, denounced the Radical Reformers and the Roman Catholics in equal terms: 'That the Radicals have publicly invited all Catholics to join their Banners is no novelty', he declared, 'for Atheism and Popery have been seen to walk hand in hand on the continent.'[1] In this spirit a petition against Roman Catholic relief was prepared in Manchester in May 1819, and the local Anglican clergy were probably among its staunchest supporters. When in 1825 the Bishop of Chester presented another anti-Catholic petition from Manchester, he claimed that it had been signed by forty-one of the forty-two Anglican clergy in the town; the absence of this single signature, he added, was only 'an accidental circumstance'.[2]

Rivalry between the Establishment and Nonconformity was thus the leading feature in the religious life of Manchester in the early nineteenth century. About the time of Peterloo this rivalry was prominent especially in two connections, over the question of new Anglican church-building and in connection with the Sunday School movement.

The government grant of one million pounds in 1818 for the erection of new Anglican churches was particularly welcomed by the leaders of the Establishment in Manchester. Here, they believed, was an excellent chance of making up the ground recently lost to the Dissenters. The Reverend C. D. Wray, assistant chaplain at the Collegiate church, had been pressing the government for some years to support just such a new church-building programme. In 1815 he had published a pamphlet on the subject, *A Statement of Facts respecting the Population of the Parish of Manchester shewing the Great Want of a New Free Church*. Wray complained of 'the yearly erection of places of worship not in unison with the ecclesiastical establishment' which (he believed) had been encouraged by the failure to provide sufficient accommodation for the lower orders in Anglican churches. Only three Anglican churches in Manchester and Salford, he noted, had any

[1] Rev. M. Horne, *The Moral and Political Crisis of England* (1820), 20.
[2] *Manchester Mercury*, May 11, 1819; *Parliamentary Debates*, 2nd ser., XII (1825), 1334.

free pews for the poor, the vast majority being let. New churches were urgently needed if the Church of England was to maintain its authority. It was over twenty years since a new Anglican church had been erected, although the population of Manchester during that time had increased by some thirty thousand; in the same period seven or eight Dissenting chapels had been opened. 'Can we wonder', Wray concluded, 'at the increase of schism?' [1]

Wray must have been very pleased, therefore, when the government grant for church-building was agreed to in 1818. The local Nonconformists, on the other hand, were not so pleased; and the attempt to implement the church-building scheme in the Manchester area occasioned strenuous resistance. The issue came to a head at two Parish Vestry meetings in 1820 at which the local middle-class Radicals, who were almost all Dissenters,[2] objected to contributing towards the cost of the new erections through the parish funds. 'It is not honourable, nor yet even common justice', declared Richard Potter (a Unitarian) at the meeting of January 27, 1820, 'to call upon the dissenters to erect places of worship for those whose creed is so essentially different from theirs.' Religion, argued J. E. Taylor, a friend of Potter who was soon to become the proprietor of the new *Manchester Guardian*, was 'a marketable commodity' and ought not to have to be sustained by artificial subsidies. In any case, concluded Potter, the existing Anglican churches were by no means filled.[3]

Because of the plural voting allowed at parish meetings the middle-class Radicals were not able at this first meeting to defeat the Anglican proposals. They began, therefore, an intensive campaign in the town designed to rouse local Nonconformist opinion against the scheme. As a result, large numbers attended the important vestry meeting of June 8, 1820, called to discuss the finding of sites for the new churches and to fix a rate. Once again the middle-class reformers contended that the present Anglican accommodation was not all taken up, and once again this was denied by the Anglicans. Whatever might be the case with let pews, declared H. H. Birley (who had led the charge of the yeomanry at Peterloo), there were few pews available for the lower orders, and new churches were urgently needed to serve

[1] Wray, *op. cit.*, 2, 9, and *passim*.
[2] See below, p. 57, n. 2.
[3] *Manchester Observer, Manchester Gazette*, Jan. 29, 1820.

their needs. This time, however, the middle-class Radicals were successful, and a hostile amendment was carried by 648 votes to 418.[1] But despite this hostile vote the plans for building still went forward, and during the early 1820's the whole issue was regularly revived as the expenses of furnishing the new churches appeared on the parish accounts. Four new churches were eventually completed under the scheme.[2]

Apart from the church-building dispute a second centre of interdenominational rivalry in Manchester about the time of Peterloo lay around the Sunday school movement. The Sunday school idea had flourished in the area ever since 1784. In their first years the schools had been administered by an interdenominational committee, but this had broken up in 1800.[3] Progress was maintained, however, and in the years before 1819 numerous new schools were founded. In 1821 almost all of the town's children appear to have been on the books of the Sunday schools.[4]

The schools had a double attraction to the 'respectable' classes. On the one hand they satisfied their desire to do 'good works', and on the other they offered a useful instrument for improving the moral standards of the poor. The former satisfied the consciences of the people of property: the latter helped to safeguard that property from attack. This last was perhaps the more important attraction; for the rise of an industrial society in Lancashire had meant the growth of a large industrial proletariat which could no longer be supervised after the old fashion. In large factories, observed one Anglican minister in Manchester just after Peterloo, it was impossible for masters to exercise the same 'patriarchal influence' over the morals of their workpeople as had the small-scale employers of the past: the work of moral improvement must now therefore be carried on in the Sunday schools on an appropriate scale. The Sunday schools in other words had a part to play complementary to the great inventions themselves. They seemed

[1] *Manchester Gazette, Manchester Chronicle*, June 10, 1820.
[2] Main, *op. cit.*, 59; Prentice, 59; R. Potter, Diaries, Correspondence and Records, XI, 90 ff.; W. R. Hay, Scrapbooks, X, 119-20.
[3] Wadsworth, *loc. cit.*, 315-19.
[4] The number of children on the Sunday schools' books appears to have been about one-sixth of the town's total population. The population of Manchester, Salford, and Ardwick in 1821 was about 137,000: in that year, according to Shuttleworth, there were some 23,000 children on the Sunday schools' books. See also S. E. Maltby, *Manchester and the Movement for National Elementary Education 1800-1870* (1918), 37.

(as one modern writer has put it) 'a short cut to the social millennium, just as the spinning frame and the steam engine seemed short cuts to a material millennium'.[1]

Both Anglicans and Nonconformists, therefore, accepted the Sunday School principle. And the Anglican clergy believed that the schools could play an important part in their religious counterattack on local Nonconformity. They strove hard to reduce the two to one lead in Sunday school attendances which the Dissenters had established by 1800. In 1801 they conceived the colourful idea of holding annual Whit Monday processions of Anglican Sunday school children to the Collegiate Church in Manchester: this has been described as 'the greatest stroke of the Church schools'.[2] They also made a striking attempt to increase their Sunday school accommodation. In 1818 they opened the Bennet Street Sunday School, described in 1821 as 'perhaps the largest School in the Kingdom'; it had nearly two thousand pupils in that year, about four times as many as the next largest Sunday school in Manchester.[3] Despite the impressive size of this school, however, and despite the Whit Monday processions, the Anglicans do not seem really to have shaken the predominance of the Dissenters in the Sunday school field; for throughout the period as population grew they consistently maintained their two to one lead.[4]

The instruction which the Sunday schools provided was not altogether the same as that afforded by their modern counterparts. In the prevailing low state of popular education the functions of the schools could not be limited to purely spiritual matters. Before religious texts could be understood the children had to be taught to read them, and in consequence all the Manchester Sunday schools in the early nineteenth century taught reading as a necessary preliminary to moral improvement, while a few taught writing and accounts also.[5]

For most poor children the Sunday schools were the only places where they could hope to receive any education. Most children had to work during the week, and in any case facilities for popular day school education were meagre. Not until 1813 were the first

[1] Rev. J. T. Allen, *A Vindication of the moral and religious Instruction of the Children of the Poor* (1820); Wadsworth, *loc. cit.*, 321; Giles, *op. cit.*, 84, 86.
[2] Wadsworth, *loc. cit.*, 318–19.
[3] *Manchester Guardian*, May 5, 1821 (Shuttleworth article).
[4] Wadsworth, *loc. cit.*, 326.
[5] *Manchester Guardian*, May 5, 1821 (Shuttleworth article).

serious attempts made to provide adequate day school facilities for the education of the children of the poor; in that year a non-sectarian Lancasterian School and an Anglican National School were both opened in Manchester. Wray and Ethelston were prominent in the foundation of the National School, which was begun in a spirit of typical rivalry with the Dissenters who had initiated the Lancasterian venture.[1]

If the poor were being taught to read it must be ensured that they read the right things. Thus in 1814 Ethelston was prominent also in setting up a Book Repository in Manchester intended to circulate cheap popular works published by the Anglican tract societies.[2] This was but one of several similar improving bodies established in the town in the years just before Peterloo: the Auxiliary Bible Society was founded in 1810, the Religious Tract Society in 1812, the Church Tract Association also in 1812, and the Ladies' Bible Society in 1816. The Wesleyan Methodists too were actively distributing improving pamphlets about the time of Peterloo. Clearly, the poor of Manchester about 1819 must have felt themselves under an increasing pressure for moral improvement.[3]

But the tract societies had their limitations. They reached out to adults who were perhaps past improvement: attention given to the children would probably be more fruitful. And as (even after the opening of the Lancasterian and National schools) the day schools in Manchester taught only a small minority of the town's poorer children,[4] it was to the Sunday schools that the greater part of Manchester's benevolent attention was being given during the years just before Peterloo.

Although the main concern of Sunday school education was

[1] See the acrimonious correspondence carried on between the adherents of the rival schools in the columns of the *Exchange Herald* newspaper in the early months of 1812.

[2] F. R. Raines, *The Fellows of the Collegiate Church of Manchester*, Chetham Soc. (1891), new series, XXIII, pt. II, 310.

[3] W. E. Axon, *The Annals of Manchester* (1886), 141–51; D. McAllum, *Memorials of the Life, Character, and Death of the Rev. H. Taft, M.D.* (1824), 125.

[4] Shuttleworth's figures for 1821 were as follows:

	Day Schools	Sunday Schools
Establishment	1,232 children	7,647 children
Nonconformist	1,271 ,,	15,461 ,,

(*Manchester Guardian*, May 5, 1821).

with the next world, inevitably it gave to its pupils the means
better to consider their condittion in this world; and in this
context the Sunday school movement in Lancashire had a direct
connection with the Radical Reform movement which culminated
in Peterloo. It was to the Sunday schools that many of the
working-class Radical leaders owed their education. 'The Sunday
schools of the preceding thirty years', remarked Samuel Bamford,
who led one of the processions of reformers at Peterloo, 'had
produced many working men of sufficient talent to become
readers, writers, and speakers in the village meetings for Parliamentary reform.' [1] It was impossible to expect of the poor their
former acquiescence, wrote the middle-class Radical, J. E.
Taylor, just after Peterloo: the Sunday schools had taught them
to take an interested part in affairs. [2]

These Sunday school educated Radical Reformers were in-
tensely critical of many of the clergy in Manchester, especially of
the Anglican clergy. The Anglicans, staunchly Tory in politics,
taught passive obedience before political abuses and passive
acceptance of economic distress. To the Radical Reformers this
seemed not merely wrong, but also hypocritical and selfish:

you are called upon to be respectful—to be *decent*—to be *moderate*—
to be patient—to be *loyal* . . . to subscribe for a bible to teach you the
shortest way to heaven—and to be very thankful to a man in black,
who every Sunday will tell you that temperance, and fasting, and
prayer, are much better than a plentiful supply of the luxuries of the
world, which he *devours himself*, lest they should do you a mischief!

The Anglican clergy, the Radicals contended, ought to cease
preaching such selfish doctrines and ought instead to teach 'the
true principles of Christianity'. [3]

The response of the Anglican clergy to these attacks was most
decided. Such views, they believed, were not merely irreligious,
they were also seditious; for the Radical religious programme
was linked to a wider programme of reform which, Anglicans
were sure, the reformers intended to achieve through revolution.
The Anglican clergy took determined action, therefore, to combat
this Radical 'sedition'; and in the four or five years before Peterloo
the Anglican religious counter-attack, which had been initiated

[1] Bamford, I, 7–8.
[2] Taylor, 163, 201.
[3] *Manchester Observer*, Jan. 16, July 17, Aug. 7, 1819.

after 1800 as a means of combating the progress of Nonconformity, began to take on a political as well as a religious colour. In this anti-Radical campaign the new churches announced in 1818 had an especially important part to play. Not only, Anglicans believed, would they check the progress of Nonconformity, they would also provide new pulpits for preaching 'loyal' anti-Radical sermons to the poor. These sermons would expound the politico-religious teaching of Archdeacon Paley and Hannah More, urging the poor to resigned acceptance of their God-given lot. As a stop-gap measure in 1817 the local Anglican clergy had published several pamphlets in this vein, Wray's *The Street Politicians*, Ethelston's *A Patriotic Appeal to the Good Sense of all Parties*, and several others, all of them attempting to persuade the working-classes to remain acquiescent and loyal to 'Church and King'.[1] But such pamphlets could not be as effective as sermons. Many of the poor could not read them, and many of those who could read them would not. What were needed, Anglicans believed earnestly, were new churches where the poor could hear the Anglican word regularly: only thus could the progress of Radical Reform be checked.

[1] Tory passive obedience teaching is discussed in greater detail below pp. 86–87.

'ORATOR' HUNT, 1773–1835
Chairman of the Peterloo Meeting

Part Two

THE POLITICAL BACKGROUND

CHAPTER FOUR

THE WORKING-CLASS RADICALS

WHO were the men who organized the Peterloo meeting? Up to the present time this important question has never been answered by historians. Any survey of the political background to Peterloo must begin, therefore, with a series of biographical sketches.

Henry Hunt (1773–1835),[1] the chief speaker at Peterloo, was not a Manchester man, but came of Wiltshire yeoman stock. Most of his early political activity was centred in London, and he did not come into contact with Lancashire Radicalism until 1817 through the Hampden Club movement. His capacities as a demagogue orator, however,—his clear and bell-like voice, and his tall and imposing personal appearance—quickly won for him a large personal following in the county; and throughout the Peterloo period (and to a lesser extent until his death) he remained the dominant, though often distant, figure in local Radicalism. Personally, Hunt was very vain and jealous of his own importance.

The most active *local* figure behind the Peterloo meeting was Joseph Johnson (1791–1872), a small-scale Manchester brushmaker.[2] Johnson first became prominent in local Radical politics in January 1819. In June he became part-owner of the *Manchester Observer*, the local Radical newspaper, and about the same time secretary of the Manchester Patriotic Union Society, the Society

[1] D.N.B.; R. Huish, *The History of the Private and Political Life of the late Henry Hunt, Esq.* (1836); H. Hunt, *Memoirs* (1820); H. W. C. Davis, *The Age of Grey and Peel* (1929), 176; Bamford, I, 202, and *passim*.

[2] *Exchange Herald*, Jan. 26, 1819; Kinsey, 14; Johnson to Sidmouth, Aug. 21, 1819, and his two voluntary examinations (H.O. 42/192); Hobhouse to Norris, Aug. 26, 1819 (H.O. 41/4); Hunt, *Memoirs*, III, 593–94, 601, 603–06; J. Johnson, *A Letter to Henry Hunt* (2nd ed., 1822), 13–14; H. Hunt, '[Letter] to the Radical Reformers' (Aug. 24, 1822), 32–34; W. Cobbett, *Rural Rides*, ed. G. D. H. and M. Cole (1930), Index of Persons; Prentice, 412; *Annual Register 1872*, Chronicle, 162.

which invited Hunt to the Peterloo meeting. After his arrest at Peterloo Johnson offered himself for two voluntary examinations before the local magistrates and expressed his 'deepest regret' for what had occurred, attempting at the same time to minimize his own connections with the local Radical cause. Clearly he was a weak character, and Hunt in his *Memoirs* denounced him (probably with justice) as 'a composition of vanity, emptiness, and conceit'. Johnson was Cobbett's host during his northern tour of 1830, and he played some part in the local agitation for the Reform Bill. For the last half of his life, however, he became (in the words of his obituary notice in the *Annual Register*) 'a Tory *sui generis*'.

John Knight (1763–1838),[1] a small-scale Manchester cotton manufacturer, was a much longer-established figure in local Radical circles. As early as 1811 he had published a reform pamphlet, and in 1812 he had been arrested for administering illegal oaths to a committee formed to prepare a reform address to the Prince Regent. He was a prominent leader of the local Hampden Club movement, and presided at the meeting in October 1816 which established a club in Manchester. By 1819 he was regarded as the elder statesman of the Radical movement in Lancashire, and he presided at the important Oldham delegate meeting of June 7th which attempted to co-ordinate the work of the Radicals and to iron out differences. Knight was arrested at Peterloo, but he continued speaking while subsequently out on bail; and it was for his part in a meeting at Burnley in November, rather than for his part at Peterloo (though found guilty on the lesser Peterloo charge), that he was eventually sentenced to two years' imprisonment. He continued an active figure in local Radical circles throughout the 1820's and '30's, and at his funeral the obituary sermon was preached by Rayner Stephens, the anti-Poor Law agitator.

Samuel Bamford (1788–1872),[2] the celebrated weaver-poet from Middleton near Manchester, has given his own vivid account of this period in his book *Passages in the Life of a Radical*. Like Knight he was active in the Hampden Club period, and,

[1] Cobbett, *Rural Rides* (ed. Cole), Index of Persons; Marshall, 133; Prentice, 76–82; Davis, *loc cit.*, doc. no. 13, and p. 16; *Wardle's Manchester Observer*, June 12, 1819; *State Trials*, 529–608; H. Bateson, *A Centenary History of Oldham* (1949), 103.

[2] Bamford, *passim;* D.N.B.; H. Dunckley, intro. to 1893 ed. of *Passages in the Life of a Radical*.

though disapproving of the Blanket meeting as the work of extremists, was arrested by the authorities and sent to London. At Peterloo he led the Middleton contingent, and was arrested for his part in the meeting. He does not appear, however, to have been one of the leading Radical circle at this time; he seems to have confined his activity to Middleton and to writing in the Radical cause.[1] He disliked Hunt for his vanity, and strongly disapproved of the low moral tone of some of the Radical leaders. In later life he became a much more moderate reformer, and enrolled as a special constable against the Chartists.

'Dr.' Healey (1780–1830)[2] was a quack-doctor friend of Bamford's who played some unknown minor part in the agitation of 1817. In 1819 his role was again a minor one; but he led the Saddleworth, Lees, and Mossley Union contingent to Peterloo headed by a black flag, and this caused great consternation in local 'loyalist' circles. It was chiefly because of this that he was arrested at the meeting. Healey, and the four other Radical leaders already noticed—Bamford, Knight, Johnson, and Hunt—were all convicted at York in March 1820 for their parts at Peterloo.[3]

J. T. Saxton (born c. 1776),[4] who was acquitted at York, was sub-editor of the *Manchester Observer*. Probably his greatest contribution to the Radical cause was the part he played at the Manchester weavers' meeting of June 21, 1819.[5] Despite his Radicalism (clearly avowed at this meeting), Saxton was acquitted

---

[1] Bamford's most celebrated poem of the Peterloo period was 'The Lancashire Hymn'. The following two verses are typical of its tone:

> Have we not heard the infant's cry,
>   And mark'd its mother's tear;
> That look, which told us mournfully,
>   That woe and want were there.
> And shall they ever weep again?
> And shall their pleadings be in vain?
>
> By the dear blood which Hampden bled
>   In freedom's noble strife,
> By gallant Sydney's gory head,
>   By all that's dear to life,
> They shall not supplicate in vain,
> No longer will we wear the chain.
>
> (*Manchester Observer*, Aug. 7, 1819.)

[2] Bamford, *passim;* Davis, *loc. cit.*, p. 19 and n. 3; Bateson, *op. cit.*, 101.
[3] See below, p. 151 ff.
[4] Kinsey, 18–21.   [5] See above, p. 23.

for his part at Peterloo, being able to claim that he was on the hustings merely as a reporter; and he was left throughout 1820-21 as the leading figure among the Manchester Radicals. His wife was secretary to the Manchester Female Reformers in 1819.[1]

From June 1819 to February 1820 James Wroe (c. 1788-1844)[2] was editor of the *Manchester Observer*. He was also the chief Radical printer—'printer-Devil to the Radical Reformers', as an opponent called him—and superintendent of the Radical Union School Rooms. His position in the Radical organization in 1819 was thus an important one. He and his family were frequently indicted by the authorities for seditious publication or distribution, and in February 1820, poverty-stricken by the cost of litigation, he was forced to give up the *Observer*. He continued nonetheless a faithful friend of reform throughout the 1820's and '30's, and in 1838 he was elected one of the Manchester delegates to the first Chartist National Convention.

In 1818 while Manchester concentrated on strikes rather than on Radical Reform, Stockport was joining the two together. This was mainly the work of four men, and in particular of the Reverend Joseph Harrison (born 1780), a local Nonconformist preacher who called himself 'Chaplain to the poor and needy'.[3] In 1818 he set up as a schoolmaster in Stockport and began teaching a mixture of Radical politics and religion to both children and adults. He quickly took over the direction of Radical activity in the town and founded a Union Society whose rules became a model for many similar societies all over the country.[4] His politico-religious sermons became regular features of Stockport Radicalism, and for two of them preached on August 15 and December 18, 1819, and for a speech at Stockport on June 28th he received a total of three and a half years' imprisonment in 1820.[5] On his release Harrison continued a zealous reformer, and he took a prominent part in the local agitation for repeal of the Combination Laws in 1824. He last appears as an active supporter of the Chartist agitation.[6]

---

[1] *Manchester Observer*, July 31, 1819.

[2] Kinsey, 14-15; *Manchester Times*, Aug. 10, 1844; *An Address to the Higher Classes in the Town of Manchester*, by An Inhabitant(1820), 11; W. H. Wickwar, *The Struggle for the Freedom of the Press 1819-1832* (1928), 104.

[3] For a brief account of the four see Giles, *op. cit.*, 143-45.

[4] See below, p. 47 ff. [5] *Manchester Observer*, April 15, 22, 1820.

[6] W. C. Taylor, *Notes of a Tour in the Manufacturing Districts of Lancashire* 2nd ed., 1842), 311-15.

Harrison's three leading associates in Stockport in 1818 were John Bagguley, Samuel Drummond, and John Johnston. Bagguley was a servant, only eighteen at the time of his arrest in September 1818; Johnston was a tailor from Salford. The three of them had been leading promoters of the March of the Blanketeers in 1817.[1] In 1818 they were active in encouraging the strikers and in trying to interest them in Radical Reform. All three were arrested for violent speeches to the strikers at Stockport on September 1, 1818, and each subsequently received two years' imprisonment.[2] They were thus out of action at the time of Peterloo; but their work, along with Harrison, had made Stockport one of the earliest and most important centres of local Radicalism.

Indicted with Harrison for violent language at Stockport on June 28th was Sir Charles Wolseley (1769-1846),[3] who like Hunt was more than a local leader. One of the founders of the original Hampden Club, Wolseley was elected 'Legislatorial Attorney' for Birmingham at a meeting on July 12, 1819. He came from an old Staffordshire family and was a man of means; he helped to provide the large sums in bail required for the release of the Peterloo prisoners after indictment, and also provided with money those reformers who needed it while in prison. He was himself imprisoned for eighteen months for a violent speech along with Harrison at the Stockport meeting of June 28, 1819. On his release he continued active in Radical affairs for some time, but after about 1826 he appears to have given up any public part in politics.

This notice of Sir Charles Wolseley completes the list of the most prominent Radical leaders in Lancashire in the year of Peterloo. Apart from the strangers Hunt and Wolsley, it will be seen that none of them held any very substantial position in society; certainly they were all lacking in that 'liberal education' which the local Tories and Pittites constantly claimed as necessary for participation in politics.[4] Their lack of social standing and training in affairs was in itself one reason for their ultimate failure. But despite their deficiencies they did contrive to develop for a time in 1819 a coherent and organized movement, a movement

[1] Davis, *loc. cit.*, docs. no. 27, 28.
[2] *Manchester Chronicle*, April 17, 24, 1819.
[3] *D.N.B.*; Hunt, *Memoirs*, III, 638; Bamford, II, 163, 210; *Manchester Observer*, April 15, 1820.
[4] See below, p. 85.

4

with clubs, meetings, and a programme of its own. These various aspects of the Radical agitation must now be studied.

The Radical programme of reform was published in its most comprehensive form in the Declaration and in the Remonstrance passed at the Manchester Radical meeting of January 18, 1819 (at which Hunt was the chief speaker),[1] and in the resolutions passed by the Union Society delegate meeting held at Oldham on June 7th.[2] From these sources it becomes clear that the Radical programme in 1819 rested on two basic and logically connected points. First, it was a protest against distress—against low wages, high prices, and unemployment; and second, it was the assertion of a theory of fundamental political rights.

The Oldham resolutions put the problem of distress in the fore-front of its grievances:

in consequence of the high price of provisions, enormous rents, excessive taxes, scarcity of employment, and lowness of wages; millions of healthy and industriously disposed Englishmen, are reduced to the deepest distress: being quite unable to procure a sufficient quantity of the meanest food, and of the coarsest raiment . . . it cannot be the duty of industriously disposed men (whether employed or not) to starve, nor submit to the degredation of becoming paupers.

This burden of distress, the Radical leaders taught, would only be removed by the people themselves taking political power into their own hands. Here was the second basic point in the Radical programme, its assertion of a theory of popular political rights, rights echoing from the days of the French Revolution. The people had a right, the Radical leaders asserted, to take control of political affairs. 'All men are born free, equal and independent of each other', claimed the Manchester Declaration; 'the only source of all legitimate power' is in the People, the whole People, and nothing but the People'. It was necessary, the Radical leaders argued, to assert these rights so as to relieve the growing burden of economic distress. The fundamental cause of distress was to be found not as the government claimed in the temporary after-effects of the Napoleonic wars, but in the corrupt borough-mongering system of government at Westminster, a system in which the rights and interests of the people had been forgotten.

[1] *Manchester Observer*, Jan. 23, 1819 (for texts, see Appendix A).
[2] *Ibid.*, June 12, 1819 (for text, see Appendix A).

As to the present distress [wrote one reformer to the *Manchester Mercury* just before Peterloo, a paper which supported the government], you and those of your kidney, say it's all owing to bad markets, want of trade with foreigners and such like . . . The root of the evil, in my judgment, . . . lies deeper by a long way. I'm come over entirely to Mr. Knight's opinion that we are unsound in the vitals.—There's the seat of the mischief—The Constitution's become rotten at the core— there's foul-play at head quarters—the Parliament! Sir, the Parliament! Corruption's at the very helm of the State—it sits and rules in the very House of Commons; *this* is the source, the true and the only one, of all our sufferings—And what's the remedy, then? Why, *reform*—a radical complete constitutional *Reform*; we want nothing but this . . . to mend our markets and give every poor man plenty of work and good wages for doing it.[1]

Thus the remedy for all the economic burdens of the operatives lay, according to Radical teaching, in political reform at the seat of government. In detail this meant three things especially— Annual Parliaments, Universal Suffrage, and repeal of the Corn Laws. These three calls (along with Vote by Ballot, which was almost as popular) were the chief rallying cries at all the Radical meetings in the area in 1819. 'Annual Parliaments and universal suffrage', declared the Manchester meeting in January, 'were formerly, and ought now, to be the Law of the Land'; universal manhood suffrage was a 'just and lawful right', and to deprive any man of this right was 'to deprive him of all security for his life, liberty, and property' and to reduce him to slavery, for a man was not free when his life, liberty, or property might be arbitrarily taken from him by laws made by others without his consent.

The Corn Law of 1815 seemed to the Radicals the supreme instance of such arbitrary legislation. It was proof, declared the Oldham delegate meeting, that 'the interest of a few Land Proprietors, preponderates in our Legislative Assemblies, over the interest of millions of labourers'. The Corn Law, the Radicals argued, not only forced up the price of food, it also reduced the demand for labour and therefore the rate of wages: the demand for manufactures slackened when food prices were high because a greater proportion of the people's income had to be spent on food, leaving less for expenditure on manufactured goods. Furthermore, the foreign as well as the home demand for our manufactures was reduced by the operation of the Law, since

[1] *Manchester Mercury*, Aug. 10, 1819.

foreign corn could not be exchanged for our products. In this way too, therefore, the demand for labour, and consequently wages and employment, was adversely affected by the Corn Law.[1] If the Corn Law were not repealed, declared the Oldham delegate meeting, the working-classes could not long survive, 'and if they must die, either by starvation, or in defence of their rights, they cannot hesitate to prefer the latter'.

Universal Suffrage, Annual Parliaments, and repeal of the Corn Laws were the three most important reforms demanded by the Radical Reformers in 1819, but there were also many others only slightly less important. There was, for example, much discussion of the state of national finances. The burden of the National Debt was a well-worn theme of Cobbett's still prominent in 1819. Opponents said that the Radicals hoped to repudiate the Debt entirely; but the reformers replied that they merely intended to make the boroughmongers pay off both principal and interest since it was for them alone that it had been so greatly inflated.[2] To support this Debt heavy taxation was necessary. The Radical cry here was no taxation without representation. Taxation without representation, asserted the Manchester Declaration, was 'as much an act of robbery as the forcible taking away a man's Property on the King's highway'. Three million pounds in extra taxes were levied in 1819, and this undoubtedly brought the reformers much fresh support.[3]

The poor rates were another burden on the distressed poor. As more fell out of work, those remaining had to carry an increasing burden, and this (as one reformer put it) overwhelmed with distress the already distressed. The rich, on the other hand, were able to pay their rates, taxes and tithes out of the profits from the labour of the poor.[4] What was needed, the Radicals contended, was cheap and efficient government: 'Cheap Land and Cheap Government', wrote the Manchester Observer, were 'the surest foundations for the prosperity of the people.'[5]

[1] 'The unjust and cruel Corn Laws', declared a Stockport Radical meeting, 'like a two-edged sword, cut both ways, by raising the price of provisions, and not only preventing the rise, but actually producing a great depreciation of wages' (Manchester Observer, Feb. 20, 1819).

[2] Kinsey, 127–28.

[3] William Howarth to Sidmouth, Aug. 4, 1819 (H.O. 42/191).

[4] Letter from a weaver in Wardle's Manchester Observer, June 5, 1819.

[5] Manchester Observer. June 26, 1819. An Ashton meeting of June 14, 1819 criticized such items as £22,000 spent 'in presents for snuff-boxes', and the

On the currency question, a topic very prominent in 1819, the Radicals based themselves on Cobbett's *Paper Against Gold*, in which 'he had argued that paper would go on increasing in quantity until death came in the shape of war prices'.[1] The Governors of the Bank of England (declared the Manchester meeting in January) were increasing distress by their unlimited issues 'without the smallest intention on their part, or means adopted by the government to compel the repayment or cancelling of their worthless notes'. The only solution which the *Manchester Observer* could offer for this financial spiral was 'the withdrawal of some genuine and more fictitious capital' from business, a drastic remedy which, it realized, would add still more to the prevailing distress.[2]

Most Radical supporters in the area were connected with industry; yet the industrial programme offered by the reformers was neither detailed nor prominent. It vaguely promised higher wages and shorter hours,[3] and the Combination Laws were attacked fairly frequently with the memory of the strikes of 1818 still fresh.[4] But though feeling against the Combination Laws may have driven some operatives to listen to the reformers,[5] the Radical leaders themselves were urging a programme which put much more emphasis on political issues: constitutional change was being stressed as a necessary preliminary to any scheme of industrial relief.

On agricultural problems the reformers were much more specific, perhaps because they felt the need to win support in this field whereas they already had a following in industry. Labourers, tenant farmers, and small landholders were carefully differentiated from the great landowners, who were charged with living on inflated rents bolstered up by the Corn Laws. The Corn Laws, it was argued, were no friend to the tenant farmers; the farmers

extra £10,000 voted to the Duke of York as custodian of his father (*ibid.*, June 19, 1819). In this context, too, a large standing army was attacked as wasteful and unnecessary: its only purpose was to 'curb the people and compel them to pay war taxes in peace time' (Kinsey, 127).

[1] Speech of William Fitton at Stockport (*Manchester Observer*, July 3, 1819).

[2] *Ibid.*, May 1, 1819.

[3] A six-hour day according to the *Manchester Observer* (July 17, 1819).

[4] See the letter from John Knight in the *Manchester Observer*, June 26, 1819.

[5] Hammond, *Skilled Labourer*, 120. The Hammonds, however, rather overestimate the importance of feeling against the Combination Laws in 1819.

merely passed on the profits from high prices to their landlords, and as prices were high owing to the operation of the Laws, so were the rents that tenants had to pay. These rents the tenant farmers had no power to alter because their landlords were in exclusive control of parliament. Tenant farmers and small land-holders, the Radicals urged, ought to align themselves alongside the industrial workers in the struggle for democratic reform of parliament: 'the struggle lies between immense property and labour; property has usurped the power of legislation'.[1]

The centrepiece in the corrupt parliamentary system attacked by the Radicals was the Crown, and royalty was not spared in the Radical attacks. The Crown, the Manchester Declaration reminded the Prince Regent, was 'a sacred trust and inheritance, held only by the free consent and for the sole welfare and benefit of the People'. The House of Brunswick, added the Manchester Remonstrance with a touch of sarcasm, had been put on the throne only in the hope of better government and not from any 'exclusive attachment or predilection for the private virtues or personal merits of the family'. Despite these attacks, however, it would be wrong to conclude that the Radical Reformers were really anti-monarchical in their views. True republicanism was merely an idea on the fringe of the movement.[2] It was the excessive expense of the Crown[3] and the abuse of its functions that was criticized, especially the inaccessibility of the Prince Regent and the use of his name as a shield by ministers.[4] The *Manchester Observer* just before Peterloo expressed 'the firmest attachment' to the royal family.[5]

The Radical attitude to religion and the church was similar in pattern to its attitude to monarchy, some extremist rejection but more criticism of abuses. The Anglican clergy were urged to follow their proper callings, 'to practice as well as preach the true principles of Christianity', and to cease upholding the Tory

[1] Letter from Joseph Johnson in the *Manchester Observer*, June 19, 1819.
[2] Kinsey, 120.
[3] 'They did not wish to meddle with the Royal Family, except to reduce their incomes' (speech of Harrison at Rochdale, *Manchester Chronicle*, July 31, 1819).
[4] 'Whereas the Ministers of this country, abusing the sacred trust reposed in them for the public welfare, have perverted the high authority assumed by the Prince Regent . . . to purposes of individual ambition and national oppression . . .' (beginning of the Manchester Declaration).
[5] *Manchester Observer*, Aug. 14, 1819.

government by preaching the doctrine of passive obedience before ministerial abuses.[1] Hunt had to admit that some of the reformers were deists,[2] but deism was probably confined to a few only of the Radical leaders and like repulicanism it was merely on the fringe of the movement.[3] The Radicals sought hard to win non-Anglican support. Tithes were attacked;[4] a Radical Sunday school was opened in Manchester for all denominations;[5] Methodists were reminded of the hostility of Lord Sidmouth, the Home Secretary, as evidenced by his Bill of 1811 for the licensing of Nonconformist preachers;[6] and Roman Catholics were offered emancipation.[7]

This by no means concludes the list of Radical grievances; the government had many other shortcomings in Radical eyes in 1819 apart from those mentioned. The Manchester Remonstrance and Declaration listed most of them. The government, complained the Remonstrance, had refused to receive petitions, it had encouraged arbitrary arrests, it had employed *agents-provocateurs*, it had suspended the laws, and much else. Also it was corrupt and boroughmongering: ministers and M.P.s had no time for popular complaints because they were 'so busy filling their pockets and bellies at the public expense'.[8]

Did all these shortcomings in government mean then that the Radical Reformers in 1819 considered themselves justified in repudiating allegiance and urging revolution? The answer to this question is of vital importance in the present context, for the Manchester magistrates rested their justification for the massacre on the contention that the Peterloo meeting was called as part of a revolutionary design. Certainly, some of the Radical language before Peterloo was very threatening in tone. The Remonstrance in January had reminded the Prince Regent that rebellion in the past had arisen not from the turbulence of the people but from the misconduct of ministers. And at a meeting a fortnight earlier J. T. Saxton had called on every man 'TO ARM HIMSELF—(applause)

---

[1] See above, p. 32.
[2] *Manchester Observer*, Nov. 13, 1819.
[3] Kinsey, 120.
[4] *Manchester Observer*, Nov. 28, 1818, May 1, 1819.
[5] See below, pp. 53–54.
[6] *Manchester Observer*, Nov. 27, 1819.
[7] *Ibid.*, May 1, Nov. 20, 1819.
[8] *Ibid.*, June 19, 1819.

—with the powerful weapons of reason. TO PRESENT—(applause)—*his firm remonstrance to the Throne*—and TO FIRE!—(applause)—*with the noble indignation of Britons determined to be free or die*[1]. But all this was merely in the realm of words, and due allowance must be made for the excitements of the moment. Radical language often outran Radical intention: the considered intentions of the Radicals were much more restrained than their occasional violent outbursts might suggest. 'Far be it from me so much as to insinuate', wrote Jeremy Bentham a month before Peterloo, 'that in anything they *do*, howsoever may be the case with some things which they *say*, there is so much as a tendency to excite in the people, as towards the said Government and Constitution, any such sentiment as *contempt.*'[2] The Radical Reformers, declared the *Manchester Observer* two days before the massacre, were 'decidedly inimical to a forcible revolution'.

Leaving aside then these occasional aberrations in language, it is clear that the Radical Reformers in 1819 were expounding a highly detailed and peaceable programme of reform, many aspects of which were linked together in quite intricate sequences of argument.[3] The Radicals believed that political science was 'no longer . . . a subject too profound and abstruse for ordinary capacities': the authority due to governors and the liberties of the governed, the prerogatives of the Crown, the privileges of the aristocracy, and the rights of the people were all now 'as familiar to the lowest as to the highest ranks in society'.[4] It was this confidence in working-class intelligence and perception which lay behind the detail of the Radical programme. The banners on the hustings at Peterloo reflected no empty platitudes: 'Annual Parliaments', 'Universal Suffrage', 'No Corn Laws', 'No Borough-mongering', and the rest of the slogans which they carried were the outward expressions of a coherent and highly developed programme of reform.

---

[1] *Manchester Observer*, Jan. 9, 1819.   [2] *Ibid.*, July 31, 1819.
[3] For example, a sequence of argument attacking distress, the Corn Laws, high taxation, and the Combination Laws: 'the master manufacturers being affected by dear bread and increased taxation, their profits must be increased to meet their increased demands, and therefore the workmen must be reduced to lower wages, and not combine, on pain of imprisonment; and if they will not work at the masters' prices, they must perish' (*ibid.*, July 17, 1819).
[4] Prospectus of the *Manchester Spectator*, Nov. 7, 1818. A short-lived Radical rival to the *Manchester Observer*.

Nor was this detailed programme merely local in its conception. It was not simply a collection of local grievances locally fought for, but was in essentials very much the same as the contemporary Radical programme in other parts of the country. Comparison with the resolutions passed at the three other great Radical meetings which preceded Peterloo, held at Birmingham on July 12th, at Leeds on July 19th, and at Smithfield, London, on July 21st, shows few differences of purpose. Annual Parliaments, Universal Suffrage, and repeal of the Corn Laws were the great goals of all the Radical meetings, large and small, held throughout the country in 1819. The Radical programme which the Peterloo meeting was called to support was a national one and the Lancashire Radicals were part of a national movement.

The Radical programme was spread abroad in 1819 through three main channels, through Union Societies, through public meetings, and through the Radical Press. The Union Societies were political clubs, groups of working-men meeting together 'for the purpose [in the words of the Oldham delegate meeting] of acquiring and diffusing political information'. They partly took as their models the Hampden Clubs of 1816–17, whose history is better known and who played a large part in Manchester in the preparation of the March of the Blanketeers.[1] The Hampden Clubs do not seem, however, to have survived the failure of this march, and none of them was left in existence by the beginning of 1819.[2] In their place had appeared the Union Societies, destined to play a vital part in the organization of the Peterloo meeting.

The first Union Society was founded at Stockport in October 1818 with the ambitious title of the Stockport Union for the Promotion of Human Happiness. Its rules were the work of the Reverend Joseph Harrison, the Nonconformist Radical preacher already mentioned. They were extremely detailed. They laid down that the town was to be divided up into twelve sections, each section to elect by ballot two members of a general committee; half this committee was to go out of office every three months, and it was to select from among its members a Union President,

---

[1] See below, p. 97 ff..
[2] At the Manchester meeting of Jan. 18, 1819, Mitchell, one of the Radical leaders, urged the formation of Union Societies in a manner which made it clear that there were no Hampden Clubs left in the area.

a Vice-President, a Secretary, and a Treasurer. The Secretary and the Treasurer were to serve during the committee's pleasure, but the President and Vice-President were to hold office for one week only, all committee members serving by rotation. Each section of the town was to be divided into classes of twelve members with class leaders elected for three months by their classes, each class meeting once a week. Members of classes were to pay one penny a week to their class leaders, and every Monday evening the class leaders were to pay these receipts to the general committee and to receive their instructions for the week. Central meeting rooms were to be provided for lecturing, reading, and conversation. They were to be open on Wednesday evenings for reading, and on Monday, Tuesday, Thursday, and Friday evenings for the instruction of adults in reading, writing, and arithmetic. On Saturday evenings the rooms were to be open for the recitation of 'moral and political pieces' learnt by the children of members. And on Sunday mornings and afternoons the rooms were to be open for the instruction of these children in the same subjects as their elders were taught during the week. A library was to be formed as soon as funds permitted, and as soon as convenient a Union representative (elected annually) was to be sent to London to conduct its business there, 'such as presenting our Petitions and Remonstrances to the Chief Magistrate', and also to 'act in conjunction with other Union delegates there'. With such an organization, the rules concluded, every member would have the chance to become adequately trained 'to promote by all just means in his power, a radical reform of Parliament, by means of suffrage in all male persons of mature age and sane minds, . . . of Parliaments having a duration not exceeding one year, and of Elections by ballot'.[1]

Such were the extremely detailed rules drawn up for the conduct of the business of political reform by the Stockport Radicals in 1818. Their significance was not merely local, for they became (and this was what made them so particularly important) the model for scores of similar societies formed throughout the country during 1819.

Set up in rivalry with Harrison's Union in Stockport was another Society following the rules of the 'Political Protestants'

---

[1] *Manchester Observer*, May 8, 1819.

of Hull. This Hull Society was established in July 1818 and so named because it proposed to protest 'against the mockery of our indisputable right to a real Representation'.[1] Its rules were not so detailed as those of the Unions following Harrison's plan. Political ignorance, the Political Protestants declared, was the cause of all present misery: 'We shall, therefore, meet once a week, in small classes, not exceeding twenty in each Class, and subscribe One Penny each, for the purpose of purchasing such means of information as may be required.' Class leaders were to meet once a month 'to report the progress of the Institution', and books and accounts were to lie open 'for the inspection of Magistrates or others'.[2]

The Hull rules were thus much less detailed and systematic than the Stockport rules. Both took up the Methodist device of class meetings,[3] but the Political Protestants concentrated mainly on the mutual acquisition of political information, whereas Unions on the Stockport model pursued a policy of nightly indoctrination with a whole hierarchy of officers and representatives. These Stockport rules clearly left much more room for the semi-professional Radical politicians; with their greater organization they were also better suited to the national effort which the Radicals were making in 1819, and it is not surprising to find them in a large majority in the Manchester area.

By the early summer of 1819 the concentration of Societies was very great. 'These Societies seem to be a principal object in the adjoining townships', reported Norris, the Manchester stipendiary magistrate, early in May.[4] The Oldham district alone had Unions in Chadderton, Lees, Mossley, Saddleworth, and Royton as well as in Oldham itself;[7] and there were similar bodies (mostly on the Stockport model) in nearly all the towns about Manchester, most of which sent contingents of reformers to Peterloo. When the meeting of local Union delegates was called at Oldham on June 7,

---

[1] *Black Dwarf*, Sept. 2, 1818.
[2] *Ibid.*, Aug. 19, 1818.
[3] 'They have adopted almost the whole Methodist economy, the terms "Class Leaders", "District Meetings", etc. etc., being perfectly current among them' (letter from a Newcastle Methodist to Jabez Bunting, President of the Methodist Conference, 1820. T. P. Bunting, *The Life of Jabez Bunting* (1887), II, 167).
[4] Norris to Sidmouth, May 20, 1819 (H.O. 42/187).
[5] A. Marcroft, *Landmarks of Local Liberalism* (1913), 43–44.

1819, no less than twenty-eight towns were represented.[1] And what was especially striking, Unions on the Stockport model were springing up far beyond Manchester, as far away as Carlisle, Newcastle, Glasgow, London, and Birmingham.[2] The rules of the Stockport Union had given a lead to Radicalism throughout the country.

What purpose, it may be asked, lay behind these many Unions? Preparation for responsibility was the purpose given by Mitchell, one of the Radical leaders, at the Manchester meeting in January 1819. If the people's strength were organized and trained, he declared, it would not be misapplied when they came to power. 'We are endeavouring most assiduously to inform ourselves, and others, by all means in our power', wrote a Union member from Oldham, 'that when we are called upon by circumstances we may be able to act as lovers of our country, and mankind.' [3] The ultimate aim of the Radical Reformers thus went far beyond the objectives mentioned in the Stockport rules, the objectives of Universal Suffrage, Annual Parliaments, and Vote by Ballot. It looked on to Universal Suffrage not only gained but operating: having come to power the people must be ready to use that power rightly.

This concern for the future explains the great stress laid by the Union Societies on education, both for adults and for children. In making careful provision for the education of children, the Stockport rules hoped to ensure that if the Radicals failed in this generation, they would succeed in the next. As for the adults, it was essential to ensure that the operatives could read the Radical Press, that they could manage the accounts of the Union Societies, and that they could speak out in the cause of reform. Instruction in public speaking and in reading, writing, and arithmetic was

[1] Representatives attended from:

Manchester	Dewsbury	Todmorden	Lees
Rochdale	Barnsley	Blackburn	Mossley
Huddersfield	Middleton	Leeds	Holmfirth
Stockport	New Mills	Wakefield	Failsworth
Oldham	Royton	Macclesfield	Heyside
Stalybridge	Bury	Ashton	Whitefield
Treaclestreet	Heywood	Gee Cross	Leigh

(*Manchester Observer*, June 12, 1819)

[2] Kinsey, 51.
[3] *Black Dwarf*, June 2, 1819.

therefore a prominent feature in the life of the Unions. Lectures or classes of some sort were held nearly every night:

The plan laid down in the rules [wrote a Stockport member] by which the Stockport Union proposes to obtain its object, is by delivering moral and political readings occasionally, moral and political readings weekly, [and] moral and political readings in the several classes.

The class meetings were the basis of this whole system of teaching and indoctrination:

in the class I belong to [went on the Stockport member] we generally read at a class meeting for about half an hour, if there is anything in the course of the reading that anyone present does not understand, it is fully explained to him . . . After reading, a general conversation takes place for about half an hour more, when each member states his opinion and ideas of government, etc. etc.[1]

Just when the first Union was formed in Manchester is not certain. James Norris, the Manchester stipendiary magistrate, reported on May 20, 1819, 'we have one Union Society', and this must have been the Patriotic Union Society, the Society which invited Hunt to Manchester for the Peterloo meeting.[2] Norris enclosed with his report a copy of the Stockport rules, which suggests (as is not surprising) that the Union was established on the Stockport model. Possibly it began on March 14th at the same time as the Union Sunday School which met in the same place, the Union Rooms in George Leigh Street, Ancoats.[3] Johnson in one of his voluntary examinations said that the George Leigh Street Union was 'the central Union Society' for 'a number' of Societies established in the Manchester area. This suggests that the Patriotic Union was either strong enough to have founded several dependent Unions of its own or important enough to have had a number of outlying Unions deliberately linked with it for operational purposes. Certainly its personnel was distinguished, for in August 1819, according to Johnson, Knight was its Secretary and Wroe its Treasurer; Johnson himself had been its Secretary before Peterloo.[4]

By the autumn of 1819 there was at least one other Union in

[1] *Sherwin's Political Register*, June 5, 1819.
[2] There is an Address from this Union in the *Manchester Observer* for May 29, 1819.
[3] See below, p. 54.
[4] Johnson's voluntary examinations (H.O. 42/192).

Manchester besides the Patriotic. This Union was ultra-Radical in tone, and its foundation was probably stimulated by the refusal of the Huntite Patriotic Union to support the calling of another meeting in the Manchester area after Peterloo. Hunt forbade this lest it should give the authorities the excuse to perpetrate another massacre.[1] The leading spirit behind the ultra Union was its Secretary, W. C. Walker; like the Patriotic Union it met in the George Leigh Street Union Rooms.[2] Just how many operatives were involved in the two Unions in Manchester or in the others elsewhere it is difficult to say, for membership figures are not easily available. Membership of the ultra-Radical Union in Manchester was probably upwards of six hundred at its highest in the late autumn of 1819 and that of the older-established and more moderate Patriotic Union considerably higher. Both these totals are striking considering the nature and origins of the Societies.[3]

Running the Unions must have been expensive. At Oldham, wrote a correspondent to the *Black Dwarf*, money for hiring a room had to be found and forms and desks had to be bought; it is not surprising, therefore, to find him admitting that the Union was not able to call many public meetings because they were 'expensive' to organize.[4] Even Harrison's powerful Stockport Union felt the strain: 'as the cause of reform advances', he wrote, 'it becomes more and more expensive, and the means more and

---

[1] See below, ch. IX.
[2] For a description by a government informant of two meetings of the ultra-Radical Union, see Appendix B.
[3] The above informant said that at the meeting of November 2nd over fifty collectors of sections were present and that each section had twenty-five members each paying one penny per week. Assuming that all the sections were up to strength, this would give 1250 members. On November 25th Norris reported to Sidmouth (H.O. 42/199) that the weekly subscriptions at the Manchester Union amounted to 'about £6'. At a penny a week per member this gives 1440 members; but unfortunately Norris did not say to which Union he referred. However, the government informant said that about two hundred members were present at the ultra-Radical Union meeting of November 2nd, and a ratio of two members absent to one present would not seem unreasonable. Thus we get a very approximate membership figure of six hundred for the ultra-Radical Union, which is well under either of the totals calculated above and may therefore be a considerable underestimate. In any case, the Huntites had a much greater following in Manchester and their Patriotic Union would certainly have a much larger membership than this.
[4] *Black Dwarf*, June 2, 1819.

more circumscribed . . . The weavers are the best givers; but, alas, they have nothing to give now'.[1]

But though their finances may have been strained, the value of the Union Societies to the Radicals is evident. Meeting together in clubs gave a corporate spirit to the movement and the opportunity for planning concerted action. The frequent calls to form Unions, and the later calls to keep them alive,[2] show how important the Union Societies were in the Radical organization: the authorities saw them as one of the greatest dangers to civil peace.

As well as Union Societies for men, similar Societies for women were being formed in Lancashire by the end of June, 1819. The first female Society was probably established at Blackburn, but Stockport and Manchester were not far behind, and female Unions subsequently spread over a wide area.[3] Even more than that of the male Unions, the purpose of these female Societies was instructional: their aim was to indoctrinate the children with Radical ideas. The rules of the Blackburn female Union (which served as a model for many others) pledged members 'to instil into the minds of our children, a deep and rooted hatred of our corrupt and tyrannical Rulers'.[4] The female Unions were thus yet another instrument devised for the spreading of instruction in Radical ways of thought.

The children were not only approached through the female Unions or through the classes held for children at the male Union Societies. Separate Sunday schools with Radical connections were also established in Manchester, Stockport, Oldham, Macclesfield, and elsewhere during 1819. In Manchester, for example, a non-denominational Union Sunday School 'for the purpose [in the words of its introductory advertisement] of instructing adults and youths of both sexes in those essential qualifications Reading, Writing, and Arithmetic' was opened on March 14, 1819.[5] From this advertisement the Radical connections of the school were not readily apparent: indeed, it was never admitted that the school had any such connections. Politics, declared J. E. Taylor, a middle-

---

[1] *Annual Register, 1820*, Appendix to Chronicle, 910.
[2] See below, p. 159.
[3] Kinsey, 66–71; *Annual Register, 1819*, General History, 104; *Manchester Observer*, July 31, 1819.
[4] *Manchester Observer*, June 26, 1819.
[5] *Manchester Observer*, March 6, 1819.

class Radical, were 'sedulously and invariably avoided' in the school;[1] the only books used, wrote P. T. Candelet, its 'Conductor', were the Bible, a Testament and a normal Sunday school spelling-book.[2] It is significant, however, that Candelet was a well-known local Radical figure, that the school met in the Radical Union Rooms in George Leigh Street, and that the monitors (as the Radical newspaper itself admitted) wore locket-portraits of Hunt round their necks in place of crucifixes.[3] Though 'loyalist' critics may have been wrong in confusing the Union Sunday School with the Patriotic Union Society which met in the same place and in denying the existence of any religious purpose at all in the school,[4] it seems certain that its proceedings were conducted in an atmosphere of political Radicalism and that the Christianity which it taught was of the kind which (as John Bagguley had put it a year before) saw Jesus Christ as 'the Greatest Reformer'.[5]

Though the Union Societies flourished in 1819 their membership cannot have been large when compared with the total number of operatives. To reach a wider public the Radical Reformers had recourse to two other channels for the dissemination of their ideas, to public meetings and to the Press.

The most important Radical meetings in 1819 apart from Peterloo were those held at Oldham on January 4th, at Manchester on January 18th, at Stockport on February 15th, at Ashton on June 14th, at Manchester again on June 21st, at Stockport again on June 28th, and at Rochdale on July 26th. The resolutions passed at all these meetings were deliberately similar. The Remonstrance passed at Manchester on January 18th was copied almost word for word at the Stockport meeting of a month

[1] Taylor, 78–79.

[2] *Manchester Observer*, Jan. 22, 1820.

[3] *Ibid.*, Jan. 29, 1819.

[4] The Hon. H. G. Bennet, M.P., the mouthpiece of the Manchester middle-class Radicals in the Commons (see below, p. 166 ff.) wrote that the Union Societies were being 'wilfully confounded' with the Union Sunday Schools (Bennet to Shuttleworth, Dec. 11, 1819. Shuttleworth Scrapbook; see also Taylor, 178–79).

For the 'loyalist' viewpoint, see [Rev. C. Burtone], *An Appeal to the Public on the Subject of the Union Sunday Schools* (1820), and his letter to Sidmouth, Jan. 19, 1820 (H.O. 42/203); *Manchester Chronicle*, Nov. 27, 1819.

[5] Lloyd to Hobhouse, Aug. 11, 1818, enclosure (H.O. 42/179).

later: the resolutions of the Stockport meeting of June 28th were almost the same as those passed a fortnight before at Ashton.[1] The speakers at the meetings were likewise similar: Knight, Harrison, and Saxton were the most active with a regular round of engagements. These same men went about reiterating the same arguments time and time again: it was their obvious purpose to publicize one coherent programme of Radical Reform throughout the area.

After the Radical meetings came the reports in the Radical Press. The role of the Radical newspapers in 1819 was an especially important one. For the already converted they had to publicize the 'Letters', 'Addresses', and speeches of the various Radical leaders giving instructions for the organization of the Radical campaign; and for the many still unconverted (who neither attended the Radical meetings nor were members of Union Societies) they had to try to expound the Radical creed.[2]

The authorities recognized the importance of the Radical Press by striving hard to suppress its publications. They tried especially hard to suppress the *Manchester Observer*, the leading Radical organ in the area. Norris, the Manchester stipendiary magistrate, arranged for copies to be sent up regularly to the Home Office for scrutiny; it was, he wrote, 'the organ of the lower classes' and its purpose was 'to inflame' their minds.[3] The paper had been founded at the beginning of 1818 and appeared every Saturday price 7d.;[4] its chief proprietor and editor at the time of Peterloo was James Wroe, a leading local Radical figure already noticed. Wroe bore the brunt of the government's suppressive policy; five indictments for seditious publication were found against him in July 1819 and two more at Michaelmas.[5] At its height in the autumn of 1819 the circulation of the *Observer* was between three and four thousand copies per week, a very large figure for the period.[6] And this circulation was not confined to Lancashire: Hunt recommended the *Observer* as 'the *only* newspaper in England . . . fairly and

---

[1] *Manchester Observer*, Feb. 20, 1819; *Annual Register 1820*, Appendix to Chronicle, 910.

[2] *Manchester Observer*, Jan. 15, 1820.

[3] Norris to Sidmouth, June 10, 1819 (H.O. 42/188).

[4] All the Manchester newspapers in 1819 were weeklies; 4d. of the 7d. in price was Stamp Duty.

[5] Kinsey, 14–15; Wickwar, *op. cit.*, 103–04.

[6] *Manchester Observer*, Aug. 28, 1819; *An Address to the Higher Classes*, 18.

honestly devoted to such a reform as would give the people their whole rights'.[1] The number of its agents in distant towns grew steadily throughout 1819[2] so that by the autumn the organ of the Lancashire Radicals was exerting an influence not only in Lancashire but throughout the country at large.[3]

A Radical Press, Radical public meetings, Radical schools and societies, a Radical political programme—the extent of Radical activity in Lancashire in 1819 was obviously very great. In itself this partly explains (though it cannot justify) the panic of the local authorities at Peterloo. And while the Manchester magistrates restricted their gaze to Lancashire, Lord Sidmouth and the government at Westminster could see a similar pattern of Radical activity throughout half the country, and were in consequence all the more concerned. The disturbed counties listed in the Arms Act passed at the end of the year included most of the Midlands, all of the north of England, and most of the industrial districts of Scotland.[4] Lancashire Radicalism was only part of this national pattern of Radical activity: we have seen how its Press, its Union Societies, and its political programme all had national connections. The Radical background to Peterloo was nation-wide.

---

[1] *Manchester Observer*, Aug. 14, 1819.

[2] The growth of the influence of the *Manchester Observer* can be illustrated from the lists it gave periodically of its outlying agents. In May 1819 it had agents at:

Bury	Chorley	Preston	Rochdale
Blackburn	Wigan	Liverpool	Huddersfield
Burnley	Stockport	London	

(May 15, 1819.)

By August it had acquired additional agents at Sheffield, Birmingham, Haslingden, and Uttoxeter (Aug. 7, 1819). By November still more agents had been added at:

Halifax	Loughborough	Leigh	Darwin
Wakefield	Hull	Carlisle	Whitehaven
Lymm	Colne	Sunderland	Glasgow
Nottingham	Bradford	Macclesfield	

(Nov. 13, 1819.)

[3] Along with the *Observer* several other Radical prints enjoyed large local circulations about the time of Peterloo; Wroe published at least three other successful Radical periodicals, the *Argus*, the *White Hat*, and the *Peterloo Massacre* (F. Leary, 'History of the Manchester Periodical Press', 131–32). London publications were equally popular: 'We have got down here bales of *Cobbetts*, *Sherwins*, *Black Dwarfs*, and *Medusas*', reported a *Times* correspondent just after the massacre (*The Times*, Aug. 25, 1819).

[4] *Parliamentary Debates*, XLI (1819–20), 1651.

CHAPTER FIVE

THE MIDDLE-CLASS RADICALS

UNLIKE the working-class Radicals, the middle-class Radical Reformers in Manchester in 1819 controlled no extensive network of agitation. They remained no more than a group of like-minded friends—'a small but determined band' [1]—who often worked together for the reform of abuses. In 1819, furthermore, even as a pressure group they were only at the beginning of their influence. Most of them were still young men, only at the outset of careers which were to have a very great influence on the life of Manchester during the first half of the nineteenth century. Most of them were Dissenters in religion, especially Unitarians, and were associated with the cotton trade in business; few of them had been born in Manchester. [2]

[1] Prentice, 74.
[2] The following were the leading members of the group:

Name	Dates Birthplace	Occupation in 1819. Remarks	Religion
Joseph Brotherton	1783–1857 Chesterfield	Master spinner. First M.P. for Salford (1832–57)	Swedenborgian
William Harvey	1787–1870 Leeds	Master spinner Mayor of Salford (1857–59)	
Thomas Potter	1773–1845 Tadcaster	Cotton merchant. First Mayor of Manchester (1838–40)	Unitarian
F. R. Atkinson	1784–1859 Leeds	Attorney	
J. B. Smith	1794–1879	Cotton dealer M.P. for Stirling (1847–1852), for Stockport (1852–74)	Unitarian
Absalom Watkin	1787–1861 London	Cotton manufacturer	Anglican
Edward Baxter	?1779–1856	Cotton manufacturer	Unitarian
J. E. Taylor	1791–1844 Ilminster	Cotton merchant	Unitarian
Richard Potter	1778–1842 Tadcaster	Cotton merchant	Unitarian
John Shuttleworth	1786–1864 Manchester	Cotton dealer	Unitarian
Archibald Prentice	1792–1857 Lanarkshire	Cotton manufacturer	Presbyterian

(Prentice, 72–74; Axon, *Annals*, *passim*; D.N.B.; Pigot and Dean, *op. cit.*; Cobbett, *Rural Rides* (ed. Cole), Index of Persons; J. T. Slugg, *Reminiscences of Manchester Fifty Years Ago* (1881), 173–75; A. Watkin, *Extracts from His Journal 1814–1856*, ed. A. E. Watkin (1920); Marshall, 224.)

By the time of Peterloo only three of the group had already achieved prominence—J. E. Taylor, Richard Potter, and John Shuttleworth.

John Edward Taylor (1791–1844)[1] was born at Ilminster in Somerset and came to Manchester with his schoolmaster father in 1805. He èarly showed a keen interest in the Lancasterian School movement and became secretary to the local committee in 1810. Soon afterwards he began also to take an interest in politics, contributing to the London newspapers and writing frequently in the *Manchester Gazette*: his articles in this latter paper were said to have nearly quadrupled its circulation. After Peterloo Taylor published a long pamphlet entitled *Notes and Explanations, Critical and Explanatory, On the Papers Relative to the Internal State of the Country, recently Presented to Parliament*. This was the most lucid exposition of the middle-class Radical response to Peterloo.

In 1819 Taylor was still listed in the Manchester directory as a cotton merchant; but his real interests lay more in writing and in politics than in trade, and in 1821, after thinking of taking up the law, he undertook the editorship of the new *Manchester Guardian*. He proved an able editor, and before his death had made the *Guardian* into one of the leading provincial papers. As its columns showed, Taylor came increasingly in later life to modify the advanced Radical attitude which he had taken up in 1819, and in consequence in the years after 1821 he gradually fell out of sympathy with his friends of the Peterloo period. Taylor's writing both in the *Manchester Guardian* and in his Peterloo pamphlet shows him to have been a man of considerable intellectual capacity and clarity of mind.

Richard Potter (1778–1842),[2] born at Tadcaster in Yorkshire, was rather older than most of the group. He and his elder brother Thomas, subsequently the first Mayor of Manchester, were engaged together in 1819 as cotton merchants. While Thomas looked after the business Richard gave much of his time to politics and he came to be known in the town as 'Radical Dick'. His particular interest about the time of Peterloo was in the exposure of abuses in local government and he was the leader of a vigorous middle-

---

[1] *D.N.B.* is the main source for details of Taylor's career. For a fuller account see my forthcoming history of the *Manchester Guardian*.

[2] G. Meinertzhagen, *From Ploughshare to Parliament* (1908), and Cobbett, *Rural Rides* (ed. Cole), Index of Persons, are the main sources for details of Potter's career.

class Radical attack in this field after the massacre.[1] In 1821 he and his brother Thomas were two of the small group which lent money to Taylor to start the *Manchester Guardian*. After the passing of the Reform Act, the local agitation for which he strongly supported, Potter became M.P. for Wigan (1832–39). His obituary notice in the *Manchester Guardian* (perhaps written by Taylor) suggests that he was a man of great application and sincerity rather than one possessed of great natural ability.[2]

John Shuttleworth (1786–1864)[3] was one of the few members of the group to have been born in Manchester where he spent his life engaged as a cotton dealer (for a time in partnership with Taylor). Like Taylor, Shuttleworth achieved prominence at an early age. He spoke at the Manchester Anti-Corn Law meeting of 1815 and served on the committee appointed to prepare the petition of protest.[4] In 1814 he had spoken in support of the Lancasterian School in Manchester,[5] and about the time of Peterloo education seems to have been his particular interest. He was a prominent defender of the Union Sunday School against charges of being tainted with Radicalism, and in 1821 he published a detailed survey of the state of Sunday school education in the town in the first number of the *Manchester Guardian*.

Shuttleworth played a very prominent part in the local agitation in support of the Reform Bill. When the final bill looked as though it was about to be lost in the Lords, he presided at the meeting which took the bold step of organizing the famous Manchester petition urging the Commons to refuse supplies until the measure was passed. He and Richard Potter were members of the delegation which took the petition up to London.[6] In 1834 Shuttleworth was appointed to the office of local distributor of stamps as a reward for his political services, and in 1838 he became one of Manchester's first group of aldermen. He was a good public speaker, 'cackling Shuttleworth' to his enemy Cobbett, 'eloquent, intellectual, and bold' according to his friend Prentice.[6] In

---

[1] See below, p. 169 ff..

[2] *Manchester Guardian*, July 16, 1842.

[3] *Ibid.*, April 28, 1864 and Cobbett, *Rural Rides* (ed. Cole), Index of Persons, are the sources for details of Shuttleworth's career.

[4] *Manchester Gazette*, March 4, 1815.

[5] *Exchange Herald*, Feb. 8, 1814.

[6] *Manchester Times and Gazette*, May 19, 1832; Prentice, 370, 396, 408.

[7] Cobbett, *Rural Rides* (ed. Cole), III, 790; Prentice, 74; Slugg, *op. cit.*, 174.

religion Shuttleworth, Taylor, and the Potters were all active Unitarians.[1]

Another member of the middle-class Radical group not yet especially prominent in 1819 but soon to become a leading figure in the political life of Manchester, was Archibald Prentice (1792–1857).[2] Prentice was born in Lanarkshire, but came to Manchester in 1815 to take charge of a muslin warehouse. He soon joined the middle-class Radical circle in the town and began writing for the *Manchester Gazette*. In 1821 he helped to found the *Manchester Guardian*, and three years later himself entered the newspaper field by purchasing the *Manchester Gazette*, the *Guardian* having become too tentative for him in its opinions. After the failure of the *Gazette* in 1828 he became editor of the *Manchester Times*, and his connection with this paper lasted until his retirement in 1847. The tone of both papers under his influence was advanced Radical, pressing especially for repeal of the Corn Laws and for parliamentary reform. During the Reform Bill agitation Prentice was a leading spirit behind one of the Manchester Political Unions, and ten years later he was a prominent supporter of the Complete Suffrage movement. In 1838 he helped to found the Anti-Corn Law League which he strongly supported throughout its career.[3]

After his retirement Prentice published two important books describing local politics during his lifetime: *Historical Sketches and Personal Recollections of Manchester Intended to Illustrate the Progress of Public Opinion from 1792 to 1832* (1851) and a *History of the Anti-Corn Law League* (1853). He was a fluent and earnest writer, and the former work is invaluable for the student of the history of Manchester about the time of Peterloo.

Personally, Prentice seems to have been rather dogmatic in his opinions and perhaps a little over-assertive. Jeremy Bentham, whom Prentice greatly admired, described him as 'juggical: Calvinistic: as descended from two parsonical grandfathers of considerable notoriety'; but his deep sincerity was also apparent, and Bentham concluded: 'My opinion of him upon the whole after

[1] Slugg, *op. cit.*, 173–74.
[2] R. Dunlop, 'Archibald Prentice, a Forgotten Page of Journalism', *Macmillan's Magazine*, LX (1889) is a useful short biographical sketch.
[3] Prentice, 368–69; A. Briggs, 'The Background of the Parliamentary Reform Movement in Three English Cities (1830–2)', *Cambridge Historical Journal*, X (1952), 304–08.

a careful scrutiny is—that he is well-intentioned, serious, generous, zealous and disinterested.' [1]

These four men were the leaders of the middle-class Radical group in Manchester about the time of Peterloo, leaders who took an interest in virtually every aspect of affairs, not only political but also literary and scientific. In the years before Peterloo this interest had been cultivated in a number of small clubs, and it was there that the middle-class Radical leaders received their early training in public expression. The chief of these clubs was the Junior Literary and Philosophical Society, founded in rivalry with the famous senior body of the same name of which only Prentice among the reformers was a member in 1819.[2] Other clubs supported by the group were the Literary and Scientific and the Sciolous.[3] It was in societies such as these that the middle-class Radicals received instruction in the principles of Adam Smith, Joseph Priestley, and Jeremy Bentham from the survivors of the Manchester reform movement of the 1790's, men like Robert Philips and Samuel Greg. Through them they carried on the tradition of reform in Manchester.[4]

A leading member of the clubs was Absalom Watkin, later prominent in the local Reform Bill agitation and a friend of John Bright. He was of a serious cast of mind, and in 1810, at the age of twenty-three, he had felt it necessary to draw up for himself a detailed plan of life. He proposed for the next eleven years to devote at least three hours every day to 'reading, meditation or composition' so as to give himself a thorough grounding in divinity, history, natural and experimental philosophy, geography, and law; then, at the age of thirty-five, to travel about the world for seven years, and finally on his return to publish an account of his travels. He would then consider how he might do most good, using the experience he had acquired to promote 'to the utmost of my power, the spread of religion, and the happiness of my fellow creatures'.[5]

---

[1] Bentham to Place, April 24, 1831 (Add. Mss. 35149 ff. 73–74).
[2] Prentice became a member of the senior society in January 1819, Taylor in April 1828, and Shuttleworth in October 1835 (*Complete list of the Members and Officers of the Manchester Literary and Philosophical Society* [1896]).
[3] Watkin, *Fragment No. I*, (1874), 25.
[4] Prentice, 73; Marshall, 131.
[5] Watkin, *Fragment No. I*, 9–16.

All this was typical of the high seriousness of the middle-class Radical group. It arose especially from a feeling among the group's members of the importance of their mission: they regarded themselves as the intelligentsia of local society, as the missionaries of a new enlightenment. They alone, they believed, understood the problems of the time and understood the remedies for them. The weight of this self-imposed burden necessarily predisposed them to seriousness.

Fundamentally, the middle-class remedy for the problems of the time was Benthamite in origin: the movement drew heavily on the Utilitarians. Bentham's writings, declared Prentice, were his 'political textbooks' and his great aim in Manchester was to be 'instrumental in popularising some of his doctrines'.[1] The whole general purpose of the group's political programme was a rational reorganization of government, national and local, along Benthamite lines. The Manchester reformers sought the removal of all monopolies of power and the equalization of opportunities for influence in political affairs, believing this to be the only way to secure the maximum possible happiness for humanity.

Believing that the object of legislation and government ought to be to produce THE GREATEST HAPPINESS TO THE GREATEST NUMBER [wrote Prentice in the *Manchester Gazette* six years after Peterloo], we shall, in all our political discussions, keep that object before us, as a land mark towards which to steer amidst the storm raised by contending parties.[2]

For support for their Benthamite programme the middle-class Radicals looked in two opposite directions, on the one side to the cotton masters, and on the other to the cotton operatives. By showing these two apparently rival classes that they really had interests and grievances in common the middle-class reformers hoped to persuade them to act together in politics, and in this way to create for themselves a substantial (indeed a preponderant) political following in Manchester. This purpose they pursued throughout the 1820's and '30's, although they were never fully successful in it.

Taylor's *Notes and Explanations* inspired by Peterloo was the earliest comprehensive expression of this dual aim. Taylor asked on the one hand for greater trust in the people, and on the other

---

[1] Prentice, 379.
[2] *Manchester Gazette*, Dec. 31, 1825.

for greater participation by the middle classes in politics. If the middle-class cotton employers could be roused from their political apathy and could at the same time be persuaded that the working classes were politically reliable, Taylor saw that the middle-class Radical group would be well on its way to achieving the desired political co-operation between the two classes. Peterloo was itself, he argued, largely the outcome of the failure of operatives and masters to act together: 'where [the middle-classes] have in any considerable proportion thrown their weight into the same scale with the labouring classes, a more conciliatory mode of conduct must be adopted, than that which has recently been in fashion'.[1]

The Benthamite political programme with which the middle-class reformers hoped to win this two-sided support had three basic points: the reform of parliament, the institution of a system of cheap and efficient government, and the introduction of a system of free trade (including in particular the repeal of the Corn Laws). This is not the place to consider this programme in its later comprehensiveness: at the time of Peterloo the middle-class reformers were only at the very beginning of their careers and their programme was not then being expressed with the detail or the cohesion which it later achieved. For the most part, only those arguments which they were already employing in 1819 can be noticed here.

On the parliamentary reform question the middle-class reformers published their views in the *Manchester Gazette* only nine days before Peterloo. Their position was somewhat difficult since they accepted most of the ends of the Huntite reformers but disapproved strongly of their means. They were 'anxiously desirous ... of a rational and moderate, but at the same time, radical reform in the representation of the people'; but they conceded that most of the recent proceedings of the popular Radicals were 'exceedingly unwise and injurious'.[2] By a moderate yet radical reform they meant something more than was subsequently given by the Reform Act of 1832 (though they later accepted that measure as 'a first step'), but something rather less than the full universal suffrage demanded by the Radicals in 1819 (even though this was supported by Jeremy Bentham). The most advanced opinions on the question were probably held by Archibald Prentice, who

[1] Taylor, 202.
[2] *Manchester Gazette*, Aug. 7, 1819.

during the Chartist period advocated a system of suffrage limited only by an elementary education test.[1]

A matter of great importance in Benthamite teaching was the need always for efficient and cheap government, and the Manchester middle-class Radicals were very active in this cause about the time of Peterloo. They regarded cheapness and efficiency in government as very closely related. Where expenditure was lavish, they believed, it was usually wasteful, in the interests not of 'the greatest number' but of only a few. In this context they were particularly opposed to the influence of the landed aristocracy, living (as they believed) on places and sinecures and opposing all reform:

'We are very well as we are,' says the Hereditary Lord, who squanders away his £30,000 a year in every species of debauchery and dissipation ...
'We are very well as we are,' say the Representatives and Aristocratical Proprietors of Rotten Boroughs.
But what say seven millions of persons in this country who are totally *unrepresented*?—What say the liberal minded—the independent—the friends of freedom—and the friends of truth?[2]

A consequence of waste in government on aristocratic sinecures and in other ways was the over-heavy burden of taxation. This burden, declared the *Manchester Gazette* in 1819, both oppressed the operatives by reducing the real value of their wages and oppressed the masters by stifling industrial enterprise, a tendency which in turn still further reduced wages.[3] Another principal cause of this heavy tax burden was the French war, fought (the reformers contended) at the instigation of the English aristocracy only for the defence of the French aristocracy. The middle-class Radicals were very anxious to return to normal peacetime rates of taxation; they therefore welcomed the decision to resume cash payments announced by the government early in 1819. The 'unnatural paper currency' of the war years, they believed, by encouraging inflation had greatly assisted the spread of economic distress.[4]

The decision to resume cash payments was taken at West-

[1] A. Prentice, *Organic Changes necessary to complete the System of Representation partially amended by the Reform Bill* (1839).
[2] *Manchester Gazette*, Dec. 26, 1818.
[3] *Ibid.*, April 24, 1819.
[4] *Ibid.*

minster: in 1819 the influence of the Manchester middle-class Radicals at the seat of national government was still small. They had much greater scope for influence in the sphere of local government; and about 1819 we find them conducting a vigorous campaign for the more efficient conduct of local affairs.

The group's members believed that the whole local government system in Manchester was out of date, a 'strange anomalous system' as Taylor called it.[1] This in itself, they argued, was a principal cause of the Peterloo outrage. The local authorities in Manchester were not in touch with the true state of local feeling as they would have been under an efficient system: they preferred to depend upon information supplied to them by a few self-appointed supporters of 'social order' and by spies. In other words, there was not any Benthamite identification of interests between governors and governed. H. G. Bennet, the spokesman of the group in the Commons,[2] asked after Peterloo for the provision of 'some better municipal form of government' for the town. The present system, he contended, was hopelessly inadequate: even apart from Peterloo the local police authorities had been engaged in 'some very atrocious transactions'.[3]

This reference to 'atrocious transactions' apart from Peterloo was an allusion to charges brought the previous year against Joseph Nadin, the Deputy Constable of Manchester. Nadin was charged with complicity in conniving at crime so that he and his beadles could win the credit for subsequent arrests and also the profits customarily given to police officers as a reward for their zeal.[4] The matter came to a head early in 1818 with the Hindley case. Nadin and his constable, Hindley, it was said, had contrived to give stolen property to two boys and had then arrested them for having the property in their possession. Both the middle-class and the working-class Radicals were vociferous in denouncing this outrage. The working-class Radical leaders Saxton, Moorhouse, and Knight (who in the next year were all three arrested for their parts at the Peterloo meeting) went round collecting depositions exposing Nadin's malpractices. The *Manchester*

---

[1] Taylor, v–vi.
[2] See below, p. 166 ff.
[3] *Parliamentary Debates*, XLI (1819–20), 859.
[4] Conviction of anyone stealing to the value of £5 might bring Nadin the reward of a Tyburn Ticket, 'average value in this town £300' (letter in *Manchester Gazette*, April 11, 1818).

Gazette, the middle-class Radical organ, demanded an immediate inquiry into this 'vile arrangement': *'if one tenth part of the charges which have been publicly and upon oath brought against Mr. Nadin be true, he ought not to be allowed to retain his situation another hour'*. An inquiry was eventually held, but not to the satisfaction of either set of reformers. Hindley was dismissed but Nadin was cleared of all charges.[1]

The middle-class Radicals decided to voice their disapproval of the findings of this inquiry by opposing the passing of the Constables' accounts in which the expenses connected with the case appeared. The *Gazette* called for 'a numerous attendance of the inhabitants of the town' at the Parish Vestry meeting of April 30, 1818, and in consequence some fifteen hundred people attended a most uproarious meeting in the Collegiate Church.[2] Taylor, Richard Potter, and Edward Baxter put forward the middle-class Radical case; Potter claimed that he had been refused access to the accounts by the late Boroughreeve and Constables on the ground that 'his wish to examine them proceeded from Presbyterian cant'. The part played by religion in the conflict between the Tory local government oligarchy and the middle-class Radical group was thus made fully apparent from the start.[3]

About this same time the middle-class Radicals also sponsored a petition to the Commons offering to expose the irregular conduct of the Manchester magistrates during the Blanket crisis of 1817.[4] This petition, and their part in the Hindley affair, may be said to mark the beginning of the full-scale participation of the middle-class Radicals in the public life of Manchester. From 1818 onwards for the next thirty years there were few issues in local politics with which some member or other of the group had not an important connection.

The growing prominence of the group in local government affairs received an especial boost from the trial of Taylor for libel early in 1819. At a meeting of the Salford Police Commissioners in

---

[1] *Manchester Gazette*, March 14, 1818; Marshall, 93–94.
[2] 'We are convinced, that many good consequences would arise and much money be saved to the ley-payers, by making the passing of the Constables' accounts, something more than a mere matter of form' (*Manchester Gazette*, April 25, 1818).
[3] *Manchester Gazette*, *Manchester Observer*, May 2, 1818.
[4] *Parliamentary Debates*, XXXVII (1818), 217–32; *Manchester Gazette*, March 18, 1818.

July 1818 called for the purpose of appointing assessors, Taylor was suggested as a suitable candidate. The Tory chairman of the meeting, however, John Greenwood, objected that Taylor was 'one of those reformers who go about the country making speeches' and also the author of a handbill that had caused the Manchester Exchange to be set on fire during the Luddite riots of 1812. Taylor, having tried in vain to get Greenwood to withdraw his false assertions, published a letter in the *Gazette* calling him 'a slanderer, a liar, and a scoundrel'. For this he was indicted for criminal libel at Lancaster Assizes, conducted his own defence, and was acquitted. The whole affair, wrote Prentice, was an indication of the rising importance of the middle-class reformers in local affairs: the attack on Taylor had been an attempt to discredit the whole group.[1]

Elated by the acquittal of Taylor, the middle-class reformers during the early part of 1819 intensified their inquiries into local government abuses. In particular, they laid bare three 'scandals'. First was the 'Bran Scandal', what looked like peculation in the provision of bran for the township's horses: the *Gazette* was aghast at 'public money thus wantonly squandered'.[2] Then came the 'Gas Scandal', the acceptance of a very high tender for work at the municipal gasworks from a firm with a partner on the Gas Committee.[3] And third came a cement scandal, irregular payment of money by Fleming, the Treasurer of the Police Commission, for cement used in the erection of the new gasworks.[4] All these attacks received full publicity both in the *Gazette* and in the *Observer*. They tended to focus on Fleming; and although none of the charges of corruption was ever completely proven, in December 1819 he felt it prudent to resign. The reformers had shaken the rule of the Tory oligarchy in Manchester even though it was by no means yet completely overthrown: the repercussions of Peterloo in local government affairs were to shake that rule still further.[5]

The third basic point in the political programme of the middle-class Radicals was their belief in the need for complete freedom

---

[1] Prentice, ch. IX.
[2] Redford, *Local Government in Manchester*, I, 262.
[3] *Ibid.*, I, 268–71.
[4] *Ibid.*, I, 267.
[5] See below, ch. X.

for trade. They were complete devotees of *laissez-faire* in commercial affairs. In particular, the group was opposed to the Corn Law of 1815. Taylor and Shuttleworth were both members of the committee appointed by the Manchester Anti-Corn Law meeting in February 1815 to prepare a petition of protest against the measure. As we have already noticed, this petition employed cheap labour arguments against the bill, claiming that higher food prices would force up wage rates and consequently the costs of manufacturing production. These, however, were not really the true middle-class Radical sentiments against the bill; they lent their support to the petition only (as Prentice wrote) 'for the sake of committing the old ruling party to an opposition to the proposed act of commercial restriction'. Their real arguments (which were set out in an advertisement in the *Manchester Gazette*) sought to appeal not only to the master class (as did the cheap labour argument) but also to the operatives. On the one hand, argued the group, the Corn Laws raised prices of bread: on the other they restricted the free exchange of our manufactures for foreign corn. For both masters and operatives both these tendencies were oppressive. In the case of the operatives the restriction of free exchange reduced the demand for labour and consequently wages, while at the same time the higher price of bread meant that a higher proportion of those diminished wages had to be spent on food. In the case of the cotton masters the restriction of free exchange gave a check to potential industrial expansion and therefore reduced potential profits. Thus for both masters and men repeal of the Corn Laws would be a great gain. Freedom of trade would bring with it an era of cumulative prosperity for both classes: foreign corn would be exchanged for our manufactures in ever increasing volume, trade would expand, and both wages and profits would rise. The cheap labour argument against the Corn Law, appealing only to the cupidity of the master class, was entirely wrong: in the trade boom which would follow the repeal of the Corn Laws the growing demand for labour would force wages steadily up. The operatives would benefit from repeal to just the same extent as did their employers. It was the duty of both classes, therefore, to act together for their common advantage, 'to give a decisive blow to the system which impoverished them both—a system which more than all the tyranny that employers had ever exercised tended to oppress the people'. The middle-class Radical attempt at a two-class appeal was never more apparent than in their arguments against the Corn Laws.[1]

The middle-class Radicals did not believe, of course, that the era of cumulative prosperity would set in simply with the repeal of the Corn Laws. Complete free trade was necessary for this end. Removal of all the restrictions and imposts under which the cotton trade laboured was essential. And in the 1820's and '30's they were staunch supporters of the movements in Manchester for their total abolition.

Much of the writing of the middle-class reformers reads like the lessons prepared by an assiduous school-teacher for his ignorant pupils. This was typical of their attitude. They believed that many of the abuses and omissions in the existing political system were the consequence simply of ignorance on the part of the people. They were keen supporters, therefore, of movements designed to develop popular education. Like their master Jeremy Bentham, both Shuttleworth and Taylor were strong advocates of the Lancasterian School movement, Taylor being appointed secretary to the local committee before he was of age. 'How should a people badly educated discern distinctly the outlines of their duty?' asked Shuttleworth in a speech in support of the movement in 1814; 'how should they learn to "know their rights—or knowing, to maintain them"?'[2] As we have already seen, the same two men were also prominent defenders of the George Leigh Street Sunday School, founded in Manchester with strong Radical associations in the spring of 1819. Though they themselves were perhaps not active in the running of the school, their inquiries into its conduct aroused their enthusiasm for it; Taylor noted approvingly that it avoided 'those anti-British and Tory principles so diligently inculcated at some other Sunday schools'.[3]

Even more important for the long-term social and political condition of the working-class than the provision of education was the more material need of the operatives for food and employment. From the point of view of general causes, the middle-class reformers believed that this economic distress was largely the product of all the abuses and shortcomings listed in their

[1] Prentice, 68–72; *Manchester Gazette*, Jan. 25, 1826, quoted Briggs, *loc. cit.*, 305.
[2] *Exchange Herald*, Feb. 8, 1814.   [3] Taylor, 79.

programme. Their long-term remedies for distress, therefore, lay
in full-scale reform. As a short-term measure of relief they were
also advocating in 1819 assisted emigration, the removal at public
expense of surplus operatives to new homes in the colonies. The
Manchester Gazette suggested this scheme more than once in the
early summer of 1819, and the announcement in July of a government grant of £50,000 to assist emigration to the Cape of Good
Hope was favourably received by the group.[1]

For those distressed operatives who remained in this country
most of the middle-class reformers supported the provision of
poor relief. Their ideal was 'the old beneficent law of Elizabeth',
the Act of 1601, which neither encouraged the poor to become
paupers, nor yet punished too severely those who were distressed
through no fault of their own. In true Benthamite spirit the group
opposed all deviations from this principle, either in the way of
making poor law administration more severe or of making it more
lax.[2]

Religion played a very important part in the lives of the middle-
class Radicals. Most of them were keen Nonconformists, and they
were highly suspicious of the claims and aspirations of the Church
of England. While not carrying their hostility to the point of
irreligion as did Bentham and his friends,[3] their attitude towards
the Establishment was far from friendly. They would have been
prepared to accept the Established Church if the Established
Church had been prepared to accept and give full recognition to
the claims of Dissent. But this was not the case. Dissenters still
suffered under disqualifying burdens and the Establishment was
still, it seemed to the group, actually attempting to extend its
privileges. Ten years after Peterloo the *Guardian* and the *Gazette*
came out strongly in favour of Catholic emancipation and of the
repeal of the Test and Corporation Acts. And as we have already
noted, about the time of Peterloo the middle-class Radicals strongly resisted the attempt of the Anglican clergy to extend their
influence by building new churches at public expense.

[1] *Manchester Gazette*, June 19, July 3, 1819.
[2] *Ibid.*, June 13, 1818.
[3] When Prentice met Bentham in 1831 the latter had to tread very carefully
on the subject of religion: 'all I gave him to understand on the score of
religion as to my own sentiments was—that I was for *universal toleration*:
and on one or two occasions I quoted scripture' (Bentham to Place, April 24,
1831. Add. Mss. 35149 ff. 73–74).

The attitude of the middle-class Radicals in Manchester to the working-class Radicals, the organizers of the Peterloo meeting was far from friendly. They disliked them on personal grounds. The Huntites, Taylor publicly declared, were deficient 'in that high tone of moral feeling which can alone dignify human nature'; their actions, wrote Prentice, gave 'little proof that [they] had any deep feeling of the responsibility they were incurring as the advocates of great national rights'.[1] For these personal reasons, therefore, the middle-class reformers were careful to dissociate themselves from the popular Radical leaders, even in the field of local government where they were usually active side by side. When, for example, the Tory *Manchester Chronicle* insinuated that at the important Parish Vestry meeting of January 27, 1820, Potter and Taylor had concerted their action with that of the popular Radical leaders, Potter published an indignant denial.[2] Middle-class and working-class Radical agitations were often parallel in Manchester, but they were never allied.

The manner of the popular Radical agitations was also unacceptable to the middle-class reformers. As might be expected from a group of intellectuals, the middle-class Radical ideal was calm rational argument, not agitation on the Peterloo scale. Reform, they believed, 'might be more easily effected by calm but spirited discussion than by violent denunciations proceeding from great assemblages'.[3] Just before Peterloo the *Manchester Gazette* denounced the Radical mass meetings: they merely gave the government 'an excuse for arbitrary measures'. They did not further the cause of reform and they were prejudicial to the poor's best interests:

The bustle and loss of time occasioned by their constant succession of meetings—the violent resolutions generally passed there—the intemperate harangues of the travelling speech-makers—the very questionable character of many, if not most of these persons—the highly objectionable matter which occasionally finds its way to the public through that part of the press which is under their controul—all these are things which do infinite mischief—which utterly preclude moderate men from wishing them success.

Hunt and the other Radical leaders, the *Gazette* concluded, were

---

[1] *Manchester Observer*, Dec. 26, 1818; Prentice, 150.
[2] *Manchester Chronicle*, Jan. 29, Feb. 5, 1820.
[3] Prentice, 202.

6

'not men by whom the intellect of the country will submit to be
led'.[1]

Though the middle-class reformers saw little good in the
characters and methods of the popular Radical leaders, this was
not to say that they approved of the means by which the Tory
authorities sought to control them. The middle-class Radicals
opposed the holding of the Peterloo meeting, but they could find
no excuse for the fashion in which it was dispersed. Though
foolishly conceived, it was, they believed, a 'perfectly peaceable' assembly. The people were indeed misguided, wrote the
Manchester Gazette, but they intended no violence despite the
agents-provocateurs sent among them by the authorities. It was the
authorities alone who purposed violence, preferring the use of
force to that of reason in checking the unwise assemblages of the
poor: 'The poor are not to be reasoned, but terrified into
quiescence.' [2] In their view of the conflict of opinion in Manchester at the time of Peterloo the middle-class Radicals pictured
themselves as standing on the middle ground. On the one side,
they believed, were the unreasoning poor, clamouring to attend
great meetings at which constructive deliberation was impossible:
on the other were the unreasoning authorities too ready to rush
in with the sword. In between stood themselves characteristically
confident that they alone were on the right path.

Whatever the middle-class Radicals might think about the
methods of the popular Radicals, their programme was a different
matter. Here there was a considerable measure of agreement
between middle and working-class reformers. That the people
had just and extensive grievances was readily conceded by
Prentice and his friends, and it was little surprising to them that
the working classes were discontented even to the point of acting
foolishly:

Our settled opinion is, that a community can never be free from disaffection to the existing form of government, while either station or
opinion excludes any part of it from the enjoyment of civil rights.[3]

On nearly all questions where these 'civil rights' were involved
the two sets of reformers in Manchester in 1819 were in agreement. Both advocated the complete removal of all religious tests;

[1] *Manchester Gazette*, June 19, Aug. 7, 1819.
[2] *Ibid.*, Aug. 7, 1819.
[3] *Ibid.*, Jan. 1, 1825.

they shared a common desire for the abolition of privilege and corruption in Government and sought the establishment of a cheap and efficient system without burdensome taxation; they shared a similar zeal for the exposure of abuses in local government and for a comprehensive reform of the local government system; they both desired a broad-based system of parliamentary representation; they both attacked the Corn Laws and the landowning aristocracy in whose interests they had been devised. In short, in nearly all fields of political discussion the two sections of Radical opinion thought alike. And having so much in common with the organizers of the Peterloo meeting the designation 'Radical' is no misnomer for the middle-class group. Significantly, when the *Manchester Observer*, the working-class Radical organ, ended its independent existence in 1821, it was to the middle-class Radical *Manchester Guardian* that its editor recommended his readers.[1] It was means not ends which separated the middle-class Radicals from the working-class Radicals. The Peterloo meeting was itself a leading illustration of this difference. If the sober intellectuals of the middle-class Radical group had had control of popular opinion in the town in 1819 there would have been no Peterloo in Manchester's history: there would still, however, have been a Radical Reform movement.

[1] *Manchester Guardian*, June 30, 1821.

CHAPTER SIX

THE 'LOYALISTS'

MANCHESTER'S self-styled 'loyalists' in 1819, those who whole-heartedly supported the action of the authorities at Peterloo, can be divided into two groups, the one High Tory, the other Pittite. The High Tories were wholly for the *status quo* in church and state: the Pittites on the other hand were mostly cotton business-men and wanted some' commercial reform in the direction of greater freedom for trade and also a limited reform of parliament so as to give Manchester some commercial representation at Westminster.[1]

The High Tories were almost all Anglicans and holders of official positions, either as magistrates or as clergy. The group thus included many of the men directly responsible for the Peter-loo Massacre. Four of the clergy—Wray, Horne, Ethelston, and Hay—have already been noticed in connection with the religious life of Manchester about 1819. They were equally prominent in political affairs, especially the two last who were also magistrates.

There were some eighteen magistrates active in the Manchester area about the time of Peterloo. All except James Norris, the Manchester stipendiary, appear to have been either landowners, clergymen, or men retired from business, it being an unwritten rule in Lancashire that no active manufacturers should be ap-pointed to the bench lest they should be prejudiced in dealing with industrial disputes.[2] This lack of connection with the local cotton trade was not taken as the virtue it was supposed to be by critics of the magistrates after Peterloo. It was one of several factors tending to separate the magistrates from local opinion. It meant, critics asserted, that the magistrates were out of touch with the true state of feeling among the majority of respectable townsmen in Manchester; it led them to act at Peterloo in a manner wholly unacceptable (as H. G. Bennet declared in parliament) to 'many eminent merchants, manufacturers, and tradesmen' in the town.[3]

[1] The position of the Pittites is discussed in greater detail below, p. 88ff.
[2] Prentice, 154; *Parliamentary Debates*, XLI (1819–20), 895 (Bennet).
[3] *Parliamentary Debates*, XLI (1819–20), 358.

Symptoms of difference between the local magistrates and the local cotton masters had appeared during the strikes of 1818. The masters had been strongly opposed to the operatives' demands, whereas the magistrates, having nothing to lose themselves, had not been unsympathetic so long as there was no violence.[1] Religious connections likewise divided the magistrates from a large part of the local population. Nonconformists outnumbered Anglicans in Manchester by about two to one, but all the local magistrates were Anglicans and two of the most active, Hay and Ethelston, were Anglican clergymen. Finally, residence was a further separating influence; of the ten magistrates who signed the warrant for the arrest of Henry Hunt at Peterloo only one, Norris, lived permanently in Manchester.[2] These three important factors all tended to divide the magistrates from both masters and men in Manchester in 1819. 'There did not exist', concluded Bennet, ' . . . that union between the magistrates and the people, which was essential to the due execution of the law.' [3]

The four most prominent magistrates during the Peterloo crisis were James Norris, W. R. Hay, C. W. Ethelston, and William Hulton. James Norris (?1774–1838)[4] was a local barrister who became stipendiary magistrate of Manchester in March 1818; early in 1819 he became also Steward of the Manor of Manchester, and in 1825 Chairman of Quarter Sessions. Personally, Norris seems to have been an amiable man (the *Manchester Chronicle* on his appointment as stipendiary spoke of 'his well-known urbanity and gentlemanly manners'), but he was not endowed with that steadiness of nerve necessary in Manchester's stipendiary magistrate at such a period as that of Peterloo. His reports to the Home Office were full of excessive alarms, and Byng, the Commander of the Northern District, accurately described him as 'timorous'.

The Chairman of Salford Quarter Sessions in 1819 was the Reverend William Robert Hay (1761–1839).[5] After attending

---

[1] For fuller discussion of this point see below, p. 89.

[2] Pigot and Dean, *op. cit.*, 226.

[3] *Parliamentary Debates*, XLI (1819–20), 895.

[4] *Manchester Chronicle*, March 28, 1818; *Manchester Guardian*, July 23, 1825; *The Court Leet Records of the Manor of Manchester* (1889), X, 220 n. 1; Byng to Hobhouse, Sept. 5, 1819 (H.O. 42/194).

[5] F. R. Raines, *The Vicars of Rochdale*, Chetham Soc. (1883), new series, II, pt. II, 284–325, is the main source for details of Hay's career.

Westminster School and Christ Church, Oxford, Hay qualified as a barrister and began to practise on the northern circuit; it was this which first brought him into contact with Manchester. He received few briefs, however, and eventually he decided to give up the law and to enter the Church. He was ordained in 1798 and in 1802 became Rector of Ackworth in Yorkshire on the presentation of his relative Bragge Bathurst, Chancellor of the Duchy of Lancaster. More important, in the same year he became also Chairman of Salford Quarter Sessions. In this office he quickly showed himself active and assiduous, and the Home Office records for the period abound with his reports which, though ever suspicious of the lower orders, were not so full of wild alarms as those of Ethelston or Norris. By contrast with his work as a magistrate, Hay's clerical labours were both tepid and unoriginal, and he never discussed religious questions outside the pulpit.

At the time of Peterloo Hay, by virtue of his position on the bench, was one of the leading members of Manchester's ruling oligarchy and he was greatly hated by the Radicals:

> Justice Hay in the Chair,
> Of the town Lord Mayor,
> And divulger of the law;
> When he winks, Heaven blinks,
> When he speaks, Hell quakes.[1]

For his part at Peterloo he was rewarded by the government with the valuable living of Rochdale, worth £1,730 a year.[2] He gave up the Chairmanship of Quarter Sessions in 1823, and thereafter lived in retirement.

The other leading clerical magistrate in Manchester was the Reverend Charles Wicksted Ethelston (1767–1830) who was born in the town and attended the Grammar School.[3] After completing his education at Trinity College, Cambridge, Ethelston entered into the living of St. Mark's, Cheetham Hill, in 1794; in 1801 he became also Rector of Worthenbury in Flintshire, and in 1804 a Fellow of the Collegiate Church, Manchester. He aspired to be an author and a poet, his publications including *A Pindaric Ode to*

[1] *Manchester Observer*, Jan. 9, 1819.
[2] *Gentleman's Magazine*, Jan. 1840, 95–96.
[3] Raines, *Fellows of the Collegiate Church*, pt. II, 305–19, is the main source for details of Ethelston's career.

the Genius of Great Britain (n.d.), *The Suicide, with other Poems* (1803), *The Unity of the Church Inculcated and Enforced* (1814), and *A Patriotic Appeal to the Good Sense of All Parties* (1817). As a magistrate he was very easily alarmed, and during the Peterloo period he seems to have believed everything told him by his spies, whom he employed on a large scale.[1] In spite of his cloth he showed little Christian charity towards the Radical Reformers: 'Some of you reformers ought to be hanged', he told two of them brought before him for drilling in 1819, 'and some of you are sure to be hanged—the rope is already round your necks.' [2]

William Hulton (1787–1864)[3] of Hulton Park, chairman of the committee of magistrates at Peterloo, was the head of a prominent local landed family. Educated at Brasenose College, Oxford, he early took part in county affairs, becoming a magistrate as soon as he was of age and High Sheriff of Lancashire in 1810. His name does not appear, however, in the Manchester directory for 1819 as one of the magistrates 'who usually attend at the New Bailey Court House' or even as one of the 'Magistrates who reside in the neighbourhood'. His interests thus seem to have been centred on county administration rather than that of Manchester, which makes it a little surprising that he should have been chosen as chairman of the magistrates at Peterloo.

In March 1820 as a reward for his part at Peterloo it was suggested to Hulton that he might stand for the representation of the county, and he agreed to take the next vacancy. 'This mark of esteem', wrote a contemporary, 'was intended to counteract the hostile deportment of his opponents.' Hulton never entered parliament, however. And when in 1831 Lord Althorp, the Chancellor of the Exchequer in Grey's Reform Ministry, commented on the 'most unjustifiable' loss of life at Peterloo, he resigned from his commission of the peace, claiming that only two people had been killed.

Such were the chief magistrates at Peterloo. The town's officers of Manchester for 1819 also require consideration. Unlike the magistrates they were probably not High Tories but rather (as businessmen) Pittites. Town's officers were generally connected

---

[1] Hobhouse to Ethelson, June 28, 1819 (H.O. 41/4).
[2] Taylor, 172.
[3] *V.C.H. Lancashire*, V, 29; *State Trials*, 263; Pigot and Dean, *op. cit.*, 226; J. Wheeler, *Manchester* (1836), 118; *Manchester Guardian*, Dec. 24, 1831.

with the cotton trade[1] and like the magistrates were always Anglicans.[2]

In 1819 Edward Clayton, the Boroughreeve of Manchester, was in business as a calico printer;[3] John Moore, jun., the first Constable, was a retired wine merchant; and Jonathan Andrew, the other Constable, was a manufacturer.[4] Clayton's part in the commotions of 1819 does not appear to have been a very public one. His Constables, however, reported after Peterloo that he was exhausted by his efforts and that his life was in danger.[5] These two Constables were much more prominent. John Moore, jun. (1774–1857),[6] the first Constable, was the more important of the two. He was a prosperous retired wine merchant, whose favourite interests were scientific not political. He was a Fellow of the Linnaean Society, President of the Manchester Literary and Philosophical Society from 1851 to 1854, and a prominent supporter in its early days of the Royal Manchester Institution. The *Manchester Guardian* at his death summed up his activities by describing him as 'one of the last survivors of that small body of men of the last century whose ardent love of science led them to promote its advancement by the establishment of associations'; revealingly, it went on to remark that 'all antagonism, all bitterness was painful to Mr. Moore'. Such gentleness of character obviously unfitted him for the office of senior Constable, head of the town's police force, in the tense atmosphere of 1819, and goes far to explain his excessive state of alarm throughout the crisis.[7]

It is clear, however, that neither the Constables of Manchester

[1] In the years 1812–20 inclusive of twenty-four identifiable men who shared the offices of Boroughreeve and Constable eighteen appear to have been connected with the cotton trade (Axon, *Annals*, x–xii, for a list of the town's officers; Pigot and Dean, *op. cit.*, for identification).

[2] 'No person has yet been allowed to fill the post of boroughreeve who would not attend at the Collegiate Church every Sunday, and thus afford his official sanction to the High Church and high Tory doctrines which are said to be promulgated from its pulpit' (R. Cobden, 'Incorporate Your Borough' (1838), reprinted in W. E. A. Axon, *Cobden as a Citizen* (1907), 48).

[3] That is if the firm of R. J. and E. Clayton was his (Pigot and Dean, *op. cit.*).

[4] *State Trials*, 1147.

[5] Constables of Manchester to Sidmouth, Sept. 16, 1819 (Papers, relative to the Internal State of the Country, *Parliamentary Debates*, XLI (1819–20), no. 44).

[6] F. S. Stancliffe, *John Shaw's 1738–1938* (1938), 103–05, 142–43, 275–76, is the chief source for details of Moore's career.

[7] See below, p. 141–42.

nor the Boroughreeve played so important a part during the Peterloo crisis as did the local magistrates, especially Norris and Hay.[1]
These two magistrates had an experience in local affairs which no
Boroughreeve or Constable holding office for only one year could
hope to rival. They were both also lawyers, and better able therefore to act with assurance in times of disturbance. Finally, they
were well-paid professionals, ready to act with a zeal perhaps not
shared by unpaid officers with private interests of their own to
attend to.[2]

Acting under the Constables and magistrates in 1819 was Joseph
Nadin (1765–1848), the permanent Deputy Constable of Manchester.[3] In the eyes of most of his contemporaries Nadin was a
notorious figure, believed by many to be (as Archibald Prentice
declared) 'the real ruler of Manchester'. He owed his appointment
to the Society for the Prosecution of Felons which had been
impressed by his skill as a thief-taker. Nadin was hated by the
working-class Radicals in Manchester,[4] but how far he was deliberately oppressive is uncertain. It may have been only that the
energy and courage which made him so admirable as a thief-taker
was less appreciated when he was acting in a political cause. Bamford, one of his victims, was certainly not hostile towards him:

He was represented as being exceedingly crafty in his business, and
somewhat unfeeling withal; but I never heard, and certainly never knew,
that he maltreated his prisoners . . . He was certainly a somewhat
remarkable person in uncommon times, and acting in an arduous
situation.[5]

Whatever the truth of the charges against him Nadin was certainly

[1] The Constables deliberately left the business of communicating with the
Home Office to Norris: 'We have avoided troubling your lordship with
frequent communications', they wrote to Sidmouth on September 16, 1819,
'knowing that our highly esteemed friend Mr. Norris was in constant correspondence with the home department' (Papers relative to the Internal
State of the Country, no. 44).

[2] Many potential town's officers thought it worth their while to purchase
a Tyburn Ticket for £300 rather than accept office to the detriment of their
business (Exchange Herald, March 17, 1818).

[3] Hammond, Town Labourer, I, 85–86; Redford, Local Government in Manchester, I, 90–92; and Prentice, 34, are the principal sources for the details of
Nadin's career.

[4] 'So great a man—so great a man—so great a man I be!!
    Why, I'm Deputy to a petty Constable! What do you think of me?'
                                    (Manchester Observer, Jan. 2, 1819.)

[5] Bamford, I, 82.

not quite the dominant force in Manchester that many of his contemporaries believed him to be. He was prominent as the principal executive agent of the local authorities, but the evidence of the Home Office records shows that it was not Nadin but Hay and Norris who were the active initiators of policy in Manchester.[1] Nadin's exaggerated importance in the eyes of his contemporaries was probably the consequence of his being, as their chief executive agent, constantly in the public notice.

One final member on the 'loyal' side in Manchester in 1819 remains to be considered, Hugh Hornby Birley (c. 1777–1845), the most prominent of the local Pittites.[2] Birley was a master manufacturer, and had been Boroughreeve in 1815. In 1819 he was second-in-command of the Manchester and Salford Yeomanry, and he led the troop which made the first fatal charge at Peterloo. Birley was active in many aspects of Manchester life, but about 1819 he was especially prominent in the agitations for greater commercial freedom. As Boroughreeve he had presided over the important anti-Corn Law meeting of February 1815 and also at the meeting for the repeal of the raw cotton duties in the same month.[3] After Peterloo he was a leading figure behind the foundation of the Manchester Chamber of Commerce and became its first President.[4] In all this he was a typical Pittite. He also shared the Pittite desire for parliamentary representation for Manchester and played a prominent part in the movements for the transfer of the Grampound and Penryn seats to Manchester in the 1820's.[5]

This completes the list of the most prominent 'loyalists' in Manchester in 1819. These nine men between them virtually controlled the local government of the town.[6] Under their direction

---

[1] A few days before Peterloo Nadin received a letter from the government-supported *New Times* newspaper asking him to supply reports of interesting local occurrences. A similar request was also sent to Hay who wrote to Hobhouse: 'Nadin seemed at a loss on the subject, and I have recommended him to take no notice of the letter—in truth, he is not quite equal to the thing.' Clearly Hay had the Deputy Constable fully under his control (Hay to Hobhouse, Aug. 14, 1819 (H.O. 42/192), quoted in A. Aspinall, *Politics and The Press, c. 1780–1850* (1949), 429).

[2] Axon, *Annals*, xii, 233–34; Pigot and Dean, *op. cit.*

[3] See above, p. 12.   [5] See below, p. 179.

[4] See below, p. 177.

[6] A very prominent part in local government was played by another 'loyalist', Thomas Fleming (1767–1848), Treasurer of the Police Commission 1810–19. Fleming was not very active, however, in purely political affairs except where they touched on local administration (see above, p. 67).

were two larger groups of supporters of 'social order', a Committee in Aid of the Civil Power and the Manchester and Salford Yeomanry.

The Committee in Aid of the Civil Power, set up early in July 1819, was composed of some sixty or seventy former town's officers and others called together by the officers for 1819 to advise them on the conduct of affairs.[1] The Manchester and Salford Yeomanry had been embodied in 1817 especially to deal with the Radical danger.[2] Its members were especially cotton merchants and manufacturers (presumably Pittites), publicans (anxious to please the magistrates for fear of losing their licences), and shopkeepers (presumably of the better class, finding their custom chiefly among the local 'loyalists').[3]

The yeomanry was a product of local 'loyalty' in its more

[1] See below, p. 116.
[2] A meeting at the Manchester Police Office on June 19, 1817, decided that 'under the present circumstances' a force of yeomanry cavalry should be embodied (*Manchester Chronicle*, June 21, 1817).
[3] A list was given in *Wooler's British Gazette and Manchester Observer*, Aug. 10, 1822, of the name of 101 members of the Manchester and Salford Yeomanry present at Peterloo. Their occupations were given as follows:

Cotton manufacturers .	7	Saddlers	2
Cotton merchants . .	4	Coachmaker . . .	1
Calico printers . . .	3	Horse-breaker . . .	1
Warehousemen . . .	3	Farrier	1
Dyers	2	Stable keeper . . .	1
Drysalter	1	Coachman	1
		Hackney writer . . .	1
Publicans	13		
Brewer	1	Ironmongers . . .	2
Brewer's clerk . . .	1	Tobacconists . . .	2
Wine merchant . . .	1	Shopkeeper	1
Butchers	7	Watchmakers . . .	2
Cheesemonger . . .	2	Tailor	1
Butter factor . . .	1	Plumber	1
Corn dealer	1	Painter	1
Flour dealer . . .	1		
		Iron-liquor merchants .	2
Attornies	3	Paper maker . . .	1
Surgeon	2		
Quack doctor . . .	1	Dancing master . . .	1
Surveyor	1	Labourer.	1
		Servant	1
		Insurance agent . . .	1

In the case of substitutes the occupation of the original member has been counted. 21 members were listed without occupations.

serious vein: the Tories and Pittites also had their more convivial and social institutions. Prominent among these was John Shaw's Club, which held regular meetings at the 'Dog and Partridge' tavern; its members were mostly cotton merchants and manufacturers, and the political tone of the club therefore was probably predominantly Pittite rather than High Tory.[1] More decidedly High Tory was the Manchester Pitt Club founded in 1812, whose chief function was the holding of an annual dinner to celebrate the birthday of the Younger Pitt. Virtually all the chief Manchester 'loyalists' were members of this club.[2] Its annual dinners appear to have been given up to deep drinking, much speechifying, and the concoction of ultra-'loyal' but sometimes improper toasts.[3] The attitude of the club to Radicalism was made amply clear by such effusions as 'Suspension to all cart-politicians' and 'May the Dream of Universal Suffrage and Annual Parliaments no longer disturb our repose'. In general, the toasts presented a solid front in favour of the *status quo*: none of them made any constructive suggestions.[4] In 1817 the club had gone a stage beyond mere toasts and speeches and had arranged for the publication of a number of cheap political tracts intended 'to counter-act the poisonous effects of the various efforts which the disaffected have so recently and fully manifested'. Five thousand copies of one pamphlet written by Wray were distributed and six thousand of another: both were given suitably 'popular' titles, *The Speech of Mr. John P—— Schoolmaster* and *The Street Politicians, or a Debate About the Times*.[5]

Pitt Clubs were to be found all over the country: more especially concentrated in Lancashire were the Orange Lodges, societies founded with the main purpose of upholding the Protestant Succession and annoying the Roman Catholics. They were a Tory

[1] Stancliffe, *op. cit.*, 59.

[2] Founder-members included Hay, Ethelston, Hulton (President in 1817), Birley (Vice-President in 1819), and Clayton; only Marriott of the magistrates chiefly active locally was not a member; seven of the nine Boroughreeves between 1812 and 1820 were members; all town's officers at the time of Peterloo were members (Pitt Club Dinner Book and Minute Books, *passim*).

[3] 'May the wives of true Britons possess two eminent Qualifications of Mr. Pitt—"A quick conception and an easy delivery".' (*ibid.*, 1817, 1819).

[4] *Ibid., passim;* Prentice, 429–30.

[5] The circulation of these two pamphlets was noted by Wray on his own copies now in Chetham's Library, Manchester.

attempt to win popular support for their cause by methods in some respects similar to those of the Radical Union Societies. Manchester had several Orange Lodges at the time of Peterloo; Colonel Fletcher, one of the Peterloo magistrates and a particular supporter of the movement, was Grand Treasurer of one of them.[1]

Such were the Tory and Pittite 'loyalists' of Manchester. Their institutions were various, their offices were many, they had power and experience behind them. What was it that caused them despite all this power and experience to panic as they did at Peterloo?

The 'loyalists' were alarmed on August 16th in part by the way the Radical Reformers assembled for the meeting and in part by the extent of the Radical organization which made possible this manner of assembling. Their dismay at the Radical organization was clearly set out in the resolutions passed by a meeting held at the Manchester Police Office on July 9, 1819, and their alarm at the particular manner in which the Peterloo meeting was brought together was expressed in a petition despatched to the Prince Regent in October 1819.[2] Both documents laid especial stress on the evil influence of the Radical Press: it had become, declared the petition to the Prince Regent, 'the instrument of daring and seditious leaders in *overthrowing the Government* of the country'. The Radical itinerant orators and the Union Societies were further causes of alarm, and also the system of 'delegates and missionaries' which helped to link these societies together. These delegates, furthermore, went about organizing the Radical meetings: the 'numerous assemblies' held throughout the area in the week before Peterloo seemed to the 'loyalists' to have only one purpose, the working up of public opinion in preparation for a revolutionary outbreak. The people's possession of pikes and other weapons was another cause of dismay: the 'loyalists' had no doubt that the people were attending the Peterloo and other meetings armed. Associated with this arming was the Radical drilling: on the morning of August 16th the marching of the reformers in order with banners was just one more addition to 'loyalist' alarms. The people arrived in 'military array', declared the petition to the Prince Regent, 'under banners of disloyalty' to

[1] *Manchester Mercury*, Feb. 4, 1817; *Manchester Observer*, Feb. 14, 1818; *Manchester Chronicle*, Nov. 13, 1819.
[2] *Manchester Chronicle*, July, 17, Oct. 16, 1819.

the 'universal consternation' of all 'loyal' citizens.[1] Many of the
men who marched in the Radical processions were strangers to
Manchester; this was yet another cause of 'loyalist' concern. 'Our
military force was slender', wrote Horne, the curate of St.
Stephens, 'and we were invaded, from twenty miles around, by
all the disloyalty of the country.'[2]

Such were the chief external circumstances which caused the
Tory and Pittite 'loyalists' of Manchester to panic as they did on
the day of Peterloo: the Radical drilling and arming, the marching,
the Union Societies, the series of meetings, the widespread network of agitation, all were inexplicable to them except as the beginning of an attempt at revolution. The symptoms were so
ominous, the 'loyalists' believed by noon on the day of the
massacre, that there was no need to let the seditious purposes of
the meeting fully reveal themselves. There was no point in waiting
to see revolution actually break out. It was against this background
of preconceived alarm that Francis Philips, a leading Pittite
'loyalist', could admit that no direct affront was offered to him on
the field of Peterloo and yet say that he felt alarmed. Matthew
Cowper, the Secretary to the Committee in Aid of the Civil
Power, shared the same feelings: he was alarmed, he declared, 'not
from what I then saw, but from previous circumstances and from
information communicated to me'.[3] Better, the 'loyalist' argument
ran, to nip insurrection in the bud before it got under weigh. In
explaining the panic of the Manchester 'loyalists' on the day of
Peterloo the actions and attitude of the Radicals on St. Peter's
Field itself are almost irrelevant. The total effect of the Radical
agitation throughout the preceding weeks (combined with the
impressive manner in which the meeting assembled on the morning of August 16th) was sufficient to convince them even before
Hunt had begun to speak that the meeting was seditious and that
it must be dispersed whatever the cost.

There is no reason to doubt the genuineness of all this 'loyalist'
alarm, excessive though it may appear in the light of after-
knowledge. Jonathan Andrew, one of the Constables of Manchester, sent his wife and family away to Liverpool a month
before Peterloo.[4] Horne gave an agonizing picture of the tension
in Tory and Pittite circles:

[1] See below, p. 128 ff.   [2] Horne, *Moral and Political Crisis*, 16.
[3] *State Trials*, 230, 233; Philips, 22.   [4] *Ibid.*, 1147.

For many months, we had suffered the terrors of siege, having enemies within, as well as without; and when we went to bed at night, we knew not, but that our town would be in flames, before morning . . . Who shall complain of Peterloo, when the *organised terrors of months of slavery and fear* had driven us to make a desperate stand for all, which Britons can value?[1]

Imaginary though the grounds for this panic may have been, it was certainly sincere.

Some slight excuse for the exaggerated fears of the 'loyalists' can be found in the novelty of much of the Radicals' manner of agitation. The manner of the Peterloo meeting was certainly something new in the sphere of political campaigning in Lancashire. The marching with banners of trained bodies of men, many of them strangers, seems to have been an innovation introduced during the strikes of 1818, and the procedure was taken over by the Radicals for their more important meetings in 1819. Philips compared the Blanket meeting of 1817 favourably with Peterloo because it lacked the latter's unusual features.[2] But though the novelty of the proceedings of August 16th may in part explain the 'loyalist' panic, it can hardly be said to justify it.

Dislike of the Radicals' manner of proceeding in 1819 was not the only reason for alarm among the Manchester 'loyalists': the persons of the reformers were also entirely unacceptable to them. The Radical leaders, wrote Horne, were 'men without name, office or property; of mean birth, education, and talents'. The 'loyalists' could not accept that such men had any right to participate in politics: statesmen needed '*capacity* and *liberal education*'.[3]

The unsatisfactory nature of the persons of the Radical leaders was only a secondary danger, however, when compared with the dangerous nature of their political principles. The conflict between the political principles of the Radical Reformers and those of the Tory and Pittite 'loyalists' underlay the whole state of tension in Manchester in 1819.

Economic distress, its origins and relief, was the basic point in

[1] Horne, *Moral and Political Crisis*, 16–18.

[2] Philips, 6. It is interesting to compare the resolutions passed at a 'loyal' Police Office meeting held on January 13, 1817 (*Manchester Mercury*, Jan. 21, 1817) with those of July and October 1819. In many respects the evils denounced were the same, but significantly in 1817 there was no mention of drilling, military array, or banners (see below, pp. 98–99).

[3] Rev. M. Horne, *A Word for My Country* (1817), 4; *An Address to the Higher Classes*, 59–63; *The Patriot*, Sept. 4, 1819.

the Radical programme. The Radicals argued that it was the outcome of the many abuses in the existing system of government: 'loyalist' teaching on the other hand denied this absolutely. All existing distress, 'loyalists' believed, was the outcome of the war with France which had upset the balance of economic affairs; time alone would restore the situation. The Reverend J. Gatliffe, a Fellow of the Collegiate Church, wrote to one of the Manchester magistrates two months before Peterloo neatly summing up this attitude:

it must be admitted [he wrote] that taxation is ponderous, and that the middle class are like enough to fall into the state of the lower, and the lower into a state of starvation. But what can Reform, or any other nostrum of political agitation do here? We are suffering from the effects of the late war and bad harvests, and must wait patiently until the tide turns. It is absurd to attribute such calamities to borough-mongering and the Bourbons.[1]

To claim that parliamentary reform would relieve distress, declared the Lancashire Grand Jury, was ridiculous: popular distress had 'no relation at all to the government or constitution of this country'.[2] As for taxes, pensions, and sinecures, so loudly complained of by the reformers, such things had no part in the present difficulties: 'We have always had Taxes, Pensions and Sinecures, and yet we have not always had bad times.'[3] And look to the United States, so often held up as a shining example by the Radicals: distress existed there too. This proved that our burdens were not the outcome of our particular system of government.[4]

Almost the only remedy for distress offered by the 'loyalists' was the remedy of patience on the part of the poor, a patience to be sustained by the charity of the rich. The argument of Paley's famous *Reasons for Contentment* was repeated time and time again, and a paraphrase of his arguments appeared in the *British Volunteer* newspaper only two days before Peterloo. Poverty, the argument ran, was an unavoidable but not a dishonourable estate: there would always be rich and there would always be poor, but Paley had proved that the latter had nothing to envy in the former. 'By

[1] Gatliffe to Farington, June 5, 1819 (Raines, *Fellows of the Collegiate Church*, pt. II, 304).
[2] Lancashire Grand Jury to the Manchester Magistrates, July 20, 1819 (Papers relative to the Internal State of the Country, no. 9).
[3] A pamphlet, no title (Manchester, ?1817).
[4] *Ibid.*

this constitution of things the *poor* are taught many useful lessons, and from it *they* derive many invaluable blessings.' They learnt especially the essential virtues of Industry, Contentment, Temperance, and Gratitude: with a knowledge of these virtues the poorest man could be as happy as the richest. And at the last the poor man had the assurance that heaven was as open to him as it was to his betters. The poor, therefore, should not complain about their poverty; they should accept their condition with resignation and also that of those placed above them. They should complain neither about distress nor about the Tory government: both distress and government were works of the Almighty.[1]

Given such resignation, the 'loyalists' were not unsympathetic towards the distressed. Indeed, their philosophy expressly ordained that they should show such sympathy. If the poor's distresses were unavoidable, the obligations of the rich to dispense charity were equally unavoidable. The Reverend John Stephens, a High Tory Methodist minister in Manchester, preached after Peterloo on the well-known text, 'For ye have the poor with you always, and whensoever ye will ye may do them good.' Though stressing Paley's passive obedience teaching for the poor, he stressed also the obligations of the rich: his text, he declared, contained two propositions, 'the perpetual existence of a class of poor people in the world—and a perpetual claim on the benevolence of the rich towards them'.[2]

This sympathy for the distress of the poor and the necessity for the provision of charity by the rich were themes repeated by nearly all the 'loyalist' writers of the Peterloo period. Nor were their readers slow in acting upon such exhortations. When a 'loyal' meeting for the poor was held in Manchester on January 5, 1820, most of the town's Tories and Pittites contributed generously. Here was a meeting, exclaimed the *Exchange Herald*, 'of the real, not the pretended friends of the poor . . . in which the Stewards who had one talent, and the Stewards who had ten talents entrusted to their care, assembled to administer comfort . . . to the more needy dependents on their common Lord'.[3]

[1] *British Volunteer*, Aug. 14, 1819; Rev. J. Stephens, *The Mutual Relations, Claims and Duties of the Rich and the Poor* (1819), *passim*.
[2] *Ibid.*, 8.
[3] *Exchange Herald*, Jan. II, 1820. Even Archibald Prentice, the middle-class Radical, had to admit that the 'loyalists' of Manchester were very generous in support of relief schemes (Prentice, 53–54).

This charity, however, was not being accepted in 1819 in the spirit in which it was given. The 'loyalists' were amazed to find that their benevolence was being increasingly spurned by the poor. Under the influence of the Radical Reformers the people had taken up the cry of the Rights of Man: and this meant that they would neither acquiesce in the silent political role designed for them in Paley's philosophy nor accept the compensating charity which he proffered them. A 'loyal' meeting in 1817 was astonished to discover that the people showed 'marked disparagement' of offers of charitable relief.[1] The Tory principle of paternalism with its expectation that the poor would humbly accept both the government and the charity of their betters was at every point directly opposed by the Radical assertion of natural political rights, especially the right of political equality. Here was the fundamental conflict of principle underlying the Peterloo Massacre.

On all the points discussed so far both Pittites and Tories in Manchester were agreed: Radical Reform spelt revolution. In certain other important respects, however, the views of the two groups differed: fear of Radical revolution did not lead the Manchester Pittites to come out in complete opposition to all reform as it did the town's High Tories. Here the two sets of 'loyalists' differed in their opinions, and it is important to elaborate these differences.

The High Tory group consisted of magistrates, clergymen, private gentlemen, and a few professional men: the Pittites were mostly cotton merchants and manufacturers. Occupationally, therefore, there was a clear division between the two groups. The Reverend Melville Horne, himself a High Tory Anglican clergyman, carefully differentiated his group from the rest of Manchester opinion including the Pittites:

With the exception of a handful of Magistrates [he wrote after Peterloo] Clergy, Gentlemen of Law, Medicine, and perhaps one hundred of private fortune, the Town is all Manufacture, or Trade. Here our enemies are of our own household, and we know not whom to trust.[2]

Horne clearly was hardly ready to trust even the Pittite masters: the gap for him between the official and professional High Tory

---

[1] *Manchester Mercury*, Jan. 21, 1817.
[2] Horne, *Moral and Political Crisis*, 16.

classes and even the 'loyal' merchants and manufacturers was pronounced.

This gap had been made very evident during the strikes of 1818 when differences of occupation and interest between Tories and Pittites led to a great difference of attitude. The cotton masters throughout the strikes firmly opposed all the wages increases demanded by the strikers: the local Tory magistrates, on the other hand, showed considerable sympathy towards the demands at least of the handloom weavers.[1] Many masters, they believed, were deliberately keeping wages low on the assumption that they would be made up out of the poor rates:

There is a *concurrence* of opinion among the English manufacturers [wrote Hay, the Chairman of Quarter Sessions, bitterly] that it serves their particular interests to have their workpeople at so low a price that they must be fed in part out of the Poor's rate which serves as a *bonus* to the Capital employed in manufacturing. The evil is growing into a system.[2]

Despite such criticisms the cotton masters refused to make any concessions to the operatives. But yet equally they refused to act decisively to put down the strikes. And here again friction developed between them and the magistrates. The masters were advised to act with energy, reported Hay, to publish a declaration saying that they would protect non-strikers from violence, but instead they remained inactive. They left everything to the authorities. They could have discovered many examples of illegal combination if they had so wished, but they would support neither a strong policy of prosecution nor a temporizing policy of conciliation. 'They, who have the means, are ready to call upon the civil power for the responsibility, while they neither take or try any effectual means to cure or meet the evil.' They merely had the effrontery to 'profess an opinion that the civil power is not only inactive but highly culpable'.[3]

These criticisms were of course levelled at the master class in general; but it seems (what is important in the present context) that many Pittite masters were included in the strictures of Hay

[1] 'I am sorry I have it not in my power to inform your Lordship that the manufacturers have granted to the weavers their demand of increase of wages . . . they are the most suffering class' (Norris to Sidmouth, Aug. 2, 1818. Aspinall, no. 242).
[2] Hay to Sidmouth, Aug. 1, 1818 (H.O. 42/179).
[3] Hay to Hobhouse, July 30, 1819 (Aspinall, no. 236).

and his High Tory friends, for in the next year we find Francis
Philips, himself a prominent Pittite merchant and manufacturer,
attacking the magistrates in his pamphlet published after Peterloo
for their 'mistaken lenity' in 1818. He seems to have adopted just
the sort of attitude complained of by Hay in the letter quoted
above, expecting the magistrates to take decisive repressive action
against the strikers without assistance from the masters and
certainly without any concessions by them; he blamed the parading
and outbreaks of violence during the strikes on the temporizing
policy of the local authorities.[1]

The High Tory magistrates and the Pittite cotton masters were
thus seriously divided in their attitudes towards the strikes of
1818. The agitation in the same year against Peel's Factory Bill
probably separated them also. We find seven magistrates and
twenty clergy signing a petition from Manchester in favour of the
bill at the same time as a petition against the measure was being
supported by 'the Owners and Occupiers of Cotton Mills in
Manchester and the vicinity'; almost certainly the latter would
include most of the Pittite cotton masters.[2] The same differences
probably existed over the Property Tax question in 1815–16.
The Manchester magistrates supported the continuation of the
tax, but some sixteen hundred inhabitants signed a petition against
it and (as businessmen) it is almost certain that this number included many Pittites.[3] The Corn Law of 1815 similarly tended to
divide the two sections of 'loyal' opinion. The committee set up
at the important Anti-Corn Law meeting held in Manchester on
February 27, 1815, included such leading Pittites as Birley,
Thomas Fleming, and Jeremiah Fielding: the local High Tory
magistrates and clergy on the other hand took no part in the opposition to the measure.[4]

Underlying these differences on economic questions between
Tories and Pittites in Manchester was an important difference of
principle. The Pittite Masters (like the rest of the cotton employers) were staunch advocates of *laissez-faire* economics: the
High Tory official and professional classes, by contrast, still inclined in their economic as in their political thinking to an attitude

[1] Philips, 59–64.
[2] *Parliamentary Debates*, XXXVII (1818), 440–41, 1188–89.
[3] *Ibid.*, XXXIII (1816), 201–04; Raines, *Fellows of the Collegiate Church*, 311.
[4] *Manchester Gazette*, March 4, 1815.

of paternal benevolence towards the industrial operatives, and this markedly qualified their acceptance of pure *laissez-faire*.

Similarly, on the parliamentary reform question the Pittite masters were inclined to differ from the local High Tories. The Tories argued either that parliament would reform itself, or (more bluntly) that the constitution was perfect and not in need of any reform. The former argument was espoused especially by Horne and Wray ('to reform Parliament is the work of Parliament'), the latter especially by Ethelston.[1] Writers of this second type were full of wonder at the self-operating perfection of the system of government which posterity had handed down:

A retrospect of the History of our Country [declared the prospectus of *The Patriot* newspaper, founded in Manchester just before Peterloo] is a proof that the British Constitution has continually progressed towards perfection, since our ancestors first boasted of its value. In itself it possesses a rectifying principle which can only be destroyed by parricidal hands.

The unrepresented state of Manchester was not the slightest obstacle to writers of this school. The town had of recent years grown immensely in wealth and size, admitted one 'loyal' placard posted up in Manchester just before Peterloo, but this was no justification for parliamentary representation: the rapid growth of the town proved on the contrary that it did not need such representation in order to prosper.[2] In any case, argued Wray, Manchester was virtually represented: 'every Member in Parliament is a Representative of the People'.[3]

This complacent view of the state of the constitution was not shared by the Pittites in Manchester. Like the rest of their fellow cotton masters they desired representation for Manchester's business interest at Westminster; and in the 1820's we find them pressing strongly for it.[4] In 1819 they accepted that the atmosphere in the town was much too unsettled to permit any agitations for limited reform; but given an end to the Radical agitations they definitely looked forward to some improvement in the electoral system. Francis Philips was quite explicit on this point in his

[1] Horne, *A Word for My Country*, 3; Wray, *Street Politicians*, 7–8; Ethelston, *Patriotic Appeal*, 6–7.
[2] *An Address to the Reformers*, by A Briton (1819).
[3] Wray, *Speech of Mr. John P——*, 5.
[4] See below, p. 179.

pamphlet defending the magistrates after Peterloo: Manchester and Birmingham should be represented, he wrote, although not of course through popular elections like those at Westminster.[1]

Thus both on the parliamentary reform question and on economic issues High Tory and Pittite opinion was quite sharply differentiated in Manchester. The Manchester Pittites never forgot their business interests and shared most of the opinions of their fellow cotton masters on these two important issues. What differentiated them from the great body of their fellow industrialists was their greater interest in more purely political affairs (as evidenced by their activity at Peterloo) in contrast to the usual apathy of the majority. The basic reason for this was probably religious: most of the Pittite masters seem to have been Anglicans, whereas the great majority of masters were Nonconformists. Anglicanism at this period, it will be remembered, was very strong in its 'loyalist' political overtones.[2] But despite their Anglican politics, the attitude of the Pittite 'loyalists' of Manchester in 1819 showed that not all who were on the side of the authorities at Peterloo were devotees of blind political negation. The circumstances of 1819 drove the Pittites to present a solid front along with the High Tories before the onrush of Radicalism: but it is important to remember that Birley, the commander of the troop of yeomanry which charged into the Radical parliamentary reformers at Peterloo, was himself in a limited way also a parliamentary reformer.

[1] Philips, xii–xiii; *An Address to the Higher Classes*, 55–56; *British Volunteer*, Oct. 9, 1819; letter in *Manchester Chronicle*, Sept. 11, 1819.
[2] Birley, Philips, Thomas Fleming, Jeremiah Fielding, and T. S. Withington, all prominent Pittite merchants and manufacturers, were all also Anglicans.

Part Three

THE MASSACRE OF PETERLOO

CHAPTER SEVEN

RIOT AND DISTURBANCE IN MANCHESTER 1789-1818

THE Peterloo Massacre, though easily the largest, was by no means the only civil disturbance in the Manchester area in the early years of the nineteenth century. The history of Manchester in the thirty years before Peterloo reveals many upsets and disturbances in the town and its environs, all of them contributing to give Manchester a particular reputation for turbulence in the eyes of contemporaries. Though some were political in form, all (it will be found on closer inspection) were really economic in origin, arising from the pressure of economic distress on the working-classes.

The period of tension began about 1789. In that year the local Dissenters and Reformers petitioned for the repeal of the Test and Corporation Acts, and this immediately aroused all the bigotry of the Anglican Tories who then dominated and ruled the town. To this old religious prejudice was soon added fear of the example of the French Revolution, which had begun in the same year. Dissenters and reformers became equated by the Anglicans with Jacobins; and Manchester publicans, anxious to display their 'loyalty' to the local Anglican and High Tory magistrates, put up notices announcing 'No Jacobins Admitted Here'. Rival clubs were formed, the Church and King Club of 'loyalists' on the one side, and the Manchester Constitutional Society of middle-class reformers on the other, the latter (to the 'loyalists' ' extreme alarm) immediately beginning to agitate for moderate parliamentary reform and for religious freedom.

The aspirations of these early reformers proved, however, to be premature. The larger part of Manchester opinion in the 1790's (insofar as it was interested in politics at all) was still strongly for 'Church and King' down even to the lowest classes, and the town's Tory ruling oligarchy was able to revel in this support. Following the example of Birmingham, where Joseph Priestley's

house had been attacked, in December 1792 the 'loyal' Manchester
mob stoned the publication office of the reformers' newspaper,
the *Manchester Herald*, and attacked the house of Thomas Walker,
the town's leading reformer. In 1794 a trumped-up charge of
conspiring to overthrow the government and assist the French
was brought against Walker and his friends. The Crown's case
collapsed when its principal witness confessed to having been
bribed; but the cause of reform was for the time being stifled.
As Archibald Prentice wrote: 'To run the risk of a trial for high
treason, or for seditious conspiracy, on suborned evidence, was,
to most persons, no trifling matter.' [1]

So ended the first period of the reform movement in Manchester. The local 'loyalist' authorities had shown that they had
little understanding of, or sympathy for, either Dissent in religion
or reform (even of the most moderate kind) in politics. In 1792,
as in 1819, they had made it clear that they believed that the best
way to combat such opinions was to suppress them, by force if
necessary. But one very important difference characterized the
events of the two years. In 1792 popular opinion was on the side
of the Tory authorities: in 1819 it was on the side of the reformers.
The mob which was shouting for 'Church and King' in 1792 was
calling for 'Universal Suffrage' and 'Annual Parliaments' in 1819.
The history of Manchester during the intervening years is to a
large degree the history of this change-over in popular opinion.

The 'loyalty' of the local working-classes in the early 1790's
was shown by the enthusiasm with which they supported the
declaration of war against France. They were completely caught
up, remarked a contemporary, in a 'universal pant for glory'. [2]
It was not long, however, before they began to feel the war's
damaging economic effects. As Archibald Prentice wrote:

Heavy taxation fell with peculiar severity upon them; and in the
general advance of prices, the consequence of a depreciated currency ...
their wages were found inadequate to their support. Their only
instruction had been, to be loyal and submissive; their reward for
loyalty and submission was unbearable distress. [3]

---

[1] Prentice, ch. I, for the above account of Manchester opinion in the early
1790's.
[2] W. Rowbottom, 'Chronology or Annals of Oldham', Giles Shaw Mss.
XCIII, 107.
[3] Prentice, 30-31.

In some years conditions approaching famine prevailed. In 1796 the Boroughreeve and higher orders of the town publicly pledged themselves to reduce their consumption of flour by one third.[1] In 1797 and again in 1799 there were food riots, and a dearth prevailed throughout 1800.[2] The handloom weavers, in particular, suffered from this distress, because at the same time as prices were rising their wages were actually falling. Their wages, which according to one magistrate had averaged 2s. 4½d. a day in June 1805, had sunk to 10½d. a day by January 1808.[3] And at the same time, reported another magistrate, 'a very considerable rise had taken place . . . in the price of flour and oatmeal'.[4]

As we have already seen, in response to the pressure of this distress the handloom weavers began to agitate for an improvement in their wage rates. They sought relief from the high price of food by pressing the government to pass compulsory minimum wage legislation. At first ministers seemed willing to support such a measure, and a minimum wage bill was introduced into parliament. It was quickly withdrawn, however, and in consequence feeling ran high all over Lancashire. A great two-day meeting of protest was held at St. George's Fields, Manchester, on May 24–25, 1808. On the second day the magistrates grew alarmed at the numbers assembled and called out the troops to clear the ground. As a result, one weaver was killed and several injured. During the dispersal Colonel Hanson, of Strangeways Hall, near Manchester, a supporter of the weavers' bill, urged the men to go home peaceably. The authorities, however, declared that on the contrary he had urged them to stand firm, and in spite of much 'respectable' evidence in his support Hanson was subsequently sentenced to six months' imprisonment and £100 fine. This injustice to one of their champions, combined with the violent dispersal of the meeting, greatly incensed the weavers. They offered to pay Hanson's fine by means of penny subscriptions, and henceforward they were no longer to incline towards the 'Church and King' loyalty of the authorities.[5]

In 1812 the extent of this change in the attitude of the working class was strikingly demonstrated. Popular distress, already great

[1] *Ibid.*, 24.
[2] C. H. Timperley, *Annals of Manchester* (1839), 64–65.
[3] Fletcher to Hawkesbury, received Feb. 24, 1808 (Aspinall, p. 95 n. 2).
[4] Farington to Hawkesbury, May 26, 1808 (*ibid.*).
[5] Prentice, 31–33; Hammond, *Skilled Labourer*, 72–81.

in 1808, had been further increased in the intervening years by the operation of the Orders in Council and by the continuing inflationary spiral. The result was (in Prentice's words) that 'the price of every commodity had risen, except the price of labour'.[1] When, therefore, the local 'loyalists' called a meeting to congratulate the Prince Regent on his investiture and on keeping the Tory ministry in office, they received a great shock; for it quickly became clear that they could no longer rely on the support of the once 'loyal' Manchester mob. At the last moment it was decided to cancel the meeting, but by this time it was too late. A mob assembled in St. Ann's Square and passed with acclamation resolutions deploring the continuance in office of the Perceval administration. The people then proceeded to the Exchange Dining Room, where the original meeting was to have been held; rioting broke out and the room was wrecked, the military being called in to restore order. It was evident that the old 'Church and King' loyalty had gone for ever. 'The occurrences of that day', wrote a contemporary, ' . . . indicated a turn in the current of popular opinion. Previously to that time "Church-and-King" was the favourite cry, and hunting "Jacobins" safe sport, but subsequently the old dominant party appeared to feel that they had an opposition to contend with, and they became less arrogant in their conduct.'[2]

A few days after the Exchange Dining Room riot, food riots broke out in Manchester and elsewhere in protest at the high price of provisions. The Luddites also were active. At Middleton a power-loom factory was attacked, and at Westhoughton another mill operating the hated machinery was burnt down completely. Alarm was widespread and very heavy sentences were imposed on the rioters. The fierceness of these sentences, combined with the improvement in trade conditions following the repeal of the Orders in Council, largely put an end to Luddism in Lancashire.[3]

It will be seen that as yet the operatives were still seeking

[1] Prentice, 42–47; G. W. Daniels, 'The Cotton Trade During the Revolutionary and Napoleonic Wars', *Trans., Manchester Statistical Society* (1915–16), 77–82.

[2] Prentice, 48–52; Taylor, 146–54.

[3] Three men and a woman were sentenced to death for their parts in the Manchester food riots, four men were hanged in connection with the Westhoughton outbreak, and fifteen men and boys were transported for adminis-

economic solutions to the economic problem of distress, solutions such as the minimum wage and the destruction of machinery (if this last can be called a solution). Though they had now thrown over their former 'Church and King' politics, they had not yet proceeded to the further stage of espousing the cause of Radical Reform. The first symptoms of political feeling began to show themselves, however, about this same time. On June 11, 1812, a group of weavers, including John Knight, the Peterloo Radical, met at a public-house in Manchester to prepare an address to the Prince Regent and a petition to the House of Commons in favour of peace and parliamentary reform. The whole group, thirty-eight in number, was arrested by Nadin, the Deputy Constable of Manchester, supported by the military, and charged with holding an unlawful meeting and with combining for a seditious purpose. Although at their subsequent trial the authorities' case was proved to be without foundation, as in 1794 the prosecution was not without its effect; of the thirty-eight men arrested only Knight was active afterwards in the cause of reform.[1]

At the end of 1816 the Radical Reform agitation revived again and soon proved that this time it was not to be so easily put down. The reformers began to attract considerable support (though not yet so much as in 1819) and began to develop an extensive net-work of agitation. Hampden Clubs were founded (under the inspiration of the famous London Hampden Club led by Major Cartwright), a Radical newspaper (the *Manchester Political Register*) was established, and numerous public meetings were called, all very much on the same lines as were followed two years later at the time of Peterloo. The very first of all the provincial Hampden Clubs seems to have been that founded at Royton, near Oldham, early in August 1816; the first Manchester club was established on October 28th. By March 1817 about forty Hampden Clubs were in existence in the area with a total membership (according to the reformers' own claims) of about eight thousand operatives. Delegate meetings were convened to co-ordinate the work of the clubs, and at one such meeting held at Middleton on December 15, 1816, four reform delegates were appointed to visit 'all parts of

tering illegal Luddite oaths (F. O. Darvall, *Popular Disturbances and Public Order in Regency England* (1934), ch. V; Hammond, *Skilled Labourer*, ch. X; Prentice, 52-57).
[1] Prentice 76-82.

the United Kingdom where the nature and cause of our distress has not been publicly asserted and its remedy insisted upon'. Thus, as in 1819, the national aspirations of the Radical Reform movement in Lancashire were quickly made plain.[1]

The extent of all this activity makes it clear that by the beginning of 1817 the Radical Reformers had gained a considerable following among the local operatives. For the first time numbers of the working-classes, especially the handloom weavers, had become associated with the reforming politicians. The pressure of economic distress was the main reason for the success of this Radical appeal, and as in 1819 the reformers exploited the distress theme to the full. In its very first number (January 4, 1817) the *Manchester Political Register* printed in detail a selection of weavers' family budgets. Their wages, it claimed, were never above 6s. per week and often less.

Both national and local authorities soon became seriously alarmed by the success of the Radical movement. In February 1817 secret committees of the Lords and of the Commons presented most alarming reports on the state of the country. The country-wide network of Hampden Clubs, they asserted, of which Manchester was a principal centre, was engaged in the preparation of a revolutionary outbreak. A week later Habeas Corpus was suspended and Acts passed to prevent public meetings, to punish attempts to seduce soldiers and sailors from their allegiance, and to protect the person of the Prince Regent.[2] This alarm was reflected by the local authorities in Manchester. On January 13, 1817 a meeting of local 'loyalists' was held to consider the 'necessity of adopting additional measures for the maintenance of the public peace'; an increased number of special constables was enrolled, the Watch and Ward was arranged to be enforced in any districts which needed it, and an Association for the Protection and Support of the Civil Authorities was formed. The list of 'loyalist' alarms expressed in the resolutions passed by this meeting shows how similar the Radical organisation of 1817 was to that of 1819. The 'loyalists' denounced 'the numerous meetings

---

[1] Davis, 'Lancashire Reformers 1816–17', *passim*, on which the following account of the Radical agitation in 1816–17 is chiefly based. See also Kinsey, 36–48; D. Read, 'The Hampden Clubs. A Lancashire Spy's Narrative', *Manchester Guardian*, Oct. 2, 1956.

[2] *Parliamentary Debates*, XXV (1817), 411–19, 438–47.

held both publicly and secretly—the organized system of committees, delegates, and missionaries', and the abuse of the freedom
of the Press. 'All these circumstances', the meeting concluded,
'afford strong manifestation of meditated disorder and tumult.' [1]

The alarms of the 'loyalists' were still further increased when
the local reformers began to organize a march on London, the
famous March of the Blanketeers. The plan was first announced
at a public meeting held in Manchester on March 3, 1817. This
meeting was adjourned until the following Monday, March 10th,
when it was to assemble again preparatory to the setting off of
the marchers. The avowed purpose of the march was to present
viginal petitions to the Prince Regent which (backed by the
presence of thousands) would, it was believed, be received with
some awe: each man was to take a blanket with him to sleep on,
hence the name given to the march. [2]

Samuel Bamford, the Middleton Radical leader, strongly disapproved of the scheme. He refused to be associated with it, and
successfully prevented any Middleton people from joining the
procession. Measures, he wrote, began to be hinted at 'which, if
not in direct contravention of the law, were but ill disguised
subterfuges for evading its intentions'. Bamford was too guarded
to say definitely that the more extreme Radical leaders intended
violence; but certainly they seem to have intended to use, if not
violence itself, at least the threat of violence, believing perhaps
that the assembling of large numbers in London would in itself
be sufficient to achieve their aims. [3] One of them, John Johnston,
made a speech at the debating hall of one of the Manchester
Hampden Clubs four days before the march which revealed this
underlying purpose and hinted at the need to go armed: 'you will
be an easy prey', he told intending marchers, 'if you have nothing
but your open hands'. [4]

[1] *Manchester Mercury*, Jan. 21, 1817.
[2] Bamford, I, 30–34. Each petition carried by the marchers was to be
signed by no more than twenty persons in conformity with an Act of
Charles II against tumultuous petitioning; ten of each twenty signatories
were to join the march.
[3] The London Radicals intended holding a meeting of Spa Fields on
March 15th. Davis suggests, though no definite evidence on this point can
be found, that the Blanketeers intended to arrive in London 'in time to
increase the confusion which the meeting was expected to produce'. The
last meeting on Spa Fields on December 2, 1816, had ended in a serious riot
(Davis, *loc. cit.*, 58).   [4] *Ibid.*, doc. no. 27.

Against this background of doubtful motives the marchers duly assembled on the morning of March 10th. The meeting-place was the same as in 1819, St. Peter's Field. Many of the men had 'blankets, rugs, or large coats, rolled up and tied, knap-sack like, on their backs; some carried bundles under their walking sticks'. At about a quarter to ten the Radical orators, led by Bagguley and Drummond, began their harangues to an audience of about twelve thousand people: both of them urged the crowd to act peaceably. At this point the magistrates decided to intervene. Bagguley and Drummond were arrested, the Riot Act was read, and the King's Dragoon Guards cleared the field. Before this, however, about three hundred men had begun to march off towards Stockport. They were pursued by a body of troops accompanied by two magistrates, overtaken just outside Stockport, and a large number of them brought back to Manchester under escort. A few stragglers went on as far as Macclesfield, twenty or so reached Leek, and a mere six got as far as Ashbourne in Derbyshire. Just one man reached London and presented his petition to Lord Sidmouth for conveyance to the Prince Regent.[1]

It is important to contrast the way the Blanket Meeting was broken up with the method employed at Peterloo two years later. Assuming the need to disperse the meeting at all, the action of the authorities was as restrained in 1817 as it was violent in 1819. For this there were probably three main reasons. First, the Blanket Meeting was much smaller than Peterloo, only one-fifth the size; this clearly made the dispersal of the assembly a much easier matter. Second, in 1817 the dispersal was effected not by ill-trained volunteer yeomanry as in 1819 but by disciplined regular cavalry used to doing such work with the minimum of violence. And finally, in 1817 General Sir John Byng, the cool-headed Commander of the Northern District, was present in person to control the situation.[2] He was not present at

[1] Davis, *loc. cit.*, 59–60, docs. no. 28, 29; Bamford, 1, 32–34; Hammond, *Skilled Labourer*, 346–47; Prentice, 92–93; Taylor, 155–56. The sources differ considerably as to the numbers of men reaching the different towns; Bamford's figures have been followed here. The sources differ also as to the numbers assembled at the initial meeting; Bamford said 'four or five thousands', Hay (the Chairman of Quarter Sessions) 'about 12,000'. Bamford disapproved of the meeting and would have some interest in minimizing numbers present.

[2] Sir John Byng (1772–1860) had served under Wellington in the Peninsular, greatly distinguishing himself at Vittoria; he was present also at

Peterloo because the magistrates had told him that he was not needed.[1]

The successful dispersal of the Blanket Meeting in 1817 did not end the authorities' alarms. They discovered a plot to make 'a Moscow of Manchester' on March 30th. Radical delegate meetings, they reported, had taken place on March 17th and 23rd at which the scheme was discussed. Whether the purpose of these meetings was really to organize such a violent outbreak is uncertain. The Radical extremists may have intended merely to release the Blanket prisoners from the New Bailey prison in Salford. In any case, the support they received was very small.

The authorities, however, were greatly alarmed. They believed that the Manchester rising was to take place simultaneously with outbreaks in other parts of the country. The magistrates therefore decided to act decisively, announcing that 'a most daring and traitorous conspiracy' had been discovered. The Watch and Ward was put into operation, special constables were enrolled in large numbers, and on the evening of March 28th the members of the Radical secret committee meeting at Ardwick Bridge, just outside Manchester, were arrested. Bamford, Knight, Benbow, and many others were also taken into custody.[2]

Waterloo. In politics Byng was a Whig, and became an M.P. in 1831. 'As one of the very few distinguished generals who supported the Reform Bill, he was looked upon with especial favour by Lord Melbourne.' He was made a baron in 1835 and Earl of Strafford in 1847 (D.N.B.).

[1] Taylor, 156. See below, p. 124.

[2] Davis, *loc. cit.*, 60–63, docs. nos. 30, 31; Bamford, I, 44–45, 79; Hammond, *Skilled Labourer*, 350–53; Prentice, 95–100; Taylor, 157–58; *Parliamentary Debates*, XXVI (1817), 949–56, 1088–98 (Second Reports of the Lords and Commons Committees of Secrecy).

The Hammonds argue that the reformers did not at any time contemplate a rising and that the scare was entirely a fabrication of the spies employed by the authorities. Davis, on the other hand, denies this. He points out that, although Bamford himself would have nothing to do with the plan, he was not apparently at all surprised to be told that it was the idea of the Manchester Committee: 'we doubted not that it had been sanctioned . . . by the Manchester Committee' (I, 39). He later went on to admit that the Ardwick committee had been 'apprehended in the act of carrying on a secret meeting for unlawful purposes' (I, 120). Furthermore, he primed them in prison to tell what he called 'the old tale', that their meetings were only 'to devise relief to persons who had fled from the suspension act, and to their families in their absence' (I, 121). The implication of this (as Davis points out) is clearly that the meetings had actually talked of other things, probably including violence.

Talk of violence is one thing, however, acting upon that talk is another;

It soon transpired, however, that the magistrates had been rather too hasty in some of their proceedings. They found it difficult to discover evidence to support in a court of law their charges of high treason against Samuel Bamford and seven others for their alleged association with the Ardwick conspiracy. On April 29th Bamford had to be discharged on his own recognizances, and in the end only four of the eight were committed to jail. The action of the Manchester magistrates was thus only partially upheld, and while publicly defending Hay and his colleagues, Lord Sidmouth, the Home Secretary,[1] privately criticized them for being over-zealous:

Upon the Minute Review of the Cases of Persons belonging to Manchester and its neighbourhood. . . . I am to request that in future, when the names of persons, whose arrest is recommended by the Magistrates, are transmitted to me, they may always be accompanied by Depositions, stating as fully and precisely as possible the grounds upon which it has been deemed expedient to advise such a measure.[2]

It was to be regretted that the Home Office did not remember in 1819 this previous evidence of magisterial shortcomings. Instead, Sidmouth and Hobhouse[3] gave the Manchester magistrates almost a completely free hand right up to the day of the massacre, offering much sensible advice but (to their own subsequent regret) no definite instructions.[4]

With the collapse of the Ardwick plot (whatever its exact nature) the Radical Reform movement dropped out of public

and certainly it seems likely that it was the government spies (who were very active in the area) who stiffened this wild talk into something approaching action. To that extent they were the principal culprits. But this is not quite the same thing as saying, as the Hammonds do, that the Radicals had no connection at all with violent remedies.

The notorious Oliver was not one of the spies involved. He came to Manchester soon afterwards, but met with no success. Prentice claimed that it was the influence of the middle-class Radicals which forestalled him in Manchester: they warned the working classes against his attempts at incitement (Hammond, *Skilled Labourer*, 357 n. 4; Prentice, 108–09, 111).

[1] Henry Addington, Viscount Sidmouth (1757–1844) was Home Secretary 1812–21. He had been Speaker of the House of Commons 1789–1801, and Prime Minister 1801–04.

[2] Davis, *loc. cit.*, 63–64.

[3] Henry Hobhouse (1776–1854) was permanent Under-Secretary of State at the Home Office 1817–27. He was later prominent in the early days of the Record Commission. He was a Tory in politics (*D.N.B.*).

[4] See below, p. 118 ff.

prominence for the time being. The arrest of the Radical leaders broke up the Radical organization and support fell away. The collapse of the Radical Reform campaign did not mean, however, the end of popular disturbance in Manchester. 1818 was as disturbed a year in the town as 1817. In 1818 the operatives turned once again to economic remedies for the improvement of their conditions, and the principal events of the year were the spinners' and weavers' strikes.[1] The spinners struck for an advance in wages early in July 1818, and by July 18th it was estimated that some twenty thousand spinning operatives were idle in the Manchester area. They claimed that their wages had been reduced at a time of serious depression in 1816 on the understanding that they would be increased again when markets improved; this improvement, they contended, had now taken place, but the masters had not increased wages. Present wages for men spinners, declared the strikers, were only some 18s. a week against 24s. before the reductions in 1816.

The cotton masters denied entirely that the spinners' wages were as low as this. 'I learn from good authority today', reported Norris, the Manchester stipendiary, on August 13th, 'that the average of earnings for the last six months, taking 40 principal mills, is 31s. 10d. for every adult male spinner.'[2] Nor in any case, even accepting their figure of 18s., were the wages of the spinners anywhere near so low as those of the handloom weavers at this period. 'The actual average rate of earnings of the journeymen spinners', observed the *Manchester Gazette*, 'is considerably above that of any other class of artisan whatever . . . in the existing state of trade, the masters really cannot afford any increase.' The paper was much more sympathetic towards the demands put forward by the weavers, who came out on strike on August 31st seeking an increase of 7s. in the £ in their rates.[3]

The strikes of the spinners and of the weavers were conducted entirely separately. The weavers, unlike the spinners, refused to have anything to do with the Radical Reformers who were

[1] Hammond, *Skilled Labourer*, 94–121, is the source for the following account of the strikes of 1818 unless otherwise stated. Many of the relevant documents from the Home Office Papers have been printed in Aspinall, ch. VII.
[2] Norris to Hobhouse, Aug. 13, 1818 (Aspinall, no. 253); *Manchester Chronicle*, Aug. 15, 1818.
[3] *Manchester Gazette*, July 25, 1818

attempting to recover their influence through the strikes. The
climax came at the end of August and the beginning of September.
An attempt was made by the spinners to organize a General Union
of Trades, and this greatly alarmed the local authorities. On
August 29th the spinners' committee of five was arrested and its
members charged with conspiracy. This shook their organization,
which was still further weakened when their treasurer absconded
with £150. In desperation they now began to threaten violent
action. A great meeting of spinners was held in Stockport on
September 1st to which five hundred men marched from Manchester. The Radical leaders Bagguley, Drummond, and Johnston
urged the strikers to violent courses,[1] and on the next day Gray's
factory in Manchester was attacked by a mob of spinners. One
man was killed, and six or seven seriously injured before the
military arrived. This violent outbreak represented a final despairing gesture; after it the strike quickly collapsed. 'Their spirit
though not their obstinacy', reported Norris three days later,
'appears broken. They have carried on their opposition as long
as they can.' [2] The obduracy of the cotton masters, the activity
of the magistrates, and their own hunger had defeated the
strikers.

The weavers meanwhile, who had come out only on August
31st, were still active. On September 1st the Stockport weavers
paraded, carefully dissociating themselves from the spinners'
meeting addressed by the Radical politicians, and throughout the
week weavers' parades and processions took place in all parts of
the Manchester area. On the 1st, bodies of men 'in regular
military order' marched into Manchester from the direction of
Middleton, Oldham, and Ashton. On the 2nd a similar procession
marched in from Stockport with a band and banners inscribed
'Seven Shillings in the Pound and no less', and held a meeting on
St. George's Fields. On September 3rd another meeting was held
in the same place, after which a procession marched to Stockport.
Finally, on September 4th came the climax to the strike. The
magistrates, greatly alarmed at all the parading, issued a 'Public
Caution' announcing that 'assemblies and processions are, in our
judgment, Illegal, and Dangerous to the Public Peace'. On this
same day the strikers of the Manchester district set out to march

[1] Giles, *op. cit.*, 202–05.
[2] Norris to Sidmouth, Sept. 5, 1818 (Aspinall, no. 289).

to a meeting at Ashton-under-Lyne. About half-way, however, they were met by Sir John Byng and a posse of troops, accompanied by the Boroughreeve of Manchester, who read the Public Caution to them. After hearing this the weavers immediately 'lowered their colours and went home'; they were 'pleased and grateful', reported Byng afterwards, 'at the kind manner they were spoken to'. Once again as in 1817 (but not in 1819) Byng's moderating presence had helped to bring success without bloodshed. Norris noticed how effective his gentle methods had been:

The conduct adopted by the magistracy [he reported on September 5th] and the valuable assistance of Sir J. Byng yesterday in pursuing and dispersing by gentle means the body of men from this place who had set out for Ashton, has much contributed, I think, to dispose the main body of weavers into a right understanding of their true interests.

Unfortunately, such 'gentle means' were not adopted a year later.[1]

After this encounter the weavers' strike gradually subsided. The movement continued for another fortnight in the Burnley area, but the Manchester Yeomanry made its appearance there and plans for strike meetings were given up.[2] Neither the weavers nor the spinners had gained anything from their turn-outs. In many places the weavers did receive small increases for a time, but these were not long maintained; and by the beginning of 1819 the pressure of distress upon them was as great as ever. As we have already seen, this was the main reason for the spread of Radicalism in the area in the first half of 1819. If the weavers' rates had been increased by even 2s. to 3s. in the £ in 1818, there might have been no Peterloo.[3]

[1] *Ibid.; Manchester Chronicle*, Sept. 5, 1818.

[2] Norris to Sidmouth, Sept. 22, 1818 (Aspinall no. 303); *Exchange Herald*, Sept. 22, 1818.

[3] 'With respect to the weavers, the main body of them, I believe, are well disposed. They naturally jump at 7s. in the £, but would be perfectly contented with two or three shillings' (Norris to Sidmouth, Sept. 5, 1818. Aspinall, no. 289).

CHAPTER EIGHT

'PETERLOO'

On January 18, 1819, Henry Hunt presided over a meeting of some eight thousand operatives held on St. Peter's Field, Manchester. With this meeting, at the same place and with the same chief speaker as the Peterloo meeting of seven months later, the political course of the year 1819 opened in Manchester.

A hint of things to come was given by the way the meeting assembled. Just as on a larger scale in August the reformers displayed flags and banners, and some of them marched in regular order with music. Hunt's speech was confident, almost threatening. A regiment of horse, he told his audience, had been sent for to attend the meeting: 'wherever I appear in public they honour me with the attendance of soldiers'; but should the day arrive when the people had to fight for their liberties he had no doubt that soldiers and people would 'act together as brothers'. Hunt advised the people not to send yet another petition to the Commons to be 'kicked out' by them, but to draw up instead a Remonstrance addressed directly to the Prince Regent. This Remonstrance, and the Declaration also passed by the meeting, have already been noticed as important statements of Radical policy in the year of Peterloo: between them they outlined virtually every aspect of the Radical reform programme. The background to Peterloo was already being filled in.[1]

After enthusiastically passing these two manifestos the meeting dispersed peaceably. No arrests were made by the magistrates, and the troops, though at the ready, remained in their barracks. Hobhouse immediately congratulated Norris on the magistrates' calm and on 'the judgment you exercised in forbearing to call for the aid of the military power while the peace remained unbroken'.[2] Right up to and during the Peterloo crisis the Home Office continued to hope that the magistrates would display such for-

[1] *Manchester Observer*, Jan. 23, 1819; Norris to Sidmouth, Jan. 18, 1819 (H.O. 42/183). For the Declaration and the Remonstrance see Appendix A.
[2] Hobhouse to Norris, Jan. 20, 1819, Norris to Sidmouth, Jan. 25, 1819. (*State Trials*, Appendix B.)

bearance. Unfortunately, by the middle of the year Norris and his colleagues, under the influence of continuous and ever-growing Radical agitation, had lost all their calm of the previous January.

Hunt remained in Manchester for several days after the meeting, and on the following Friday visited the Theatre Royal. He was received there with great applause from his supporters in the audience, and this aroused the feeling of the 'loyalist' sections. They called for 'God Save the King', and when (as they claimed) Hunt hissed the anthem, he was forcibly removed from the theatre by a group of 'loyal' enthusiasts led by some officers of the 7th Light Dragoons. Hunt's vanity was now touched. He sent for Bamford and told him that he intended to go to the theatre again on another night and that he would need a bodyguard. Bamford accordingly collected from Middleton a party of ten men, including himself, armed with sticks. 'Our business', he wrote, 'was to attend the play,—to protect Mr. Hunt, if requisite, and to retaliate with punishment, any insult that might be offered to him or any of his friends'. The magistrates soon got to hear of this scheme and not surprisingly they ordered the theatre to remain closed. On discovering this, Hunt addressed the crowd outside the theatre and then returned to his inn. There, later in the evening, about a dozen 'loyalists' roughs 'in the garb of gentlemen' forced their way into his private room and challenged him and the three or four friends with him to a fight.[1]

So ended Hunt's visit to Manchester. The dangerous tendencies on both sides had been amply displayed. The reformers' language had grown wild, wilder probably than they meant. Remonstrance had replaced petition: 'resistance to earthly tyranny' had become the call.[2] Much of this was certainly only intended for effect and had no connection with any intended Radical revolution; but the appearance was there to alarm 'loyal' minds. These 'loyalists' too had shown an unfortunate tendency, a distressing readiness to use physical violence against the reformers. Violence on the Peterloo scale was probably far from their minds, but an unhappy beginning had been made. As yet, however, the magistrates remained calm.

[1] Bamford, ch. XXIX; Prentice, 147–50; *Manchester Observer*, Jan. 23, 30, 1819.
[2] Manchester Declaration.

The next important event locally was the Stockport Radical meeting of February 15th. Harrison was the chief speaker, and a remonstrance to the Prince Regent was passed similar to that at Manchester. A Cap of Liberty was displayed which some mounted constables unsuccessfully attempted to seize. After the meeting there was considerable disturbance in the town and the Riot Act had to be read three times. Norris, the Manchester Stipendiary magistrate, regretted the attempt on the Cap of Liberty 'as it gave the multitude an apparent triumph'. His fears were beginning to rise now: 'if these meetings are continued to be held with impunity', he wrote, 'it is quite impossible but that in a few months it must lead us to the same state in which we were last year'. The weavers' wages, he added significantly, 'are at present *extremely low*'.[1]

March and April saw a lull in the Radicals' public activities, no important meetings being held until one at Stockport on April 22nd to protest against the sentences passed on Bagguley, Drummond, and Johnston.[2] Behind the scenes, however, the reformers were probably very busy, for by the end of April the rules of the Stockport Union Society had been published by Harrison, and Unions on the Stockport model had begun to spring up all over the area. These included the Patriotic Union Society at Manchester.

The successful establishment of many new Unions was almost certainly one reason for the intensified Radical activity which began to get under way during May. Another probable reason for this increased agitation was the refusal of Lord Sidmouth to present the Manchester and Stockport Remonstrances of January and February to the Prince Regent. Hunt asserted in a letter sent to Sidmouth on May 29th that he would find 'some other means of making the prayers and complaints of the suffering people' known to the Regent. The result, declared the Manchester magistrates, was the spate of Radical meetings.[3]

Before the appearance of Hunt's letter Norris had still been comparatively calm. Although one of his spies had promised to produce a Radical pike, he was not too disturbed: 'it had more of a

[1] Norris to Sidmouth, Feb. 20, 1819 (H.O. 42/184); *Manchester Observer*, Feb. 20, 1819.

[2] Giles, *op. cit.*, 219.

[3] Magistrates of Lancashire and Cheshire to Sidmouth, April 23, 1820 (*State Trials*, Appendix B); *Manchester Observer*, June 12, 1819.

threat than anything real in it', he wrote on May 26th, 'and I consider at present that it is chiefly used to keep alive the spirit of their adherents—in other words that they are not by any means *ready for action*'.[1] Within less than three weeks, however, under the influence of the spate of Radical meetings, his whole attitude had changed. By June 15th he was reporting that 'a very short period of two *Months* at the longest is spoken of as the great Day of Trial . . . a few weeks may blow this wicked conspiracy into a Flame'.[2]

The number of meetings was indeed impressive. 'Meetings took place about the same time', wrote Prentice, 'at Oldham, Bolton, Royton, Bury, Heywood, Stockport, Ashton-under-Lyne, Failsworth, Gee Cross, Lees, Middleton, Rochdale, Todmorden, Barnsley, Holmfirth, Leeds, and other towns, all unrepresented in parliament.'[3] The extent of the new organization of which these meetings were the public reflection was emphasized at the important delegate meeting which the Radicals were able to call at Oldham on June 7th. Delegates from twenty-eight towns attended, the most important part of their work being to lend the support of the Lancashire Radicals to a proposal for a national meeting of Radical delegates in London. The national connections and aspirations of the local reform movement were once more made clear.[4]

The new power of the Radicals was strikingly demonstrated by what happened at the meeting (already noticed) held on St. Peter's Field on June 21st. This meeting, called by the distressed weavers to petition either for relief for their distresses or for assisted emigration to North America, was won over by the Radicals Saxton and Walker to the cause of Radical Reform. Resolutions were passed urging the election of delegates in readiness for the national Radical delegate meeting in London and supporting the principle of abstention from the use of exciseable articles.[5]

From now on the magistrates' alarms were to be given no time to cool. A week after the meeting of June 21st another great assemblage was held at Stockport on June 28th, probably the

[1] Norris to Sidmouth, May 26, 1819 (H.O. 42/187).
[2] Norris to Sidmouth, June 15, 1819 (H.O. 42/188).
[3] Prentice, 150–51.
[4] *Manchester Observer, Wardle's Manchester Observer*, June 12, 1819. For the resolutions passed by the Oldham delegate meeting see Appendix A.
[5] *Manchester Observer, Manchester Chronicle*, June 26, 1819.

greatest of the Radical meetings in the area in 1819 apart from
Peterloo itself. As at Manchester, the last of the Stockport handloom weavers had recently gone over in despair to the Radicals,[1]
and their numbers helped to swell the audience to 'upwards of
20,000' according to the *Observer*. The Radicals assembled in much
the same manner as they did at Peterloo, coming in from all the
surrounding towns in processions with banners bearing Radical
slogans. When the meeting was assembled a Cap of Liberty was
hoisted. The chief speakers were Sir Charles Wolseley and Joseph
Harrison; both of them made speeches for which they were later
imprisoned on charges of attempting to bring the government
into hatred and contempt:

I was at Paris during the taking of the Bastile [declared Wolseley] and
I can assure you I was not idle on that glorious occasion—I therefore
think, that it is a pretty fair presumption, that the man who has been
engaged in the destruction of Bastiles in a foreign land will not be
inactive in endeavouring to annihilate those dungeons of despotism
in his own.

The people of England [asserted Harrison] have a right to approach
the throne with their complaints, but the avenues have been stopped
by the very men who had an immediate interest in screening their own
misdeeds from public investigation—this was a barrier of corruption
and the people must blow it up or blow it down.

A long Appeal to the Nation was passed by the meeting, asking
for a Radical Reform and supporting the calling of a national
delegate meeting in London.[2]

Some new Radical gesture was now being made almost every
day. On July 1st Sir Francis Burdett introduced a Radical parliamentary reform motion in the Commons,[3] and two days later the
first step in the sequence of events which led directly up to Peterloo was taken when Joseph Johnson on behalf of the Patriotic
Union Society asked Hunt to visit Manchester. He seems to have
feared a popular outbreak irrespective of what the Radicals might
do:

Trade here is not worth following [he told Hunt]. Everything is
almost at a stand still, nothing but ruin and starvation stare one in the
face. The state of this district is truly dreadful, and I believe nothing

[1] See above, pp. 22–23.
[2] *Manchester Observer*, July 3, 1819; *Annual Register, 1820*, Appendix to
Chronicle, 911; Giles, *op. cit.*, 221.
[3] *Parliamentary Debates*, XL (1819), 1440–504.

but the greatest exertions can prevent an insurrection. Oh, that you in London were prepared for it! The Manchester Patriotic Union Society have requested me to inform you that it is their intention to call a public meeting [in] this town next Monday four [weeks]. They at the same time particularly request your attendance . . . I trust therefore you will not deny us your company.[1]

On the 6th Hunt privately accepted this invitation, asking that it should be made 'rather a meeting of the county of Lancashire, etc. than of Manchester alone . . . I think by management the *largest assemblage* may be procured that ever was seen in this country'. He desired a public invitation to be sent to him which should be published in the *Manchester Observer* and in the London papers. 'This will raise a public feeling and a desire to know whether I accept or not.' Hunt's vanity and his power of stage management are apparent, and also his intention of making Peterloo an especially impressive meeting.[2] Johnson dreamed not only of a huge assemblage of Radical followers but also of the greatest possible display of Radical leadership: Wolseley and Major Cartwright had promised to attend, he wrote to Hunt on July 10th, and he was inviting Wooler (the editor of the *Black Dwarf*) also.[3]

Two days later the national ramifications and ambitions of the Radical movement were made still further apparent when Wolseley, fresh from his wild speech at Stockport, was elected 'Legislatorial Attorney' at a great Radical meeting in Birmingham. He was to take his seat, the local Radicals intended, as the popularly elected representative of Birmingham in the House of Commons. Cartwright and Wooler were present at the meeting along with (according to the *Birmingham Recorder*) not less than sixty thousand people. Although in reality the audience was probably considerably smaller than this, the Birmingham meeting was clearly on a much larger scale than most previous Radical meetings, and its importance needs to be stressed.[4] It was the first of four Radical assemblages in the summer of 1819 of much more than local importance of which the Peterloo meeting was the last and greatest. All of them were intended by the Radicals to attract national attention to their agitation.

[1] Johnson to Hunt, July 3, 1819 (*State Trials*, Appendix B).
[2] Hunt to Johnson, July 6, 1819 (*ibid.*).
[3] Johnson to Hunt, July 10, 1819 (*ibid.*).
[4] *Manchester Observer*, July 24, 1819, quoting from the *Birmingham Recorder;* Spooner to Sidmouth, July 13, 1819 (Papers relative to the Internal State of the Country, no. 5).

After Birmingham the next meeting in this series was held at Hunslet Moor, near Leeds on July 19th. Knight, Fitton, and the local middle-class Radical, Edward Baines, were the principal speakers. The meeting agreed to 'the election of a representative to parliament, whenever a proper one could be met with'. The numbers attending were perhaps not so large as the reformers had expected, only four or five thousand according to *The Times*; but despite this, the decision to prepare for the election of a Legislatorial Attorney on the Birmingham model made the meeting an important event in the progress of the Radical agitation.[1]

Two days after the Leeds meeting the Radicals held a rally in London itself, at Smithfield. Some ten thousand people were present according to *The Times*, and Hunt was the principal speaker. Among the other Radical leaders present was Harrison from Stockport who was actually arrested while the meeting was in progress for his speech at Stockport on June 28th. The meeting passed eighteen resolutions, and these assumed an especial importance later because they were used by the prosecution at Hunt's trial as evidence of his dangerous intentions at Manchester. The most important point which they made was to claim that because the House of Commons had 'not been fairly and freely nominated or chosen by the voices or votes of the largest proportion of the members of the State', any laws which it enacted or taxes which it imposed were not in equity obligatory upon those who were unjustly excluded from the franchise. The meeting resolved therefore

that from and after the 1st day of January 1820, we cannot conscientiously consider ourselves as bound in equity by any future enactments which may be made by persons styling themselves our representatives, other than those who shall be fully, freely, and fairly chosen by the voices or votes of the largest proportion of the members of the State.[2]

Such language as this certainly seemed to threaten anarchy: and the government and magistrates were not disposed to believe, as Bentham suggested a few days later in the *Observer*, that the language of the reformers far outran their intentions.[3]

[1] *The Times*, July 22, 1819; *Leeds Mercury*, July 24, 1819; Fitzwilliam to Sidmouth, July 21, 1819 (Papers relative to the Internal State of the Country, no. 10); Resolutions passed at the Hunslet Moor meeting (*ibid.*, no. 8).

[2] *Manchester Observer*, July 31, 1819; *State Trials*, 463–65.

[3] See above, p. 46.

The authorities' worst fears seemed only to receive confirmation when on July 23rd Birch, the constable bringing Harrison back under arrest from Smithfield, was shot at and seriously injured in Stockport. A reward was immediately offered for the discovery of the intended assassin and the Radicals were naturally accused of the deed.[1] In fact, the culprit was a silk weaver who had acted entirely on his own initiative. Hunt wrote to Johnson saying he was 'very sorry for the Act; it will give the Villains of the Press such a handle'.[2] After being concealed in the neighbourhood for some months the culprit was eventually captured and executed. Birch recovered and was given a pension by the government.[3]

A week after the Birch affair appeared the first public announcement of the intended Peterloo meeting. The present intention was to hold the meeting on August 9th:

The public are respectfully informed, that a MEETING will be held here on MONDAY the 9th of AUGUST, 1819, on the Area near ST. PETER'S CHURCH, to take into consideration, the most speedy and effectual mode of obtaining Radical Reform in the Commons House of Parliament; being fully convinced, that nothing less can remove the intolerable evils under which the People of this Country have so long, and do still, groan: and also to consider the propriety of the 'Unrepresented Inhabitants of Manchester' electing a Person to represent them in Parliament; and the adopting Major Cartwright's Bill.

H. HUNT, Esq. *in the Chair.*

Major Cartwright, Sir Charles Wolseley, Mr. Charles Pearson, Mr. Wooler, and Godfrey Higgins, Esq. have been solicited, and are expected to attend.

[Names of eleven signatories]

The Boroughreeve, Magistrates, and Constables are requested to attend.[4]

The influence of the Birmingham 'Legislatorial Attorney' meeting was very apparent in this notice. The Birmingham meeting had been the great rally of Radicalism in the Midlands; the Hunslet Moor meeting had been an attempt to display Radical strength in Yorkshire; the Smithfield meeting had been an exhibition of Radical power in the metropolis. There remained now the

---

[1] Lloyd to Hobhouse, July 27, 1819 (H.O. 42/190).
[2] Hunt to Johnson, July 29, 1819 (H.O. 42/190).
[3] Giles, *op. cit.*, 224; *Manchester Observer*, April 15, 1820.
[4] *Manchester Observer*, July 31, 1819.

Manchester meeting, intended, as Hunt had written, to be 'a meeting of the county of Lancashire', to be a concentration of the supporters of Radical Reform in what was probably its most important centre. 'We have nothing to do', he wrote to Johnson deprecating any violent policies, 'but concentrate public opinion, and if our Enemies will not listen to the voice of a whole People, they will listen to nothing, and may the Effects of their Folly and Wickedness be upon their own Heads'.[1]

So the month of July came to an end with the Radicals preparing for the great meeting which was to be the climax of their campaign. The authorities, meanwhile, were watching their activities very closely. Ethelston had for months been supplying the Home Office with reports from his spies of intended Radical risings. 'I am not an Alarmist', he wrote on July 24th, reporting the shooting of Birch, 'but I think I foresee in this only a prelude of future Bloodshed.' [2]

The lower classes [reported Norris on June 30th] 'are repeatedly heard to murmer threats that in a few weeks some explosion is to take place . . . for which I fear there is little doubt numbers are preparing themselves with Arms of various descriptions.

The same general date for the expected Radical effort—the first fortnight in August—was given in several letters to the Home Office.[3]

The magistrates admitted to being short of specific intelligence on which to base their alarms, but this did not cause them to question their soundness:

We feel a difficulty [confessed five Lancashire magistrates to Sidmouth on July 1st] in stating to your lordship, any specific facts upon which legal responsibility will attach to any particular individuals at present; but upon the general view of the subject, we cannot have a doubt that some alarming insurrection is in contemplation.[4]

The magistrates were quite sure that the people would attend the

[1] Hunt to Johnson, July 29, 1819 (H.O. 42/190).
[2] Ethelston to Sidmouth, July 24, 1819 (H.O. 42/190). See also his letters of April 24 (H.O. 42/186), June 17 (H.O. 42/188), and July 19 (H.O. 42/189).
[3] Norris to Sidmouth, June 15, June 30, 1819 (H.O. 42/188); Ethelston to Sidmouth, June 26, 1819 (*ibid.*).
[4] Five Lancashire Magistrates to Sidmouth, July 1, 1819 (Papers relative to the Internal State of the Country, no. 1).

proposed Manchester meeting armed with pikes and other weapons. For months they had been reporting their manufacture, though at first they seem to have been doubtful about the extent of the danger: 'although arms have been repeatedly spoken of', reported Norris on May 10th, 'only two have been produced and it seems very difficult to procure more'.[1] By the time of Peterloo, however, his attitude had entirely changed: 'very many of them', he wrote on August 11th 'I have little doubt will come secretly armed'.[2]

Even more dangerous than the Radical pikes, it seemed to the magistrates, was the Radical Press. This, they believed, was the basic evil, urging the people to arm and to all the other Radical excesses. The Radical meetings and 'the unbounded liberty of the press' were the principal causes 'of the evil which we apprehend', reported five Lancashire magistrates.[3] 'The *Manchester Observer* has an incalculable circulation', regretted Norris, 'so also have all the London political publications'.[4] In this connection, however, an immediate remedy lay in the hands of the magistrates; and on July 24th five bills for seditious libel were found against Wroe, the editor of the *Manchester Observer*.[5] This prosecution was probably the work of the select committee of magistrates from Lancashire and Cheshire which had been set up the day before: it was this select committee which was in charge of the military and civil power at Peterloo.[6]

There was only one man in important office who did not share the excessive alarms of the magistrates: this was Sir John Byng, the Commander of the Northern District. As during the Blanket period and during the strikes of 1818, he used his influence continually to restrain the magistrates. In the second week of July Norris visited Byng at his headquarters in Pontefract to discuss the best disposition of forces 'for the suppression of the intended revolutionary insurrection'.[7] On this occasion Byng

---

[1] Norris to Sidmouth, May 10, 1819 (H.O. 42/187). See also Norris to Sidmouth, May 26, 1819 (*ibid.*), and Lloyd to Hobhouse, March 8, 1819 (H.O. 42/185).
[2] Norris to Sidmouth, Aug. 11, 1819 (H.O. 42/191).
[3] Five Lancashire Magistrates to Sidmouth, July 1, 1819 (Papers relative to the Internal State of the Country, no. 1).
[4] Norris to Sidmouth, July 4, 1819 (H.O. 42/189).
[5] See above, p. 55.
[6] Narrative of the Peterloo Proceedings by the Rev. W. R. Hay (H.O. 42/196).   [7] Norris to Sidmouth, July 14, 1819 (H.O. 42/189).

probably tried hard to calm Norris's fears, though clearly without much success. The commander-in-chief did not expect any
trouble:

I have . . . but little expectation [he wrote] from the united strength
of the Civil and Military Force in readiness, that Mr. Hunt or His
Associates will either say or do that which will authorize any interference. They will be too cautious and fearful to try our strength.[1]

Unfortunately, Byng was almost alone in his calm appraisal of
the situation. The local magistrates were fully supported in their
alarms by the local 'loyalists'. On July 9th they met at the Police
Office in Manchester and passed the series of alarmist resolutions
which has already been discussed. They also established a Committee in Aid of the Civil Power. This Committee, consisting
chiefly of former town's officers, was very active in Manchester
in the weeks just before Peterloo: its members (rather than the
magistrates) were 'the original instigators' of the massacre, wrote
Taylor, 'men of the most violent party feelings'.[2] At a meeting of
the Committee on July 16th it was resolved to form an 'Armed
Association' for the protection of life and property in the town.
This was intended as a kind of 'loyal' Home Guard. Arms for a
thousand men were requested from the government.[3]

While all this activity was going on locally, the government at
Westminster was also busy. On July 7th Lord Sidmouth sent a
circular to all the Lords-Lieutenant telling them that because of
the large number of Radical meetings which were being called
they must repair to their counties.

It is earnestly hoped [he wrote to Lord Derby, the Lord Lieutenant of
Lancashire] that the power of the civil authorities will be fully sufficient,
but as a measure of precaution, your Lordship is desired to give
immediate direction to the several corps of yeomanry cavalry in the
county of Lancaster to hold themselves in readiness to attend to any
call for support and assistance, which in case of necessity they may
receive from the magistrates.[4]

As a result of this letter, the Manchester and Salford Yeomanry
were put in a state of readiness and their sabres were sent for

---

[1] Byng to Hobhouse, July 21, 1819 (H.O. 42/190). See also his letter of
August 14 quoted below, p. 124, n. 4.
[2] Taylor, 173–74.
[3] *An Address to the Higher Classes*, 44.
[4] Sidmouth to Derby, July 7, 1819 (*State Trials*, Appendix B).

sharpening.[1] On July 30th the government acted again. A proclamation was issued in the name of the Prince Regent condemning seditious assemblies and libels and the practice of drilling. This proclamation was posted up by the magistrates in Manchester on August 3rd.[2]

The magistrates seem, however, to have acted against the proposed Radical meeting of August 9th even before they knew of the proclamation, for on the same day as its first announcement (July 31st) they pronounced the intended meeting illegal:

Whereas it appears by an Advertisement in the *Manchester Observer* Paper of this day, that a PUBLIC and ILLEGAL MEETING is convened for *Monday the 9th day of August next*, to be held on the AREA, NEAR ST. PETER'S CHURCH, in Manchester; We, the Undersigned Magistrates, acting for the Counties Palatine of Lancaster and Chester, *do hereby Caution all Persons to abstain*, AT THEIR PERIL, from attending such ILLEGAL MEETING.

It will be noticed that the magistrates' grammar was at fault and that strictly speaking the announcement reads as an instruction to *attend* the meeting: the Radicals immediately pounced on this error.[3]

The reformers' next move was interesting. Saxton was despatched to take the opinion of counsel in Liverpool as to the legality of the action of the magistrates. Counsel's opinion was 'that the intention of choosing Representatives, contrary to the existing law, tends greatly to render the proposed Meeting seditious'. Therefore, announced Saxton in a public notice, the proposed meeting was abandoned: no Legislatorial Attorney would be elected for Manchester.[4]

The Radicals were not seriously discomfited by this setback, nor by the Prince Regent's proclamation. They were immediately ready with plans for another meeting. Johnson wrote to Hunt on August 3rd:

To day they have posted a proclamation from London in consequence of which I shall alter the advertisement for the meeting. and call one for the purpose of taking into consideration the *propriety of petitioning* the House of Commons, or something else . . . I suppose it is con-

---

[1] *Manchester Observer*, July 17, 1819; Philips, 17.
[2] *Manchester Observer*, Aug. 7, 1819; Johnson to Hunt, Aug. 3, 1819 (*State Trials*, Appendix B).
[3] *Manchester Observer*, Aug. 7, 1819.
[4] *Ibid.*

sidering the propriety of electing a member for Manchester that they call 'illegal'. We must therefore alter it.[1]

Clearly acting under Johnson's instructions, on the next day the signatories of the original requisition gave up the proposed meeting for the 9th:

Our Guardians of the public peace having in massy placards and large letters declared the said meeting to be illegal . . . although these Guardian Angels did not deign to inform the Public wherein such illegality consisted: yet in compliance with their mandate, and to give them no general cause of complaint or offence, it has been deemed advisable, NOT to hold such Meeting: but to request the Boroughreeve and Constables, to convene another.[2]

Not surprisingly, the Boroughreeve failed to call this requested substitute meeting, and on August 6th therefore the Radicals called another one on their own initiative:

A REQUISITION having been presented to the Boroughreeve and Constables of Manchester, signed by above 700 Inhabitant Householders in a few hours, requesting them to call a PUBLIC MEETING *'To consider the propriety of adopting the most* LEGAL *and* EFFECTUAL *means of obtaining a* REFORM *in the Commons House of Parliament'* and they having declined to call such Meeting therefore the undersigned Requisitionists give NOTICE that a Public Meeting will be held, on the area, near St. Peter's Church, for the above mentioned purpose, on Monday the 16th instant—the Chair to be taken by H. Hunt, Esq. at 12 o'clock.

Major Cartwright—Mr. Wooler—Mr. Pearson—Mr. Carlisle—Dr. Crompton—Mr. E. Rushton—Mr. J. Smith—Mr. Thomas Smith—will be invited to attend this Meeting.[3]

An analysis of the signatories to this announcement suggests that most of them were handloom weavers.[4]

While these final preparations were being made in Manchester the government continued to watch the situation closely. Apart from their public pronouncements in the circular of July 7th and in the proclamation of July 30th the ministers also sought to influence developments through the private channels of the Home Office correspondence with the magistrates. In this correspondence the attitude of the government was much less panic-stricken than its two public statements inclined contemporaries (and has since inclined historians) to assume. The Home Office was by

---

[1] Johnson to Hunt, Aug. 3, 1819 (*State Trials*, Appendix B).
[2] *Manchester Observer*, Aug. 7, 1819.
[3] *Ibid.*
[4] See above, p. 24.

no means so excessively alarmed as were the magistrates of Manchester and on many occasions both Sidmouth and Hobhouse set out to restrain the magistrates. As early as February 24th Sidmouth was writing to Lord Derby, the Lord-Lieutenant of Lancashire, defining the nature of the relations between magistrates and military 'which have not been very clearly understood'. Magistrates, Sidmouth stressed, should make every effort to act without the military and even when called to be present at a meeting troops were not to be used 'until the Peace had been actually broken'.[1] This letter showed how little liking the Home Office had for the use of the military, in contrast to the attitude of the magistrates who (not only in Manchester but generally) tended to rely too much on the threat of armed force.[2] The use of troops for the maintenance of civil order, it seemed to the Home Office, was an exceptional proceeding beyond the normal application of the law. When Norris regretted the lapsing of the coercive legislation of 1817, Hobhouse reminded him that 'the powers of the Conservators of the Peace for the suppression of riots and unlawful assemblies are strong by the Common Law'.[3] Ominously Norris continued to press for coercive powers and began to fear that 'martial law' would be needed:[4] the Home Office could not wean the Manchester magistrates from their love of military gestures.

How far the attitude of the Home Office differed from that of the Manchester magistrates responsible for the Peterloo massacre was shown in a letter written by Hobhouse to Norris twelve days before Peterloo. Hobhouse urged the magistrates simply to gather evidence of what took place at the meeting, to ignore any illegal proceeding for the time being, and not to use force:

Lord Sidmouth has no doubt that you will make arrangements for obtaining evidence of what passes; that if anything illegal is done or said, it may be the subject of prosecution. But even if they should utter sedition or proceed to the election of a representative, Lord Sidmouth

---

[1] Sidmouth to Derby, February 24, 1819 (H.O. 41/4).
[2] Norris as late as August 8th was pressing for still more troops. Byng refused and wrote to Hobhouse: 'the Police there will soon be afraid to move without soldiers with them' (Byng to Hobhouse, Aug. 1819. H.O. 42/191).
[3] Norris to Sidmouth, June 17, 1819, Hobhouse to Norris, June 18, 1819 (*State Trials*, Appendix B).
[4] Norris to Sidmouth, July 10, 1819 (*ibid.*).

9

is of opinion that it will be the wisest course to abstain from any endeavour to disperse the mob, unless they should proceed to acts of felony or riot. . . . His Lordship [concluded Hobhouse in a similar letter to a Rochdale magistrate eight days later] considers that on various Accounts this mode of proceeding is far preferable to an attempt to disperse the Assembly by force.[1]

Exhortations such as these to gather evidence of Radical meetings and plottings were a constant theme in the letters sent out from the Home Office in the fortnight before Peterloo. Sidmouth and Hobhouse clearly had the very sensible idea of getting the Radical leaders quietly into prison by using the normal processes of the law and without making any spectacular gestures. Unfortunately their policy met with little response from the Manchester magistrates: they did not think a policy of accumulating evidence sufficiently vigorous. 'The remedy for the present state of things', wrote Norris six weeks before the massacre, 'must be (*in the first instance*) more violent than informations or indictments.' [2]

There was thus a great and very important difference between the attitude of the Home Office and the attitude of the Manchester magistrates before Peterloo. Both sincerely believed that the Radicals were plotting eventual revolution, but their ways of thwarting that revolution were very different. Hobhouse pressed for the collection of damaging evidence: Norris on the other hand had given up all hope by the end of June of putting down the reformers by mere informations or indictments. The Home Office expressed the need for the greatest caution in the use of the military: Norris was for putting his trust in 'martial law' and more troops. The Home Office suggested 'a monitory and conciliatory Address to the lower Classes': the magistrates made no such gesture.[3]

Different however as were their attitudes, contact between the magistrates and the Home Office was close. In particular, the Law Officers of the Crown gave detailed advice to the magistrates through the Home Office as to their legal position. The most

[1] Hobhouse to Norris, Aug. 4, 1819 (*ibid.*); Hobhouse to Crossley, Aug. 10, 1819 (H.O. 41/4).
[2] Norris to Sidmouth, June 30, 1819 (*State Trials*, Appendix B).
[3] Hobhouse to Norris, Aug. 7, 1819 (H.O. 41/4). Byng suggested as a counter to the Radical meetings a meeting of the clergy, gentry and master manufacturers to receive deputations from the distressed operatives (Byng to Hobhouse, Aug. 5, 1819. H.O. 42/191).

important of their opinions was communicated by Hobhouse on
July 17th:

> With reference to what I yesterday stated, on the expected meeting at
> Manchester on Monday, I have now to acquaint you that the Attorney
> and Solicitor-General have given their opinion that the election of a
> member of Parliament without the King's writ is a high misdemeanour
> ... Lord Sidmouth therefore hopes that, if such an election should be
> attempted at Manchester, measures will be taken for bringing the
> offenders to justice. From the opinion of the Law Officers it follows
> that a meeting held for the purpose of such election is an unlawful
> assembly. But if the meeting is not convened for the unlawful purpose,
> the illegality will not commence until the purpose is developed, and of
> course after the crowd has been collected; when it must be a question
> of prudence and expediency, to be decided by the magistrates on the
> spot, whether they should proceed to disperse the persons assembled.[1]

Thus meetings which were not for the purpose of electing Legislatorial Attornies were legal in the eyes of the Law Officers at
least until they had assembled and an illegal purpose had developed.
The magistrates of Manchester were much influenced by this
letter. On the strength of it they condemned the meeting proposed
for August 9th, which was 'to consider the propriety of ...
electing a Person to represent them in Parliament'; and equally
because of it they felt themselves bound to let the meeting of
August 16th assemble, which was merely a meeting '*to consider the
propriety of adopting the most* LEGAL *and* EFFECTUAL *means of obtaining
a* REFORM'. There was in this second instance no mention of
electing a member of parliament on which the magistrates could
pounce as an illegal purpose: they therefore had to wait on events,
and it was not (as hostile critics said afterwards) that the magistrates preferred to let the Peterloo meeting assemble so that they
could attack it. Similarly, when Hunt offered to surrender himself
on the Saturday before the meeting the magistrates were not being
dishonest when they told him that they had no grounds for
arresting him: until his intentions revealed themselves on the
Monday the magistrates, following the advice of the Law Officers,
really did believe that they had none.[2] They feared the worst, but
they felt that they could not stop it beforehand: 'the magistrates,
as at present advised', wrote Norris on the day before Peterloo,
'do not think of preventing the meeting ... I hope the peace may

---

[1] Hobhouse to Norris, July 17, 1819 (*State Trials*, Appendix B).
[2] See below, p. 182.

be preserved; but under all circumstances, it is scarcely possible to expect it'.[1]

The legal basis of the attitude of the Manchester magistrates before Peterloo was thus a sound one. But it was nonetheless most unfortunate; for by allowing the people to assemble on St. Peter's Field the magistrates gave them the impression that they accepted the meeting as legal and that they would not interfere. But once the meeting had assembled the magistrates were no longer bound by the detailed moderating advice of the Law Officers. They were left much more to their own discretion. And because, as we have seen, fundamentally they were far out of touch with the desire of the Law Officers and of the Home Office for moderation, this discretion was not exercised with the restraint which their superiors clearly desired. In the weeks before the Peterloo meeting moderation had been forced upon the Manchester magistrates from above, but on the day of Peterloo itself they were left free to give full rein to their own immoderate alarms. Ominously, on August 3rd the 'loyalist' *Manchester Mercury* newspaper reported that the Cheshire magistrates had 'come to a determination to act with decision, and to *suppress all Seditious Meetings immediately as they assemble*'. It was this policy, not the one advocated by the Home Office, which produced the Peterloo Massacre.

While behind the scenes the magistrates and the Home Office made their regrettably ill-attuned preparations for the great meeting, an atmosphere of great excitement was developing in Manchester. The local 'loyalists' were terrified by the popularity of Hunt, the Radical leader, and in an attempt to lessen his influence they posted up handbills blackening his character. Suggestions were made that he was a coward: 'in his absence he writes boldly, and urges you to *action* and *resistance*; and yet when he

[1] Norris to Sidmouth, Aug. 15, 1819 (Papers relative to the Internal State of the Country, no. 32).

The Home Office was not too happy even about the banning of the meeting of August 9th. The Attorney-General agreed with Hobhouse that as the proposed meeting was called only to *consider* the election of a representative, it was not really correct for the Manchester magistrates to pronounce it illegal (Hobhouse to Attorney-General, Aug. 2, 1819, Attorney-General to Hobhouse, Aug. 3, 1819, Hobhouse to Norris, Aug. 3, 1819. *State Trials*, Appendix B). Norris was 'sorry to find . . . that any doubts are entertained as to the propriety of declaring the intended meeting on Monday to be illegal in consequence of the peculiar wording of the advertisement' [Norris to Sidmouth, Aug. 4, 1819 (*ibid.*)].

speaks in public, he advocates *peaceable demeanour and obedience to the laws.* This looks like personal fear, if it is not double dealing.' [1] Despite such attacks, however, Hunt's popularity in Manchester remained unabated and he received a rapturous welcome from the people when he arrived in the town on August 9th.[2] On the 11th he issued an address from Johnson's cottage at Smedley, just outside Manchester, where he was staying. It gave instructions for the conduct of the people on the following Monday.

You will meet on Monday next, my friends, and by your *steady*, *firm* and *temperate* deportment, you will convince all your enemies, that you feel that you have an *important* and an *imperious public duty* to perform . . .

Our Enemies will seek every opportunity by the means of their sanguinary agents to excite a Riot, that they may have a pretence for Spilling our Blood, reckless of the awful and certain retaliation that would ultimately fall on their heads . . .

Come, then, my friends, to the meeting on Monday, armed with no other Weapon but that of a self-approving conscience: determined not to suffer yourselves to be irritated or excited, by any means whatsoever, to commit any breach of the public peace.[3]

On the next day Hunt wrote a private letter which showed that he was sincere in this public expression of his desire for peace. He regretted that many of the weavers passed their time in 'playing soldiers' and remarked that he was doing all he could 'to dissuade them from continuing such foolish measures':

I have no doubt but we shall conduct the proceedings with great quietness and order, although I dread any mad attempt to produce disturbance, as the people here, although disposed to peace, are much more determined to resist any illegal attack made upon them: however, I shall do my duty, and I hope to keep them firm and quiet.[4]

On Saturday the 14th Hunt offered to surrender himself to the magistrates so that (as he later put it) 'they should not have any . . . pretence for interrupting the proceedings'.[5] Hunt's critics, however, put a less favourable interpretation on his gesture, claiming that he had volunteered to surrender himself only 'in order that his bail might be accepted on Monday before the meeting assembled'.[6]

The committee of magistrates sat in continuous session over this final weekend. Tension in 'loyalist' circles was growing with

[1] Huish, *op cit.*, II, 178–80.   [2] *Manchester Observer*, Aug. 14, 1819.
[3] *Ibid.*   [4] *Manchester Gazette*, Aug. 21, 1819.
[5] *Manchester Observer*, Aug. 28, 1819.   [6] *The Times*, Aug. 17, 1819.

every hour and on Thursday, August 12th, the Watch and Ward
was enforced.[1] Finally, at eleven o'clock on Sunday night, some
thirteen hours before the meeting was due to begin, Norris sent a
last pessimistic report to the Home Secretary:

The magistrates, the military, and the civil authorities of Manchester
[he wrote] have been occupied nearly the whole day in concerting the
necessary arrangements for the preservation of the peace to-morrow,
and for the safety of the town in case riot should ensue. We have been
much occupied in taking depositions from various parts of the country;
and although the magistrates, as at present advised, do not think of
preventing the meeting, yet all the accounts tend to show that the worst
possible spirit pervades the country; and that considerable numbers
have been drilling to-day at distances of four, six and ten miles from
Manchester; and that considerable numbers are expected to attend the
meeting. I hope the peace may be preserved, but under all circumstances
it is scarcely possible to expect it; and in short, in this respect we are
in a state of painful uncertainty.[2]

Despite this 'painful uncertainty', however, Hay had written to
Lord Sidmouth only five days before saying that there was now
no need for the presence of General Byng in Manchester as the
situation had improved.[3] Thus almost on the eve of the great
meeting the magistrates, either through folly or through vanity,
had dispensed with the assistance of the man who had restrained
their alarms at the Blanket meeting and who had peaceably dispersed the weavers' parade in 1818. This was perhaps the most
important single decision leading to the bloodshed at Peterloo.[4]

The drilling referred to in Norris's letter was the final addition
to the magistrates' many alarms. This, it seemed to them, in
association with the arming which had long been going on, was
certain proof that violent insurrection was intended: the Home
Office was deluged with depositions collected by the magistrates

[1] Gorst to Derby, Aug. 13, 1819 (Papers relative to the Internal State of the
Country, no. 31).
[2] Norris to Sidmouth, Aug. 15, 1819 (Papers relative to the Internal State
of the Country, no. 32).
[3] Hay to Sidmouth, Aug. 10, 1819 (H.O. 42/191).
[4] Byng, at his headquarters in Pontefract, had no expectation of trouble at
Manchester: 'I have no fear of any disturbance on Monday', he wrote to
Hobhouse; 'on the contrary they are much alarmed at our precautions'
(Byng to Hobhouse, Aug. 14, 1819. H.O. 42/192). His attitude contrasts
with that of Norris as expressed in his letter of the 15th quoted above.
There seems little doubt that if Byng had been present at Manchester on
the 16th the arrests would have been made without bloodshed.

to prove that drilling was taking place.[1] And certainly the Radicals did drill: they made no attempt to conceal the fact. But their drilling, wrote Bamford and Taylor, was only for the purpose of appearing at the meeting in better order, no revolutionary violence was intended:

It was deemed expedient that this meeting should be as morally effective as possible, and, that it should exhibit a spectacle such as had never before been witnessed in England. We had frequently been taunted by the press, with our ragged, dirty appearance, at these assemblages; with the confusion of our proceedings, and the mob-like crowds in which our numbers mustered; and we determined that, for once at least, these reflections should not be deserved . . . 'CLEANLINESS', 'SOBRIETY', 'ORDER', were the first injunctions issued by the committees; to which, on the suggestion of Mr. Hunt, was subsequently added that of, 'PEACE'. The fulfilment of the two first was left to the good sense of those who intended to join our procession . . . the observance of the third and of the last injunctions.—ORDER, PEACE,—were provided for by general regulations. Order in our movements was obtained by drilling; and peace, on our parts, was secured by a prohibition of all weapons of offence or defence.[2]

Taylor made the point, which certainly tends rather to support Bamford's interpretation of the drilling, that the magistrates obtained no evidence of drilling until a short time before Peterloo.[3] The clapping of hands by the drillers in simulation of firing particularly disturbed the magistrates; Bamford admitted that 'when the men clapped their hands in "standing at ease", some would jokingly say, it was "firing".'[4] The Radicals, however, were definitely not armed at the Peterloo meeting: this was subsequently admitted by Hay himself in his report of the proceedings.[5] Hunt was strongly against all appearance at St. Peter's with arms. Bamford, indeed, wanted some weapons to be taken 'to keep the specials at a respectful distance from our line', and suggested at a meeting of the Middleton reformers on the day before the massacre that at least 'a party of men with stout cudgels

[1] A selection was printed in the Papers relative to the Internal State of the Country, nos. 17–24, 28, 29.

[2] Bamford, I, 176–77.

[3] Taylor, 36. The first mention of drilling in the magistrates' reports to the Home Office appears to have been in Norris's letter to Sidmouth of July 14, 1819 (H.O. 42/189).

[4] Bamford, I, 180.

[5] 'There was no appearance of arms or pikes' (Hay to Sidmouth, Aug. 16, 1819. Papers relative to the Internal State of the Country, no. 34).

should be appointed to take care of the colours'. But he was over-ruled, and no arms were taken.[1] Even Chippendale of Oldham, the leading government spy in the area, was convinced of the peaceable intentions of the reformers:

I have been particularly fortunate [he wrote on the day of the massacre] in obtaining correct Information of the Plans of the Leaders. . . . My Information was derived from the Committee at Royton [acting under orders from Manchester]. The Orders are not to break the Peace on Any Account whatever. They are to bear any Insult upon themselves or even to suffer any or all of their Speakers to be taken. . . . They are enjoined not to bring any Weapons of any Kind whatever, and to keep their Flags furled till they receive orders from the Committee to display them.[2]

Armed or not armed, however, peaceable or not peaceable, the magistrates of Manchester could not by this stage have been calmed by any assurances. The seal was set on their fears when early on the morning of the 15th two of their spies were beaten up while watching drilling on the White Moss near Middleton. Taylor afterwards pointed out that one of the spies, Murray, had been one of the gang which had broken into Hunt's private room in January. It was for this, he argued, and not because the Radicals were dismayed at their sedition being discovered, that Murray had been attacked: the Radicals had no seditious intentions.[3] This explanation of the White Moss incident was not known to the magistrates however, and it would not have been believed by them if it had. The White Moss affair, Bamford believed, caused the magistrates finally to decide 'to return a full measure of severity to us on the following day'.[4] Their worst fears had been confirmed, 'it being considered', wrote a contemporary, 'as a presage of what might be feared, when the many thousands who were expected should actually assemble'.[5]

The morning of the 16th dawned fine and warm,[6] 'well calcu-

---

[1] Bamford, I, 191–92, 196–97.
[2] XY [Chippendale] to Byng, Aug. 16, 1819 (H.O. 42/192).
[3] Bamford, I, 193–96; Taylor, 66.
[4] Bamford, I, 196.
[5] An Impartial Narrative, 31.
[6] Unless otherwise indicated, this account of the events of August 16th is taken from F. A. Bruton, 'The Story of Peterloo', Bulletin of the John Rylands Library, vol. 5 (1919), and from Three Accounts of Peterloo by Eye-

lated to produce the attendance of an immense assemblage'.[1] As early as nine o'clock the people began to assemble on St. Peter's Field. The magistrates met first at the Star Inn and then at eleven o'clock moved to the house of Mr. Buxton overlooking the meeting place. By this time the troops engaged had been posted out of sight in the streets round about. One troop of the Manchester and Salford Yeomanry was in Byrom Street, and another, the troop under Captain Birley which later charged into the crowd, was concealed in Pickford's Yard off Portland Street. The Cheshire Yeomanry, totalling some four hundred men, were stationed in St. John's Street; two squadrons of the 15th Hussars, over three hundred strong, were in Byrom Street, and a troop of the same regiment was in Lower Mosley Street, acting as escort to a troop of the Royal Horse Artillery with two long six-pounders. Apart from these mounted troops, the whole of the 31st Infantry was concealed in Brasenose Street, and several companies of the 88th Infantry were in the neighbourhood of Dickenson Street. The whole military force was commanded by Lieutenant-Colonel L'Estrange. It was his intention, he reported afterwards, to use the cavalry in the first instance and not to employ the infantry (who would have had to use their firearms) except in case of 'urgent necessity'. And so it turned out, no infantry being used to disperse the meeting.[2]

As well as the military between three and four hundred special constables had been enrolled by the magistrates for the day.[3] About two hundred of them were stationed on St. Peter's Field itself, some of the others were scattered about the town to protect the factories, and the rest were employed to watch on horse-back the approaches to the town and to bring back reports to the magistrates.

witnesses (1921), edited by the same writer. See his plan reproduced on p. 235. for topographical details.

[1] *Manchester Observer*, Aug. 21, 1819. Baines (*History of the County Palatine and Duchy of Lancaster*, II, 351) gives the meterological readings for the period in Manchester. It is interesting to notice that August was the hottest and driest month of 1819, the hottest and driest August of the whole period 1819–32, and the third hottest of any month during the period. The heat of the day no doubt played its part in straining the nerves of the authorities at Peterloo.

[2] L'Estrange to Byng, Aug. 16, 1819 (Papers relative to the Internal State of the Country, no. 36).

[3] *State Trials*, 1164.

On the field over which the committee of magistrates looked
out, the hustings, made of deal planks 'with vacancies so that all
but the speaker might be seated', had been erected towards the
southern edge.[1] From the magistrates' house to these hustings the
two hundred special constables formed a double line through
which, it was hoped, the magistrates could communicate with the
speakers. Nadin, the Deputy Constable, moved up and down this
line until Hunt made his appearance.[2] When Hunt arrived he
found that the position of the hustings was such that he would be
speaking against the wind; they were therefore moved a few yards
and apparently out of contact with the line of constables. This was
afterwards claimed by the authorities as a most sinister development.[3]

Long before Hunt's arrival processions of reformers from the
surrounding towns had been pouring into Manchester from all
directions. This was an important part of the day's happenings,
for a majority of those actively engaged at Peterloo were not
Manchester people but strangers from the surrounding towns.
'The active part of the meeting may be said to have come in
wholly from the country', reported Hay, ' . . . it did not consist
of less than 20,000 men, etc.' [4] 'From Bolton, Oldham, Stockport,
Middleton, and all the circumjacent country', exclaimed the
Manchester Observer; 'from the more distant towns of Leeds,
Sheffield, etc. etc. came thousands of willing votaries to the shrine
of sacred liberty.' [5]

One of the most important processions came in from Middleton
and Rochdale, consisting of about six thousand men as well as
numerous women and children. Samuel Bamford, who led the
Middleton contingent, has graphically described its march.[6] By
eight o'clock in the morning all Middleton was astir and the procession forming. It was arranged with a body of youths in front
wearing laurels 'as a token of amity and peace', then some of the
men marching five abreast, then the band and the colours (inscribed with the slogans 'Unity and Strength', 'Liberty and

[1] G. Swift, *Narrative*, 12.
[2] *State Trials*, 1164.
[3] *Ibid.*, 191, 354, 1151.
[4] Hay to Sidmouth, Aug. 16, 1819 (Papers relative to the Internal State
of the Country, no. 34).
[5] *Manchester Observer*, Aug. 21, 1819.
[6] Bamford, chs. XXXIII–IV.

'raternity', 'Parliaments Annual', and 'Suffrage Universal'), and hen finally the rest of the men again five abreast. Every hundred nen had a leader distinguished by a sprig of laurel in his hat, and controlling the whole was a principal conductor, Bamford himself, who headed the column with a bugleman to sound his orders. Bamford does not definitely say so but almost certainly his careful organization was the work of the local Union Societies.

Before they set off Bamford addressed his men:

I reminded them, that they were going to attend the most important meeting that had ever been held for Parliamentary Reform, and I hoped heir conduct would be marked by a steadiness and seriousness befitting the occasion . . . [They were] not to offer any insult or provocation by word or deed. . . . If peace officers should come to arrest myself or any other person, they were not to offer any resistance, but suffer hem to execute their office peaceably . . . I also said, that in conformity with a rule of the committee no sticks, nor weapons of any description, would be allowed to be carried in the ranks; and those who had such, were requested to put them aside.

Bamford then described the beginning of the march:

My address was received with cheers . . . we opened into column,— he music struck up,—the banners flashed in the sun-light,—other nusic was heard,—it was that of the Rochdale party coming to join as,—we met; and a shout from ten thousand startled the echoes of the woods and dingles. Then all was quiet save the breath of music; and with intent seriousness, we went on.

A similar procession was meanwhile setting out from Oldham. The various contingents met at nine o'clock on the village green where they were received by John Knight. As well as from Oldham itself divisions of reformers came in from Crompton, Royton, Chadderton, Saddleworth, Lees, and Mossley. In this case the people, some six thousand in number, were definitely organized by Unions, each Union marching together with its leaders and banner. The Saddleworth, Lees, and Mossley Union banner was black, inscribed with the slogans 'Equal Representation or Death', 'Unite and be Free', 'No Boroughmongering', 'Taxation without Representation is Unjust and Tyrannical', 'No Corn Laws', and 'Universal Suffrage'. This black banner, with its ambiguous cry of 'Equal Representation or Death', was captured at Peterloo and used as evidence against the reformers at their trial, especially against 'Dr.' Healey the leader of the contingent. The

Royton Female Union also carried a banner which figured at the
trials; it was inscribed 'The Royton Female Union—Let us DIE
like Men and not be SOLD like slaves'. Women, totalling nearly a
thousand altogether, seem to have been especially prominent in
this procession: two hundred of them dressed in white escorted
the Oldham committee.[1]

As the Radical contingents approached Manchester special constables on horseback rode out in various directions to meet them
and then returned to report to the magistrates. One of these special
constables was Francis Philips. In his *Exposure* he described how
he rode along the turnpike road towards Stockport and met at
Ardwick Green a 'regiment of reformers' marching three abreast.
This was the procession of the Stockport Radicals. Philips
reckoned that it was composed of some fourteen or fifteen
hundred people, including about forty women. They 'marched
extremely well, preserving the step, though without music' and
carried two colours inscribed 'No Corn Laws' and 'Universal
Suffrage'. Philips was careful to add that nearly half the men
carried 'stout sticks'.[2]

There were yet other processions marching into the town.
Stanley[3] saw the Ashton contingent come in, and evidence at the
trials after Peterloo gave details of the Bury formation, five
abreast and three thousand strong with many women, and also
of that from Pendleton.

All these various processions converged on St. Peter's Field.
Archibald Prentice, standing at a window, watched the crowds
streaming down Mosley Street. He had never seen, he wrote, 'a
gayer spectacle'; the majority of the processionists, he noted,
were young people dressed for the most part in their Sunday best.[4]

It seemed to be a gala day with the country people [wrote J. B. Smith[5]
watching from a window of a house next to that of the magistrates]
who were mostly dressed in their best and brought with them their
wives, and when I saw boys and girls taking their father's hand in the

---

[1] Bateson, *op. cit.*, 99–101; Marcroft, *op. cit.*, 42–45.

[2] Philips, 20–21.

[3] The Rev. Edward Stanley (1779–1849), father of Dean Stanley and an
eyewitness of Peterloo, was Rector of Alderley in 1819; he later became
Bishop of Norwich. Bruton (*Three Accounts of Peterloo by Eyewitnesses*) prints
a description of Peterloo which he wrote soon after the massacre.

[4] Prentice, 159.

[5] For Smith see above, p. 57. Bruton (*Three Accounts of Peterloo by Eyewitnesses*) prints an account of Peterloo which he wrote in old age.

procession, I observed to my Aunt: 'These are the guarantees of their peaceable intentions—we need have no fears'.

The people themselves certainly had no fears: they expected no violence from either side. Prentice 'occasionally asked the women if they were not afraid to be there, and the usual laughing reply was—"What have we to be afraid of?"' [1]

For two hours the yeomanry and hussars remained at their stations dismounted. Occasionally a few of the hussar officers would ride up to Deansgate to watch the processions go by. Lieutenant Jolliffe of the 15th Hussars was one of them. [2]

During the greater portion of that period [he noted] a solid mass of people continued moving along. . . . They marched at a brisk pace in ranks well closed up, five or six bands of music being interspersed . . . Mr. Hunt, with two or three other men, and I think two women dressed in light blue and white, were in an open carriage drawn by the people. . . . As soon as the great bulk of the procession had passed, we were ordered to stand to our horses.

Jolliffe was correct in thinking that he saw at least one woman in Hunt's carriage: this was Mrs. Mary Fildes, the President of the Manchester Female Reformers. The female committee dressed in white walked behind the carriage.

At about quarter past one the carriage made its way across the field with Hunt standing up. A great shout arose from the crowd and the reformers' bands struck up 'See the Conquering Hero comes', 'God Save the King', and 'Rule, Britannia'. The numbers present to welcome Hunt have been variously estimated: Hunt himself claimed afterwards that 150,000 people were on the field, but probably the actual figure was nearer 60,000. This was still a remarkable total. [3]

Arrived at the hustings, the Radical hero was at once voted into

[1] Prentice, 159.

[2] William Jolliffe (1800–1876) later became Lord Hylton. Bruton (*Three Accounts of Peterloo by Eyewitnesses*) prints a description of the massacre which he wrote a quarter of a century later for inclusion in Dean Pellew's biography of Lord Sidmouth.

[3] The report of the meeting in the *Manchester Observer* (August. 21, 1819) said that 153,000 people were present at Peterloo; Hunt claimed 150,000 (*ibid.*, Sept. 18, 1819), and the *Annual Register* gave 80,000 (*Annual Register, 1819*, General History, 106). Hulton, however, the chairman of the committee of magistrates, gave the total as 50,000–60,000 (*State Trials*, 255) and this latter figure was accepted by Prentice (159), in most other respects a severe critic of the magistrates.

the chair, and taking off his white hat he began his speech. Spectators were packed all around him, some on rising ground behind the hustings but more stretching out in front as far back as the Friends' Meeting House on the northern edge of the field. The magistrates were in Buxton's house overlooking the eastern edge, with a gap between them and the fringe of the crowd where the Manchester Yeomanry was soon to rein up before its charge. Above the heads of the people at intervals could be seen the various banners and Caps of Liberty. All around the field in the side streets (but not visible to those at the meeting) were posted the regular troops and the yeomanry; for communication with them mounted messengers were in attendance at the magistrates' house. On the hustings sat several press reporters, John Tyas of *The Times*, Edward Baines, jun., of the *Leeds Mercury*, John Smith of the *Liverpool Mercury*, and several others. This was the first time that newspapers from distant towns had ever sent special reporters to cover a political meeting.[1]

Now that the meeting had assembled the magistrates were left to their own discretion rather than bound by the advice of the Law Officers, and the restraint hitherto forced upon them by the Home Office quickly disappeared. They became convinced that they must take drastic action. They 'felt a decided conviction that the whole bore the appearance of insurrection; that the array was such as to terrify all the king's subjects, and was such as no legitimate purpose could justify'.[2] They decided to secure the appearance of support for strong measures by getting a few of the 'loyal' inhabitants of the town to put their names to a statement saying that they believed Manchester to be in danger. Accordingly Richard Owen and some thirty other 'loyalists' (including Francis Philips) signed the necessary sworn affidavits and a warrant for the arrest of Hunt and his colleagues was drawn up stating that

Richard Owen hath this day made oath before us, His Majesty's Justices of the Peace . . . that Henry Hunt, John Knight, Jos. Johnson, and —— Moorhouse, at this time (now a quarter past one o'clock) have arrived in a *car*, at the area near St. Peter's Church and that an immense mob is collected, and that he considers the town in danger.[3]

---

[1] W. H. Mills, *The Manchester Guardian. A Century of History* (1921), 28.

[2] Hay to Sidmouth, Aug. 16, 1819 (Papers relative to the Internal State of the Country, no. 34).

[3] *Manchester Observer*, Aug. 28, 1819.

Nadin, the Deputy Constable of Manchester, was instructed by the magistrates to serve the warrant and to arrest Hunt. This he set out to do, but (as he subsequently claimed) found it impossible without the aid of the military.[1] Messengers were therefore despatched calling for the assistance of the troops, and the special constables in the line to the hustings were ordered to withdraw from the field. One messenger was sent to Colonel L'Estrange and another to Pickford's Yard, where Birley's troops of the Manchester Yeomanry waited. The soldiers were now quickly brought into action. L'Estrange ordered the infantry to close on the field from several directions, while he himself led the hussars and the Cheshire Yeomanry by a necessarily rather circuitous route to the magistrates' house. Meanwhile, from the other side of the town the troop of the Manchester Yeomanry in Pickford's Yard was also bearing down on the scene, and having much less far to go, it arrived easily the first. As the yeomen galloped quickly along the back streets a woman carrying a two-year-old child was knocked down by one of their stragglers. The child was killed and became the first casualty at Peterloo.

That the Manchester Yeomanry appeared first on the field was the last link in the chain of events leading up to the massacre. These were local men, ardent in their politics, who had suffered much from the taunts of the Radicals. There was thus a strong presumption from the first that they would not show much moderation in a crisis. Their prejudices had been further aggravated by the fact that during the morning, while gathering in the taverns to have their boots cleaned and their horses curried, they had become half-drunk.[2] The employment of these troops to arrest Hunt was the final misfortune; if experienced hussars had been used instead, men skilled in manœuvring into and breaking up a crowd without violence, there would probably even then have been no bloodshed, for as Bamford said, the Radicals had been instructed not to oppose the arrest of any of their leaders. Regular troops would therefore have had no occasion to use their sabres. The Manchester Yeomanry however, unskilled as they were, soon got into difficulties in the crowd and began striking out. The magistrates themselves seem to have half-realized that

---

[1] *The Whole Proceedings before the Coroner's Inquest at Oldham, &c. on the body of John Lees*, ed. J. A. Dowling (1820), 459.
[2] Marshall, 168.

this would happen, for there was some discussion among them
whether to wait until the hussars arrived before proceeding with
the arrests. It was decided, however, that as many of the special
constables had already been withdrawn, the gap down which the
troops were to pass might fill up if there were any delay.[1] After
only a brief pause, therefore, the yeomanry wheeled and (accompanied by Nadin) rode through the crowd towards Hunt and the
hustings.

Hunt had been speaking for only a few minutes. It had been
decided by the Radicals beforehand that he should take the chair
and speak first, that Johnson should move the resolutions and a
remonstrance, and that Knight should second him.[2] There was no
intention, Hunt declared later, of electing a Legislatorial Attorney
for Manchester:

The Royal Proclamation had declared it illegal, and though I did not
think it illegal, I thought it a foolish and absurd scheme. It was my
opinion, that to follow such an example at such a time, would have
been unjust to the people of Manchester—that an election should not
have been proceeded in till its inhabitants had three months' notice.
I had declared that I would not have put such a question as chairman
long before the first meeting was prohibited. . . . it was intended first to
pass a strong vote of censure, for refusing to present the petitions of
Manchester and Stockport; and then to make a solemn appeal to his
Royal Highness the Prince Regent on the distressed state of the country
and on the necessity of immediately reviving the connection between
the people and the throne.[3]

In other words, the reformers intended to follow much the same
course of action at Peterloo as they had followed at most of the
previous Radical Reform meetings in Lancashire in 1819.

Hunt was not allowed to speak for long before the yeomanry
interrupted him; but what he said even in those few minutes later
caused great dispute.[4] He appears to have declared (in accord
with his frequently reiterated peaceful intentions) that he hoped
that 'if any person would not be quiet, that they would put him
down and keep him quiet', referring (as he subsequently claimed

[1] Narrative of the Proceedings of the Manchester and Salford Yeomanry
(H.O. 42/192); Inquest . . . on the body of John Lees, 460.
[2] Hunt, Memoirs, III, 611.
[3] Bamford, I, 270.
[4] Few of the huge numbers assembled could hear clearly what Hunt was
saying: 'I should think no-one beyond ten yards from the hustings could
hear', remarked Stanley.

at his trial) to 'idle boys' and 'drunken fellows' who might interrupt the meeting. By the authorities, however, his words were given the most sinister interpretation. His 'exhortation to order', reported *The Times*, was interpreted by the magistrates as 'the watchword of unlawful resistance against authority'.[1] The *Quarterly Review* even went so far as to compare Hunt's speech with that of Antony on Caesar: 'the burden of his speech', it commented, 'amounted to this: "Good friends, sweet friends, let me not stir you up to mutiny." '[2]

Hunt had not done much more than make this disputed exhortation to peace when the yeomanry arrived on the field. An alarmed cry of 'The soldiers! the soldiers!' spread throughout his audience and some of the crowd began to panic. Hunt saw this and called out to steady his followers: 'Stand firm, my friends! you see they are in disorder already. This is a trick. Give them three cheers.' The people responded, a great cheer went up, and confidence was restored.[3] Unfortunately this gesture added only still further to the alarms of the authorities, who saw it as a symptom of 'most marked defiance'.[4] This, as Lord Milton remarked in parliament later, was the sum total of positive evidence against the people which Hay was able to muster for his report to the Home Office written on the evening of the massacre.[5]

The cavalry, the special constables, and the 'loyalists' in general replied to the Radical cheer with one of their own. Then the Manchester Yeomanry began to move into the crowd to make the arrests.

At first [wrote Stanley] . . . their movement was not rapid, and there was some show of an attempt to follow their officer [Captain Birley] in regular succession, five or six abreast; but, as Mr. Francis Philips in his pamphlet observes, they soon 'increased their speed', and with a zeal and ardour which might naturally be expected from men acting with delegated power against a foe by whom . . . they had long been insulted with taunts of cowardice, continued their course, seeming to vie individually with each other which should be first . . . As the cavalry approached the dense mass of people they used their utmost efforts to escape: but so closely were they pressed in opposite directions

---

[1] *The Times*, Aug. 25, 1819; Taylor, 177–78; Philips, 6, 57.
[2] *Quarterly Review*, XXII (1820), 500.
[3] Hunt, *Memoirs*, III, 615; *State Trials*, 1119–20.
[4] Hay to Sidmouth, Aug. 16, 1819 (Papers relative to the Internal State of the Country, no. 34).
[5] *Parliamentary Debates*, XLI (1819–20), 545.

by the soldiers, the special constables, the position of the hustings, and their own immense numbers, that immediate escape was impossible . . . On their arrival at the hustings a scene of dreadful confusion ensued. The orators fell or were forced off the scaffold in quick succession; fortunately for them, the stage being rather elevated, they were in great degree beyond the reach of the many swords which gleamed around them.

These swords were soon to be in use, by the hussars unintentionally, by the yeomanry less so. 'The Hussars drove the people forward with the flats of their swords', wrote Jolliffe, 'but sometimes, as is almost inevitably the case when men are placed in such situations, the edge was used.' Furthermore, the yeomanry did not restrict the use of their weapons to driving the people back. As soon as Hunt had been arrested the cry went up amongst them: 'Have at their flags!' In consequence, they dashed not only at the flags on the hustings but also for those in the crowd, 'cutting most indiscriminately to the right and to the left in order to get at them'.[1]

The actual arrest of Hunt and Johnson proceeded comparatively smoothly. Birley went up to the hustings and said to Hunt: 'Sir, I have a warrant against you, and arrest you as my prisoner.' Hunt, after briefly exhorting the people to tranquillity, turned round and replied: 'I willingly surrender myself to any civil officer who will show me his warrant.' Nadin then came forward and said: 'I will arrest you: I have got information upon oath against you.' The same formality was gone through with Joseph Johnson. They then leaped from the waggons and surrendered themselves to the civil power.

The crowd now began to attempt to break up. 'The square was now covered with the flying multitude', wrote Stanley; 'though still in parts the banners and caps of liberty were surrounded by groups.' By this time the hussars and other troops had arrived, and the fleeing mob found its escape impeded by the presence of the military blocking the exit ways.

The climax of the whole day had now been reached. The arrests had been made and Hunt removed: but on account of its poor horsemanship the troop of Manchester Yeomanry, already dis-

[1] *Peterloo Massacre, containing a Faithful Narrative of the Events which preceded, accompanied, and followed the fatal Sixteenth of August 1819* . . . edited by an Observer [J. E. Taylor] (1819), no. 5; *Annual Register, 1819*, General History, 106–07.

organized even before it set out for the hustings, was by now completely broken up and enveloped in the fleeing crowd. The magistrates could see this from their window. Hulton, their chairman, took the surging of the hemmed-in crowd to be a symptom (as he declared later) of 'a general resistance': 'seeing sticks flourished in the air as well as brickbats thrown about', he conceived the Manchester Yeomanry 'to be completely defeated'. This question of the use of sticks by the reformers was a topic on which the evidence was later to conflict hopelessly. Bamford, as already indicated, had ordered his Middleton men not to bring sticks: other contingents, however, appear to have done so. They were only such sticks as country people often carried with them when out-of-doors and they were mostly borne by old people,[1] but the authorities and 'loyalists' were immediately convinced that they had been brought to the meeting for violent purposes.

One thing was conceded by the authorities: no pikes, about which they had been so busy collecting evidence before Peterloo, appeared on the scene. 'There was no appearance of arms or pikes', admitted Hay, 'but great plenty of sticks and stones.' [2] To what extent stones were really used was another point of dispute. Bamford admitted that when a number of Middleton people were pressed back by the yeomanry they defended themselves with stones. This, however, was excusable. *The Times* reporter said emphatically that not until the yeomanry attacked the flags were any brickbats or stones thrown, and then only a few.[3] On the other hand, the authorities made a great point of stressing that they had had the field cleared before the meeting but yet that afterwards a load of brickbats and stones was removed from it.[4] This seems to confirm that a few stones at least were thrown by the crowd and that some at least had been specially brought to the meeting by the reformers.

Virtually no firearms were used by the people. One shot was fired from a window near the Meeting House and some men on the roof of a house had a gun. The infantry fired a shot or two over the spot and cleared it.[5]

[1] *State Trials*, 348, 351.
[2] Hay to Sidmouth, Aug. 16, 1819 (Papers relative to the Internal State of the Country, no. 34).
[3] *Peterloo Massacre*, 5.
[4] *State Trials*, 1187.
[5] *Ibid.*, 1200–02.

Another question which gave rise to much discussion at the trials and elsewhere was whether the Riot Act had been read before the second body of troops was ordered to charge the crowd. The reformers and their friends doubted whether it had been read at all, and declared that if it had been read then certainly the people had never heard it.[1] There seems little doubt that the Act was read: it was emphatically stated by the magistrates at the trials that it was read twice.[2] Admittedly few people probably heard it, and the statutory hour was not allowed to elapse before the meeting was dispersed. But the whole discussion was somewhat academic since, if the action of the magistrates was justifiable at all, it could be justified without benefit of the Riot Act: an illegal assembly can be dispersed under the common law without any of the Riot Act formalities.[3]

We now return to the scene at St. Peter's at the moment when the new troops arrived. Colonel L'Estrange halted his men in Mount Street, rode up to the magistrates' house, and looking up at the window where Hulton was standing asked what he was to do. Without consulting his fellow magistrates Hulton immediately replied: 'Good God, sir! do you not see how they are attacking the yeomanry? Disperse the crowd.'[4] Stanley described what now happened:

[The 15th Hussars] then pressed forward, crossing the avenue of constables, which opened to let them through, and bent their course towards the Manchester Yeomanry. The people were now in a state of utter rout and confusion, leaving the ground strewed with hats and shoes, and hundreds were thrown down in the attempt to escape. The cavalry were hurrying about in all directions, completing the work of dispersion, which . . . was effected in so short a space of time to appear as if done 'by magic' . . . During the whole of this confusion, heightened at its close by the rattle of some artillery crossing the square, shrieks were heard in all directions, and as the crowd of people dispersed the effects of the conflict became visible. Some were seen bleeding on the ground and unable to rise; others, less seriously injured but faint with the loss of blood, were retiring slowly or leaning upon others for support . . . The whole of this extraordinary scene was the work of a few minutes.

[1] See, for example, the Declaration and Protest quoted below, p. 174.
[2] *State Trials*, 1076–77, 1179–80; 1184; Hay to Sidmouth, Aug. 16, 1819 (Papers relative to the Internal State of the Country, no. 34).
[3] See below, p. 182.
[4] *State Trials*, 256.

Bamford noticed 'several mounds of human beings remaining where they had fallen, crushed down and smothered'.

The charge of the Hussars [wrote Jolliffe] swept this mingled mass of human beings before it; people, yeomen, and constables, in their confused attempts to escape, ran one over the other; so that by the time we had arrived at the end of the field the fugitives were literally piled up to a considerable elevation above the level of the ground.

So the field was cleared, sixty thousand people swept aside in some ten minutes. Little wonder that hundreds were hurt, and many more by crushing than by sabring. The carnage might have been even worse if all the troops at the magistrates' disposal had been used: but fortunately neither the Cheshire Yeomanry nor the infantry took any direct part in the dispersal.

The crowds now streamed out into open country, back to their homes in the outlying towns. Archibald Prentice, who had left the meeting to go to his home in Salford just as Hunt was mounting the hustings, described their flight:

I had not been at home more than a quarter of an hour when a wailing sound was heard from the main street, and, rushing out, I saw people running in the direction of Pendleton, their faces pale as death, and some with blood trickling down their cheeks. It was with difficulty I could get any one to stop and tell me what had happened. The un-armed multitude, men, women and children, had been attacked with murderous results, by the military.[1]

Meanwhile Hunt, Johnson, and the other prisoners were hurried away to the New Bailey prison in Salford. On their way from the hustings to the magistrates' house they had been hissed and belaboured by the special constables. One prominent 'loyalist' knocked Hunt's hat down over his face with a stick. Hay was forced to address the constables, urging them to restrain themselves.[2]

Altogether eleven persons, including two women, were imprisoned with Hunt as the main culprits of the day: thirty others were also imprisoned on lesser charges.[3] According to the report

---

[1] Prentice, 160.
[2] Hunt, *Memoirs*, III, 617–19.
[3] They were Johnson, Knight, Saxton, Bamford (not arrested until Aug. 26), Healey, Moorhouse, Jones, Swift, Wild, Mrs. Gaunt, and Mrs. Hargreaves. The only leading Radical present on the hustings who was not arrested for his part in the meeting was Richard Carlile. He helped four women down from the hustings and then fled from the field and sheltered in

of the Metropolitan Relief Committee eleven people were killed or died as a result of injuries sustained at the meeting: these included one special constable.[1] By the time this report was published in January 1820 the committee had relieved about four hundred people injured at the massacre: one hundred and forty of these were the victims of sabre cuts, the rest were crushed or thrown down as a result of the pressure of the crowd. As one hundred and forty cases of injury still remained to be investigated Dr. G. M. Trevelyan has suggested that these hundred and forty can perhaps be balanced off against deceptions practised on the committee, thus leaving the number of persons genuinely injured at Peterloo as about four hundred.[2] According to the report of Colonel L'Estrange the number of military casualties at the meeting was sixty-seven men struck by stones and sticks and twenty horses injured.[3]

For the rest of the day troops and special constables patrolled the streets. The atmosphere in the town was tense: 'all the working people were athirst for revenge', wrote Bamford. Stanley, who praised the quiet demeanour of the people before the meeting, remarked that afterwards they were in 'a very different state of feeling': he heard 'repeated vows of revenge'.

On the evening of the 16th a riot broke out at New Cross, the most turbulent part of Manchester. One of the shopkeepers there was supposed by the mob to have been a special constable at Peterloo and to have exhibited a captured Radical flag. For this his shop was attacked. The Riot Act had to be read, and one person was killed by shots from the military.[4]

Whatever the case before, there was now no question that some of the people were preparing arms:

a house (A. Watkin, *Fragment No. II* (1878), 11-12). Proceedings were already under way against Carlile for publishing the works of Tom Paine, for which he received three years' imprisonment in November, 1819. The authorities may have decided that further action against him was unnecessary.

[1] The special constables suffered as much from the attack of the yeomanry as the reformers: 'I saw several of those fellows', wrote George Swift, one of the Peterloo prisoners, 'showing their Staves and begging them to observe they were constables. Not so: they slashed amongst them, and they squeaked out like your Irish pigs' (Swift, *op. cit.*, 16).

[2] G. M. Trevelyan, 'The Number of Casualties at Peterloo', *History*, VII (1922-23).

[3] *State Trials*, 1261n.

[4] *The Times*, Aug. 24, 1819

Many of the young men had been preparing arms [wrote Bamford] and seeking out articles to convert into such. Some had been grinding cythes, others old hatchets, others screw-drivers, rusty swords, pikels, and mop-nails; anything which could be made to cut or stab was pronounced fit for service. But no plan was defined,—nothing was arranged,—and the arms were afterwards reserved for any event that might occur.[1]

But even now it will be seen that nothing like a systematic rising was being contemplated.

The Radical Press increased its circulation immensely: 'odious and blasphemous publications', declared the Cheshire Grand Jury, 'poured forth throughout the country'.[2] Such 'garbage' Taylor commented, would not have flourished if the people had not been so ill-treated.[3] Hay, realizing the mediocre standard of the local 'loyalist' Press, appealed to the Home Office for help in getting good 'loyal' articles from newspapers in other parts of the country published locally. In this way he hoped to check the upsurge of the popular Press.[4]

As well as a flourishing Radical Press schemes were underfoot among the people to boycott 'loyal' shopkeepers and publicans.[5] In short, as Taylor wrote, 'the dispersion of the Manchester meeting had produced no other effect, than an increased irritation among the people'.[6] The Cheshire Grand Jury noticed at the beginning of September that 'the danger had, within the last fourteen days, assumed a more formidable character'.[7]

The day following Peterloo was one of great panic in Manchester. About eleven o'clock in the morning Moore, the senior Constable, came upon the Exchange (Tuesday being the principal

[1] Bamford, I, 216.

[2] Resolutions of the Cheshire Grand Jury, Sept. I, 1819 (Papers relative to the Internal State of the Country, no. 41).

[3] Taylor, 68–69.

[4] One article, for example, originally published in a Scottish newspaper was copied by the *Yorkshire Gazette* and subsequently by 'the several well-affected papers' in Manchester. Hay was also anxious to get good articles disseminated throughout the country at large 'for the question is not local but general' (Hay to Hobhouse, Sept. 27, 1819 (H.O. 42/195), Hobhouse to Hay, Sept. 29, 1819 (H.O. 79/4), quoted in Aspinall, *Politics and the Press*, 352, 418).

[5] Statement of the Lancashire Grand Jury, Sept. 1819 (Papers relative to the Internal State of the Country, no. 43); Taylor, 74–75.

[6] *Ibid.*, 67.

[7] Communications of the Cheshire Grand Jury, Sept. 3, 1819 (Papers relative to the Internal State of the Country, no. 40).

market day for cotton goods) and reported that thirty to fifty
thousand men armed with pikes were marching upon the town
from the direction of Middleton and Oldham. The Exchange was
immediately closed and the Boroughreeve and Constables posted
up a ñotice ordering all persons to stay indoors 'otherwise their
lives will be in danger'.

All seemed in a state of confusion [wrote Bamford]; the streets were
patrolled by military, police, and special constables: the shops were
closed and silent; the warehouses were shut up and padlocked; the
Exchange was deserted; the artillery was ready.

Moore's story was entirely untrue: there had been no Radical
uprising. The whole affair had, as Prentice put it, been conjured
up in the consciences of the guilty. After an hour this began to be
realized and business partly recommenced.[1]

Further wild alarms seized the 'loyalists' a few days later. On
the 23rd there was an accidental explosion in a gunsmith's shop
and the cry was immediately raised that the Radicals were coming.
Again on September 1st the town was much agitated by the
rumour, spread by Moore, that a Watch and Ward man had been
killed the previous evening. Once more the report was entirely
without foundation.[3]

There were, indeed, a few more genuine outbreaks of violence,
though not on the large and premeditated scale imagined by the
authorities. On the 17th a special constable was fatally injured in
the New Cross district of Manchester, and there were riots in
Stockport and Macclesfield on the same evening. On the 19th
houses in the New Cross area were attacked, and on the 20th the
mob of this locality fought a pitched battle with the cavalry.[4]

The authorities and 'loyalists', full of alarms, were feverishly
active for several days after the massacre. On the 17th Hay, the
Chairman of Quarter Sessions, and Thomas Hardman, a former
Boroughreeve and a leading 'loyalist', were sent off to London to
justify the massacre to the government.[5] On the same day a notice
was put up by the magistrates thanking the yeomanry for their

[1] Taylor, 188–89; *Manchester Obersver*, Aug. 21; 1819; Bamford, I, 214,
Watkin, *Journal*, 79; Prentice, 169.

[2] Taylor, 189.

[3] *Newcastle Chronicle*, Sept. 11, 1819.

[4] *The Times*, Aug. 24, 1819.

[5] Norris to Sidmouth, Aug. 17, 1819 (Papers relative to the Internal State
of the Country, no. 37).

part in dispersing the meeting: it expressed gratification at 'the extreme forbearance exercised by the Corps, when insulted and defied by the rioters'.[1] On the same day also the magistrates published a notice against drilling, declaring it to be 'contrary to Law'.[2] On the 18th a meeting of the Committee in Aid of the Civil Power was held and letters were sent out to known 'loyalists' asking them to give the committee 'the earliest information of any *extraordinary* appearances in their respective neighbourhoods'.[3] Finally, on the 19th the 'loyalists' of Manchester met, first at the Police Office, then at the Star Inn, to express formally their thanks for the action of the authorities at Peterloo. The meeting was described as a public one, but in fact great care seems to have been taken to ensure that only 'loyal' opinions were heard. The middle-class Radicals immediately replied to this meeting with a Declaration and Protest which condemned it as private and which attacked the manner of the Peterloo dispersal. A great volume of local opinion rallied to their side, a significant percentage of it coming from the 'respectable' classes in the town.[4]

The middle-class Radicals J. E. Taylor and Archibald Prentice, who were prominent in support of this Declaration and Protest, had also been very active in other respects. In particular, knowing that Tyas, *The Times* reporter, had been arrested for being on the hustings, they had both written reports of the meeting and sent them off to two London papers. As a result, a full and honest account of the massacre was quickly available in the capital; when released Tyas confirmed the accuracy of the two accounts.[5]

The Times gave a very full coverage to the situation in Manchester. In the issue of August 23rd a report appeared describing the state of military control in the town after Peterloo. 'Manchester', it declared, 'now wears the appearance of a garrison, or of a town conquered in war.' During the alarms of August 17th 'soldiers were posted at all the commanding position of the town, and were to be seen at full length on the flags in various directions'.[6] Service at the Collegiate Church on the 29th 'exhibited a singular appearance', the soldiers who attended all carrying their muskets with bayonets fixed.[7] On the 20th Hobhouse agreed to

---

[1] *Manchester Chronicle*, Aug. 21, 1819.   [2] *Ibid.*
[3] Taylor, 174.   [4] See below, pp. 165, 174–75.   [5] Prentice, 163.
[6] *Peterloo Massacre*, 6.   [7] *Newcastle Chronicle*, Sept. 11, 1819.

the request of the panic-stricken Norris that permanent infantry barracks should be erected in Manchester.[1]

While all this was going on, the Radical prisoners languished in the New Bailey prison. The Home Office was quickly active in arranging the prosecution against them. Bouchier, the assistant solicitor to the Treasury, was sent to Manchester, avowedly to assist in taking evidence against the prisoners, but clearly with the real purpose of supervising the magistrates.[2] Before he arrived, however, the examinations had been proceeding, and Johnson had his two important voluntary examinations on August 19th and 20th. On the 20th also the preliminary public examination of the prisoners was made but was quickly adjourned because the magistrates, prompted by the Home Office, were not yet ready with their case. On the 27th the prisoners were at last brought up for their final examination. Norris addressed them and told them that the original charge of high treason had been dropped and that instead they were to be charged with conspiracy.[3] The bail required of the prisoners was very heavy: Hunt and Johnson themselves in £1,000 with two sureties of £500 each, the rest themselves in £500 with two sureties of £250. At Lancaster a few days later the bail was reduced somewhat: Hunt, Johnson, Knight and Moorhouse themselves in £400 with two sureties of £200 each, the others themselves in £200 with two sureties of £100 each. It was clearly hoped that some of the prisoners at least would not be able to find this heavy bail: as Saxton said, some of them were 'mere labourers, and their friends are labouring men themselves'. But Sir Charles Wolseley came to the aid of those prisoners who could not find bail otherwise, and all the Peterloo Radicals had to be freed.[4]

As well as organizing the prosecution of the Peterloo prisoners the government also acted in support of the magistrates in a more public fashion. On the 21st congratulations in the name of the Prince Regent were conveyed to the authorities for their action at Peterloo. The Prince Regent spoke of his 'great satisfaction' at

[1] Norris to Sidmouth, Aug. 18, 1819 (H.O. 42/192); Hobhouse to Norris, Aug. 20, 1819 (H.O. 41/4).

[2] Hobhouse to Norris, Aug. 19, 1819 (H.O. 41/4).

[3] *State Trials*, 173–74; Bamford, I, 251, 272.

[4] Bamford, I, 272–72, II, 18; Huish, *op. cit.*, II, 237; Hunt, *Memoirs*, III, 638.

their prompt, decisive and efficient measures for the preservation
of the public tranquillity'.[1] On this same day, it is interesting to
notice, the word 'Peter-Loo' first appeared in print in the columns
of the *Manchester Observer*.

On the day following Sir Francis Burdett, the Radical member
of parliament for Westminster, published a strongly-worded
address to his constituents:

This, then [he declared], is the answer of the boroughmongers to the
petitioning people—this is the proof of our standing in no need of
Reform . . . What kill men unarmed, unresisting and Gracious God!!
women too, disfigured, maimed, cut down, and trampled on by
dragoons! Is this England? This a Christian land? A land of freedom?
Can such things be and pass by us like a summer cloud unheeded?
Forbid it every drop of English blood in every vein that does not
proclaim its owner bastard. Will the gentlemen of England support or
wink at such proceedings? . . . They never can stand tamely by as
lookers on, whilst 'bloody Neroes' rip open their mother's womb. They
must join the general voice, loudly demanding justice and redress and
head public meetings throughout the United Kingdom.[2]

Such a meeting was held at Westminster on September 2nd with
Burdett and Cam Hobhouse as the chief speakers. It was entirely
peaceable and (according to the *Manchester Observer*) attracted an
audience of some thirty thousand persons. Resolutions were
passed declaring the Manchester meeting to be entirely legal and
asserting that the attack upon the people was the natural consequence of having a non-representative parliament; a Radical
Reform was therefore called for, and an address to the Prince
Regent was drawn up in these terms. Arrangements were also
made for the setting up of a Peterloo relief committee. This was
the origin of the Metropolitan and Central Relief Committee
which seems to have co-ordinated all the work of relieving the
Peterloo injured and imprisoned.[3]

Hunt, meanwhile, was still in Lancashire, and while at Lancaster
settling his bail, he and his friends attempted to bring charges
against two of the Manchester police for perjury and against
several of the Manchester Yeomanry for maiming and cutting.
The Grand Jury, however, refused to find true bills against any
of them. The only true bill was found against Richard Owen, the

[1] *Manchester Observer*, Aug. 28, 1819.
[2] *State Trials*, 5–6.
[3] *Manchester Observer*, Sept. 11, 1819.

chief of those who had deposed as to their alarm on the 16th, and even this eventually came to nothing.[1]

On his departure from Lancaster Hunt met with a triumphal reception as he proceeded through Lancashire back to Manchester. 'There could not have been fewer than 40,000 spectators betwixt Pendleton and the New Bailey', declared the *Manchester Observer* rapturously.[2] The authorities were greatly disturbed by this evidence of the ever-growing popularity of the Radical leaders:

If Hunt and Sir Chas. Wolseley be bold villains [Norris wrote to Sidmouth] we shall be in a civil war in a fortnight or three weeks—they have I solemnly believe thousands at their command who are even panting to be led on.[3]

On the day after his return to Manchester Hunt issued an address to the reformers of Lancashire urging them to abstain from the use of all exciseable articles. He then departed for London.[4]

His arrival in the capital on September 13th was an affair of great pomp carefully organized by the London Radicals. His carriage was preceded and followed by whole hosts of Radical horsemen and banners, and *The Times* estimated that he was welcomed by no less than three hundred thousand people.[5] In his speech to the crowd Hunt urged them to be peaceable and to abstain from the use of exciseable articles 'until public justice is done to the community, and the blood of the sufferers at Manchester is avenged'.[6]

Meanwhile, four days before Hunt's return to London the Court of Common Council of the city had passed an address to the Prince Regent asking for an inquiry into the proceedings at Peterloo. The rejoinder of the Prince Regent to this address was uncompromising: 'with the circumstances which preceded the late meeting', he replied, 'you must be unacquainted; and of those which attended it, you appear to have been incorrectly informed'. If the laws had been violated the normal tribunals were open for the people to obtain redress: any special inquiry 'would be manifestly inconsistent with the clearest principles of public justice'.[7]

---

[1] *Manchester Observer*, Sept. 18, Nov. 13, 1819.   [2] *Ibid.*, Sept. 11, 1819.
[3] Norris to Sidmouth, Sept. 2, 1819 (H.O. 42/194).
[4] *Manchester Observer*, Sept. 11, 1819.   [5] *The Times*, Sept. 14, 1819.
[6] *Manchester Observer*, Sept. 18, 1819.
[7] *Annual Register, 1819*, General History, 110–112. The Lord Mayor refused to call a Common Hall 'to take into consideration the late violation of the law at Manchester' although requested to do so by nearly a hundred liverymen.

Radical protest meetings similar to that at Westminster were now beginning to be held all over the country. A meeting of the Paisley Radicals was held on September 11th,[1] of the Leeds Radicals on the 20th,[2] of the Birmingham Radicals on the 23rd,[3] of the Newcastle Radicals on October 11th,[4] and many more. Despite these widespread critical demonstrations, however, the magistrates felt confident in the support of the government. A private meeting of magistrates, town's officers, and some leading 'loyalists' held on September 21st decided to send a deputation to ministers urging them to strengthen the law, and the Manchester magistrates and 'loyalists' clearly had some influence upon the framing of subsequent repressive legislation.[5] On October 8th Hunt attempted to bring a criminal information against the magistrates for their action at Peterloo, but the attempt was unsuccessful.[6]

The approach of winter brought little relaxation of the tension in Lancashire. The inquest on one John Lees of Oldham, who died on the morning of September 7th from injuries received at Peterloo, was a particular cause of continued excitement.

Lees, of course, was not the only victim of the massacre: several other persons had also been the subjects of inquests. But the verdicts in these other cases had all been quickly arrived at, and were not such as to make legal proceedings possible. Some had been 'accidental death', another (on a child) 'died by a fall from his mother's arms', and another 'died by the pressure of the military, being under the civil power'.[7] In the case of Lees, however, the Radicals determined to make a special effort to secure acceptance in a court of law of the illegality of the action of the magistrates at Peterloo. Harmer and Dennison, two leading Radical solicitors, engaged themselves on the case without charge

This occasioned 'much turbulence' when the next Hall was eventually called for the purpose of electing a new Lord Mayor (*ibid.*, 112–13).

[1] *Manchester Observer*, Sept. 25, 1819. This meeting ended in an outbreak of violence which lasted for three days.

[2] *Ibid.*, Oct. 2, 1819.

[3] *Ibid.* The Radical leaders (including Sir Charles Wolseley) rode to this meeting in a mourning coach.

[4] *Ibid.*, Oct. 23, 1819.

[5] See below, p. 188.

[6] *Manchester Observer*, Nov. 13, 1819.

[7] *Annual Register, 1819*, General History, 107.

to Lees' family.[1] Harmer's particular purpose was to prove that the meeting was peaceable and that the military cut down the crowd. The authorities were naturally anxious to prevent this, and it was around this issue that the long drawn-out squabbles, which aroused national interest, principally turned, with Ferrand, the coroner, doing his best to foil the Radicals at every stage.

On the first day of the inquest proper, September 25th, Ferrand quickly made his bias clear by declaring that no notes of the proceedings were to be published until the inquest and any subsequent legal proceedings had been concluded. Here was an attempt to prevent any publicity being given to the inquiry. Because they ignored this ruling the reporters of both *The Times* and the *Morning Chronicle* were subsequently excluded from the court. The Boroughreeve and Constables of Manchester briefed Ashworth, a barrister, to appear for them. Ashworth vigorously countered the attempts of the Radicals to prove that the military attacked the crowd by arguing that until it could be settled exactly who had struck Lees (which it proved impossible to do), it was not permissible to bring in more general evidence: 'shew me a principal', he declared, 'and then I will accede to the possibility of there being accessories'. In this way the authorities at Manchester sought to prevent any general discussion of their actions at the meeting. Despite all Ashworth's efforts, however, revelations prejudicial to the authorities began to be made, and on October 13th Ferrand stepped in and adjourned the proceedings until December 1st. His excuse for this excessive adjournment was that the jury was fatigued by the long-drawn-out nature of the proceedings: almost certainly, however, his real purpose was to prevent the accumulation of any further damaging evidence against the authorities.

The Radicals were determined not to be baulked in this way, and they immediately applied to the Court of King's Bench for a mandamus to compel the coroner to proceed without further delay. Denman, later Lord Chief Justice, put their case. Events in the King's Bench, however, took an unexpected turn. It was discovered that the coroner and the jury had not viewed the body of Lees at the same time, and this, the court ruled, made all the

[1] The inquest and the subsequent proceedings in the Court of King's Bench were reported in *The Whole Proceedings before the Coroner's Inquest at Oldham, etc. on the body of John Lees*, ed. J. A. Dowling (1820). A useful summary of this report is contained in Sir Gerald Hirst, *Lincoln's Inn Essays* (1949), ch. V.

proceedings at the inquest null and void. This error in procedure was entirely the fault of Ferrand, the coroner, the person against whom the mandamus was desired to be directed, but nonetheless he was in this way relieved from having to proceed further. 'The coroner', as Prentice put it, 'by omitting to observe the law, had placed himself above the law!' [1]

The manner in which the Lees inquest was conducted aroused a storm of indignation not only in Radical circles but in all liberal circles in the country. Its mismanagement was one of the most frequent criticisms voiced at the many Whig meetings held during the autumn to protest against the massacre and subsequent events.[2] Signatures were collected in Manchester protesting against the employment of Ashworth and saying that the signatories would not permit his fees to be paid out of the poor rates.[3] Seven of the jurymen on the case subsequently wrote to the coroner telling him that, had a verdict been asked for, they would have submitted one of murder.[4]

While the Lees inquest was still in progress another legal conflict between the authorities and the reformers was also taking place. On October 2nd Meagher, trumpeter of the Manchester Yeomanry, who had become very unpopular on account of his prominent part at Peterloo, fired shots from his window while in a drunken condition at a crowd hooting him in the street. For this (most surprisingly) the Manchester magistrates merely bailed him for a misdemeanour, and a month later acquitted him of all guilt on the grounds that he had been 'in great danger' from the crowd and therefore justified. 'We are not likely to be surprised at any thing nowadays', commented J. E. Taylor in the *Peterloo Massacre*.[5]

A fortnight after the Meagher affair came the final and formal vindication of the attitude of the 'loyalists' in their petition to the Prince Regent already noticed. This document was important as revealing the nature of 'loyalist' opinion in Manchester after Peterloo.

The last two months of the year saw feeling return almost to the level of August. The working-class Radicals had now split into two factions, the more moderate Huntites inclining to

[1] Prentice, 175.   [2] See below, pp. 192–93.
[3] *Inquest . . . on the body of John Lees*, 471–72.
[4] *Manchester Observer*, Jan. 8, 1820.
[5] *Ibid.*, Oct. 9, 23, Nov. 12, 1819; *Peterloo Massacre*, 145.

peaceful courses and the ultra-Radical supporters of Thistlewood openly contemplating violence. In particular, they agitated for a series of simultaneous reform meetings to be held throughout the country on the same day and including one at Manchester. Abortive attempts to call such meetings were made for November 1st, November 15th, and December 13th.[1]

The authorities were, of course, much disturbed by these schemes. A circular from the Committee in Aid of the Civil Power was sure that 'the Radicals probably may attempt some measures of violence'.[2] These fears were further strengthened by an alleged attempt to assassinate Nadin, the Deputy Constable of Manchester, on November 11th.[3] Fearing that the Radicals might seize and use old ornamental pieces of artillery 'which are laying about', Sidmouth sent a curious circular to the Lords Lieutenant urging their immobilization by the magistracy. This oddly phrased circular aroused 'considerable amusement' in Manchester.[4]

Parliament met on November 23rd, and on the 29th the Hon. H. G. Bennet, Whig-Radical M.P. for Shrewsbury, presented a petition from Manchester respecting the conduct of the magistrates. This important document listed the principal middle-class Radical criticisms of the action of the authorities both at the Peterloo meeting and subsequently. It was signed by a significant number of the Manchester middle classes.[5] On the 29th and 30th petitions were also presented from Hunt and Bamford denouncing the authorities.[6]

The end of November in Manchester saw preparations being made by the Radicals to receive a visit from William Cobbett, the great Radical hero who had just landed at Liverpool from his self-imposed exile in America. The authorities, however, were determined to thwart any further Radical demonstrations in Manchester, and the Boroughreeve and Constables addressed a letter to Cobbett condemning the proposed 'unusual procession and multitude of people, as well strangers as inhabitants' and warning

[1] See below, p. 157.
[2] Taylor, 175.
[3] *Manchester Observer*, Nov. 20, 1819; Boroughreeve and Constables of Manchester to Sidmouth, Nov. 12, 1819 (Papers relative to the Internal State of the Country, no. 79).
[4] Prentice, 176–77.
[5] See below, p. 176.
[6] *Parliamentary Debates*, XLI (1819–20), 370–77, 509–13.

him not to enter the town. The authorities clearly had no intention of permitting any more processions of the Peterloo type to assemble. In view of the Boroughreeve's letter Cobbett thought it prudent, lest he should provoke another massacre, not to visit Manchester at all.[1]

With the coming of December the atmosphere in the town was made yet more tense on account of the meeting called by the advanced Radicals for December 13th as part of the scheme for simultaneous meetings. The authorities alarmedly prepared their counter-measures. On December 7th the Boroughreeve and Constables sent out a private circular to the leading local 'loyalists' warning them that 'the Disaffected Spirit which was long prevailed in this and other Districts, is on the Eve of breaking out into open violence'. The most extensive military preparations were made. The New Bailey prison was greatly strengthened and converted into 'a regular fortress': deep trenches were cut to defend the outworks and a strong bulwark of old hogsheads filled with earth and stones was put up. The temporary barracks near New Cross were also strengthened.[2] 'This town is in such a state of disorder and distrust occasioned by the wickedness and folly of the powers that be', wrote a local Radical rent-collector, 'that a complete stagnation [of business] has been occasioned and still continues . . . I have not yet been able to collect one farthing.'[3] In the event, the fears and preparations of the authorities proved unnecessary, for at the last moment the ultra-Radicals called off the meeting, though not before the Boroughreeve and Constables had issued a notice instructing all inhabitants to remain indoors and to continue at work.[4]

This turned out to be almost the last throw of the Radicals in Manchester. A scheme for a general fast on January 1, 1820, came to nothing, and it soon became clear, even to the authorities, that the reformers were fast losing their influence. By the middle of 1820 the Radicals, although still active in a small way, no longer possessed a movement with the powerful and widespread ramifications of the year before.[5]

The trial of Hunt and his associates began at York on March 16,

[1] *Manchester Observer*, Dec. 4, 1819. [2] *Ibid.*, Dec. 11, 1819.
[3] *Manchester City News*, Jan. 7, 1911 (letter of Thomas Leech).
[4] *Manchester Observer*, Dec. 18, 1819. [5] See below, ch. IX.

1820.[1] They were charged with conspiring to disturb the peace, to excite discontent and disaffection, and to arouse hatred and contempt of the government and constitution, and with unlawful assembling.

As expected, the nature of these charges excluded discussion of the manner in which the meeting was dispersed. The court was concerned only with the motives of the reformers in calling the meeting and the manner in which it assembled. As Scarlett, the chief prosecuting counsel, stressed, it was 'no part of the facts to be tried' whether the yeomanry charged the crowd or whether the crowd resisted the yeomanry, 'for the original formation of the meeting and the object of those who assembled it, cannot depend on what the result was'.[2]

The case was heard before Mr. Justice Bayley. His summing up was for an acquittal, and before the verdict was announced there was a general expectation in political circles in London that Hunt would go free.[3] Bayley himself believed that Hunt would have been acquitted if he had rested his case after making his speech in his own defence which was very well managed. Sydney Smith, who heard Hunt, was 'much struck with his boldness, dexterity and shrewdness'.[4]

The summing up of the judge largely narrowed the case down to a discussion of the fourth count, the charge of unlawful and seditious assembling for the purpose of exciting discontent. In this context the drilling and the inscriptions on the Radical banners were all-important. Bayley drew the attention of the jury to these circumstances particularly in dealing with Bamford.

The inscriptions upon his flag are 'Parliaments Annual, Suffrage Universal'. I cannot say that I see anything wrong in either of those. 'Unity Strength', 'Liberty and Fraternity'. Now are these or are they not calculated to produce dissatisfaction and contempt and hatred to

[1] *State Trials*, 171–496. A slightly fuller contemporary account is contained in Dolby's version of 1820.

[2] *State Trials*, 401. Scarlett, who was a Whig M.P., wrote to Lord Fitz-william shortly before the verdict was announced: 'If there is a conviction it will not touch the case of the Magistrates or the Yeomanry. The nature of the charges did not involve the propriety of *their* conduct, which will be still open to inquiry and in my opinion will call for inquiry as much as ever if all the defendents are found guilty' (Wentworth Woodhouse Papers, 52e).

[3] *State Trials*, 489n.

[4] Smith to Davenport, April 10, 1820, Smith to Grey, May 10, 1820 (*The Letters of Sydney Smith*, ed. N. C. Smith (1953), nos, 355, 364).

His Majesty's Government? If they are not, why then, unless the meeting was in its nature illegal, what is there to make out a clear case against him? His people had been drilled, . . . but the existence of that drilling would not make it illegal in him to go at the head of a party who had been so drilled, unless he meant that they should go to the meeting for the illegal purpose . . . of, by the appearance of strength, and the existence of strength, securing to those persons who might be disposed to deliver doctrines of discontent and disaffection a patient hearing; and unless there was the additional purpose also of securing confidence to those persons who might be disposed to unite in that conduct which discontent, disaffection and a belief that they had not the benefit of equal laws was calculated to produce.

This drilling and these banners, it will be remembered, were particular causes of 'loyalist' alarm in Manchester, and they seem to have had the same effect on the jurymen at York; for despite Bayley's obvious desire for an acquittal, they found the principal defendants—Hunt, Johnson, Knight, Healey, and Bamford— guilty on this fourth count. Saxton, Moorhouse, Jones, Swift and Wild were acquitted. After a motion for a new trial had failed sentence was passed on May 15th. Hunt was sentenced to two and a half years' imprisonment at Ilchester jail, and Johnson, Bamford and Healey to one year's imprisonment at Lincoln: all four prisoners had to give security for their good behaviour for five years after their release. John Knight was not sentenced on the Peterloo charge: instead he received two years' imprisonment for attending an armed meeting at Burnley on November 15th.[1]

The legal consequences of Peterloo did not come to an end with Hunt's trial. As already indicated, the conduct of the yeomanry had not been discussed there. In 1822, therefore, a test case was brought to compel a discussion of their conduct by a certain Thomas Redford, one of the injured at Peterloo. He brought an action against H. H. Birley, Richard Withington, Edward Meagher, and Alexander Oliver of the Manchester Yeomanry who had all taken part in the charge on August 16th.[2] A justification was pleaded to the effect that the assault was properly committed by the defendents in dispersing an unlawful assembly: this argument was accepted by the jury and the yeomen were found not guilty. The government paid their expenses.

Apart from the Peterloo Radicals most of the other Radical

---

[1] *State Trials*, 529–608.
[2] *Ibid.*, 1071–1262. Farquharson's contemporary report is slightly fuller.

leaders also found themselves imprisoned or under threat of imprisonment by the middle of 1820. Burdett was sentenced to three months' imprisonment and fined £2,000 for his address to the electors of Westminster occasioned by Peterloo.[1] Wolseley and Harrison were sentenced to eighteen months' imprisonment for conspiring to cause a riot by their speeches at Stockport on June 28, 1819, with an additional two years for Harrison on two other charges of seditious utterance,[2] Wroe was imprisoned for twelve months with a £100 fine for seditious publication,[3] and Carlile received a three-year sentence with a fine of £1,500 for publishing the works of Tom Paine.[4] Finally, in 1821 after long legal delays Wooler received a sentence of fifteen months' imprisonment and Cartwright was fined £100 for their parts in the Birmingham 'Legislatorial Attorney' meeting of July 12, 1819.[5]

The great working-class Radical effort of 1819 thus ended with most of its leaders in prison. The calm with which the people accepted the prosecution and conviction of their erstwhile heroes was due in part no doubt to the sudden engrossing of public interest in 1820 in the Queen's Affair. But even more it showed how superficial had been much of the working-class Radical influence over the popular mind. It held its grip only so long as economic distress was at its very worst: with a slight easing of popular suffering in 1820 came an immediate slackening of interest in Radical Reform.

[1] *State Trials*, 1–170.   [2] *Manchester Observer*, April 15, 22, 1820.
[3] Wickwar, *op. cit.*, 104.   [4] *D.N.B.*; *State Trials*, Appendix D.
[5] *State Trials*, 785–948.

Part Four

THE AFTERMATH OF PETERLOO

CHAPTER NINE

THE WORKING-CLASS RADICALS

THE story of popular Radicalism in the Manchester area after Peterloo is a story of decline. In the early autumn of 1819 the Radicals appeared to be in a position of great strength: Hunt was given an enthusiastic popular reception during his progress through Lancashire early in September. Yet by the end of the year the reformers had lost almost all their popular support and influence. What were the reasons for this surprising change of circumstances?

A principal cause of the Radical decline was the growth of internal dissension within the ranks of the reformers; this had a very damaging effect on the movement in Lancashire. In the main, the local Radical disputes reflected divisions within the Radical ranks in London. Throughout the autumn of 1819 in London the various factions of Radical Reformers were quarrelling among themselves as to what their response to the massacre should be. A meeting held at the Crown and Anchor Tavern on August 21st, attended by the moderate Radicals Cartwright and Wooler, pledged itself to raise a subscription for those imprisoned after Peterloo.[1] This gesture was not strong enough, however, for the ultra-Radicals led by Thistlewood and Watson, and on August 25th they held a public meeting of protest against the massacre at Smithfield. Wolseley and Cartwright declined to take part and Wooler's *Black Dwarf* regretted that it had been called before Hunt was free to attend. Hunt, it declared, was 'the only man, perhaps, who could preside with effect at such a meeting'.[2]

The Radical quarrels thus began only a few days after the massacre, and as soon as he returned from Lancashire Hunt

[1] *Manchester Observer*, Aug. 28, 1819.   [2] *Ibid.*, Sept. 4, 1819.

became deeply involved in them. He quarrelled with Watson over the choice of route for his triumphal procession and also on the choice of chairman for the subsequent dinner. When Watson was imprisoned for non-payment of expenses connected with this dinner, he blamed Hunt. Hunt's conduct, Watson declared, had destroyed all 'harmony and unanimity' in Radical circles and had unjustly left him to foot the bill alone.[1] About this same time James Wroe, the Manchester Radical leader and editor of the *Manchester Observer*, also began to quarrel with Watson. Thistlewood and Watson published letters saying that Wroe had paid their expenses when they visited Manchester in October to advocate their scheme for calling simultaneous reform meetings. Wroe vehemently denied this, claiming that he had merely lent Thistlewood four pounds to pay for his return to London.[2] This simultaneous meetings question was the most important point of difference between the ultra-Radicals and the Huntites, and Wroe would have lost his position of influence among the latter if he had not vigorously dissociated himself from the plans of Thistlewood and his group. Within less than a month of Peterloo the ultra-Radical organs, such as *The Republican* and *The Cap of Liberty*, had begun calling for such meetings, held on the same day 'in every Shire in England' and including one at Manchester.[3] They recommended the people to attend with arms lest the authorities should again attempt to disperse a meeting by use of force, and it was generally in this connection that the Huntites began their arguments opposing the scheme. Any meetings, Hunt agreed, would have to meet armed in case the authorities should attack again: it would be best, therefore, not to hold them at all.[4] The wisdom of this argument was widely appreciated in Lancashire and Hunt retained most of his following in the area: 'the Manchester Reformers', wrote Joseph Johnson, 'see the necessity of resting on their oars, and waiting the decision of Parliament on that subject, before they meet again'.[5] The Huntites seem indeed to have had great hopes of parliamentary redress; the

[1] Letters from Watson in the *New Times* dated Dec. 16, 21, 24, 1819 (in Hay Scrapbooks, VIII, 143, 153–54, 160); *Exchange Herald*, Sept. 28, 1819.

[2] *Manchester Observer*, Nov. 6, 1819; *Exchange Herald*, Nov. 2, 1819.

[3] *The Cap of Liberty*, Oct. 13, 1819; *The Republican*, Sept. 10, Nov. 12, 1819.

[4] *Manchester Observer*, Oct. 23, 1819.

[5] *Ibid.*, Nov. 6, 1819.

Manchester Observer strongly urged its readers to sign the petition got up by the local middle-class Radicals complaining of the conduct of the magistrates at Peterloo.[1]

Not quite all the Lancashire Radicals followed Hunt, however: Lancashire too had its hotheads. These more extreme elements could clearly hope for no support for simultaneous meetings from the Huntites and their Unions; they therefore began to form—sometime in the autumn of 1819, and probably during the visit of Thistlewood and Watson—a new ultra-Radical organization devoted to their own more extreme courses. In Manchester a rival Union to the Patriotic was set up under the leadership of W. C. Walker, described by Norris, the Manchester stipendiary, as 'the Thistlewood of this part'.[2] This new extremist Union was soon busy trying to arrange public meetings. A meeting for November 5th was discussed at the Union on November 2nd and 4th, simultaneous meetings for November 23rd were considered at a local delegate meeting on November 12th, and Walker attended a delegate meeting at Nottingham called to organize simultaneous meetings for December 13th.[3] None of these schemes came to anything, although the meeting of December 13th was nearly held and, as already noted, caused the authorities considerable alarm.

The Manchester Huntites opposed the ultra-Radicals at every stage. The *Observer* used its influence strenuously to oppose the idea of simultaneous meetings: 'Stay at Home and spare the effusion of blood', it urged its readers on December 11th. Chippendale, the Home Office informer, reported that the Unions in the circumjacent towns' had decided not to co-operate with the Manchester extremists on the 13th, either by attending a Manchester meeting or by holding simultaneous meetings of their own.[4] The final gesture of the ultra-Radicals was to call for a general fast on January 1, 1820. Delegate meetings were held in the area in an attempt to arrange this, but this scheme also came to nothing.[5]

That the ultra-Radicals met with so little success is not surprising if their Union at Manchester was typical of their organization

[1] *Ibid.*, Nov. 20, 1819. For the petition see below, p. 176.
[2] Norris to Sidmouth, Oct. 30, 1819 (H.O. 42/197).
[3] Norris to Sidmouth, Nov. 7, 1819, enclosure, Nov. 16, 1819, enclosure H.O. 42/198); Norris to Sidmouth, Nov. 29, 1819 (H.O. 42/199).
[4] Chippendale to Sidmouth, Dec. 12, 1819 (H.O. 42/200).
[5] Kinsey, 93.

and leadership. A magistrates' spy reported on their meetings on November 2nd and 4th in the George Leigh Street Union Rooms supposedly called to consider holding a public meeting on the 15th. On November 2nd instead of discussing this question the meeting developed into a squabbling argument as to whether Walker, the Union Secretary, was fit to continue in office while he kept two wives. It was argued in his defence that morality was not relevant to politics; but Walker resigned, only to be reinstated in time for the meeting of November 4th to which the original business had had to be left. This meeting (with only about a hundred members present as against two hundred on the 2nd) finally decided not to call a meeting for the 15th. During the proceedings Wroe, the Huntite Superintendent of the Union Rooms, came in and announced that in future the Union must meet elsewhere: 'Mr Bradbury and Mr W. C. Walker', he declared '. . . were of so bad Characters that the Union would never prosper whilst they had anything to do with it.' There was obviously much truth in this: 'their boasted Union', commented the magistrates' spy with justice, 'is a Mass of Disunion.' Unfortunately for the Huntites, the contemptible nature of such proceedings could not help having a detrimental effect on their own standing in the area.[1]

Apart from opposing the ultra-Radicals the only activity among the Huntites in the last quarter of 1819 had to do with preparation for the intended visit of William Cobbett, already noticed and with advocacy of abstinence from the use of excisable articles. This idea of abstinence had first become prominent in the area just before Peterloo. The Manchester meeting of June 21st passed a resolution in favour of the scheme,[2] and Joseph Harrison in a sermon at Stockport on August 15th, supported it in language which was to cost him an extra prison sentence: 'the Government have starved the people', he asserted, 'and therefore it is fit that the people should starve the Government'.[3] Cobbett calculated that three-quarters of the whole revenue came from wine, spirits, tea, coffee, and tobacco: if even one-third of this were withheld the consequences would be 'the most beneficial that can be

[1] The spy's description of the two meetings (Norris to Sidmouth, Nov. 7, 1819, enclosure. H.O. 42/198) is printed in Appendix B.
[2] *Manchester Observer*, June 26, 1819.
[3] *Ibid.*, April 22, 1820.

imagined'.[1] Hunt strongly supported the scheme, frequently mentioning it.[2] He produced a coffee substitute made from roasted corn; but this proved to be undrinkable, and the reformers concentrated mainly on abstinence from spirits and ale. At Oldham wakes after Peterloo the Radicals brewed their own beer and drank it in tents.[3] Despite all these efforts, however, the scheme does not seem to have secured any extensive support. As a method of coercing the government it never looked like succeeding, and by the end of the year the *Observer* was stressing its value more as a gesture of solidarity than as a practical means of embarrassing the authorities.[4]

By this date the Radicals, Huntites as well as extremists, were fast losing ground. At the end of January 1820 Wooler in his *Black Dwarf* felt it necessary to call for support for the Union Societies,[5] and even the easily alarmed local authorities began to be hopeful. Sharp, the Boroughreeve of Manchester, reported on the 'declining influence' of the Unions: he detected 'a favourable change in the temper and conduct of the lower classes'. Norris too noticed that 'the great body of the radical reformers seem to retire from their work of disturbing the public peace'.[6]

At the last this collapse had come quite suddenly, but several factors had been working towards it for some time. The disputes between the Huntites and the Watsonites undoubtedly lost both factions much support. Critics were not slow to make capital out of their squabbles. The 'loyalist' Press printed the letters of the disputants with glee. 'These letters', declared the *Manchester Chronicle*, 'are merely echoes of the gross abuse which each of these friends to reform throws upon the other . . . not one of them has a claim to integrity of character.'[7] Though they did not agree with the *Chronicle* on other things, many of the working-men of Lancashire probably came to the same conclusion.

Developments in Radical policy may not have pleased some of the operatives. Notorious for their heavy drinking, abstinence

[1] *Ibid.*, Dec. 11, 1819.
[2] *Ibid.*, Sept. 11, 18, Oct. 23, Dec. 18, 1819.
[3] Marcroft, *op. cit.*, 61–62.
[4] *Manchester Observer*, Jan. 1, 1820.
[5] *Black Dwarf*, Jan. 26, 1820.
[6] Sharp to Sidmouth, Jan. 8, 1820 (H.O. 42/203); Norris to Sidmouth, Jan. 10, 1820 (*ibid.*).
[7] *Manchester Chronicle*, Nov. 6, 1819.

campaigns and fast-day schemes may have asked too much of their Radicalism. Norris, the Manchester stipendiary magistrate, noted that '*very many* were in a state of inebriation' in Manchester on New Year's Day 1820, the day set aside by the ultra-Radicals for a solemn general fast.[1] The Six Acts, too, hurried through Parliament at the end of 1819, undoubtedly accelerated the Radical collapse. Sidmouth, the Home Secretary, arranged for their immediate enforcement: 'as soon as this Act [against seditious meetings] comes into operation', he instructed the Lord-Lieutenant of Cheshire on December 24th, 'it should be enforced with vigilance and activity'.[2] In the event, however, there was little need for rigorous enforcement, for the Radicals allowed their organization to be set outside the law with surprisingly little demur. The threat of the Six Acts was enough: enforcement was hardly necessary. In his last address before they came into force Hunt wrote to his followers in a spirit of resigned acceptance; he offered no more stirring encouragement to the movement than a renewed charge to abstain from the use of excisable articles, to 'cherish the principles of Liberty', and to exercise 'patience, fortitude, and forbearance'. The government was devising 'unheard of laws' so that it could rule by the sword and frustrate the cause of Radical Reform: 'But despair not, my friends; if our cause be just, Heaven will yet assist us in obtaining that cause.'[3] Apart from violence, there was perhaps no other course left for Hunt to recommend but this: nonetheless, it meant that his last call was in a very minor key. And if anything showed that the Huntite Radicals never intended violence, it was the acquiescent spirit in which they accepted parliament's will as expressed in the Six Acts.

Another factor tending to encourage the withdrawal of support from the Radicals was the gradual but steady improvement in trade conditions which began early in 1820. Only the most extreme depression had driven many of the weavers to Radicalism: when the depression eased a little they reverted to their distrust of all politicians. The *Manchester Mercury* detected the first symptoms of this trade revival as early as January 4, 1820, and a few days later, William Rowbottom, an Oldham weaver, noted in his journal that trade was now 'Brisk' even though wages were still

[1] Norris to Sidmouth, Jan. 2, 1820 (H.O. 42/203).
[2] *Manchester Chronicle*, Jan. 8, 1820.
[3] *Manchester Observer*, Dec. 18, 1819.

ow.[1] By Whitsuntide the improvement was becoming more pronounced: 'trade seems progressively improving and the poor weavers . . . begin to feel the good effects by an increase . . . in their too scanty wages', remarked the *Exchange Herald*; 'the gloom and ferocity', it added significantly, 'which deformed the human countenance on the famous 16th of August . . . were no longer to be seen'.[2]

As a result of all these weakening influences, by the middle of 1820 Radicalism in the Manchester area had declined very far from the widespread popular movement of a year before. Though the Cato Street Conspirators claimed to have acted 'to avenge the innocent blood shed at Manchester', the Manchester Radicals had no connection with their proceedings.[3] And though the Queen's Affair later in the year produced some temporary effusions of Radical feeling it made no permanent impression.[4] Even the demonstrations arranged for the first anniversary of Peterloo were not very impressive. In Manchester, Saxton harangued a meeting on St. Peter's Field, but little more than a thousand people took part altogether.[5] At Oldham it had been intended to march in procession to the grave of Lees, the Peterloo victim, but only a few 'idle persons' made the trip and (as the *Annual Register* put it) 'the unity of the grand design was entirely lost sight of'.[6]

These demonstrations at Manchester and Oldham still centred round the Union Rooms there; but whether Union *Societies* were still in existence at this date is very doubtful. The *Manchester Observer* in describing the demonstrations does not mention them and probably very few were still in existence. The extent of the Union collapse was shown by the need to set up new bodies in some respects similar. Thus, early in the summer of 1820 the *Observer* was urging the establishment of a 'Permanent Fund'

[1] Rowbottom, *op. cit.*, IC, 106.
[2] *Exchange Herald*, May 30, 1820.
[3] *Annual Register, 1820*, Appendix to Chronicle, 949. The Boroughreeve of Manchester tried hard to find 'arrangements for active operations of a similar nature [in Manchester], had the plot unhappily succeeded'; but he could find none (Sharp to Sidmouth, Feb. 27, 1820. *State Trials*, 335n.).
[4] Addresses from the Artisans and Mechanics of Manchester were voted to the Queen on her arrival in England and on the collapse of the case against her, and on each occasion meetings were held in the Union Rooms (*Manchester Observer*, Sept. 9, Dec. 2, 1820).
[5] *Manchester Observer, Manchester Chronicle*, Aug. 19, 1820; *Annual Register, 1820*, Chronicle, 376–77.
[6] *Annual Register, ibid.*, 377.

organization to provide financial support for the imprisoned
Radical leaders; Manchester was eventually divided into twenty-
four districts with subscription classes of twenty within each
district.[1] The influence of and similarity to the Union Society
organization was obvious here; if those bodies had still been
flourishing there would have been no need for these new crea-
tions. This new activity eventually merged into Hunt's Great
Northern Political Union, which had numerous branches in the
area by 1822 and whose central committee for Lancashire met in
Manchester.[2]

In Stockport, the original centre of the Union movement, the
collapse was probably more protracted than elsewhere. After the
conviction of Harrison and of all the other prominent Radical
leaders only William Perry, a veteran of the days of the Hampden
Clubs, was left to carry on. During 1820 the Union got into
financial difficulties through trying to keep up its payments to its
imprisoned leaders, and at the end of the year Perry had to appeal
for funds in the *Black Dwarf*.[3]

By about 1824 even the Radical Indian Summer under the
Great Northern Political Union was at an end.[4] The Union Room
at Stockport was sold up to meet debts;[5] the *Black Dwarf* ceased
publication, as the *Manchester Observer* had already done three
years before;[6] and after 1821 no Peterloo memorial meetings were
reported in the Press.[7] In 1826, when trade was again depressed,
there was a plan for a meeting on St. Peter's Field of all those who
had been at Peterloo, but the attendance was small.[8]

Thus the great popular movement begun in Lancashire in 1816,
and reaching its climax in 1819, ended its days in gradual decline.
The Union Societies, the public meetings, the banners, the

[1] *Manchester Observer*, May–June, 1820, Jan. 6, 1821; Wearmouth, *op. cit.*,
44–45.
[2] *Wooler's British Gazette and Manchester Observer*, Oct. 6, 20, 1821, March 1,
30, 1822; Wearmouth, *op. cit.*, 45–49.
[3] Giles, *op. cit.*, 228–31; *Black Dwarf*, Dec. 13, 1820.
[4] Wearmouth, *op. cit.*, 47–48.
[5] Giles, *op. cit.*, 231.
[6] The *Manchester Observer* ceased publication in June, 1821. It was revived
in the following August with the help of T. J. Wooler and became associated
with (although not merged into) his existing London paper *Wooler's British
Gazette*. *Wooler's British Gazette and Manchester Observer* survived for about
a year.
[7] Main, *op. cit.*, 66.
[8] *Ibid.*, 78.

extensive organization and the detailed programme of what had been the first large-scale political movement of the new industrial working-class had achieved no direct results. Only the memory of Peterloo remained to act as a spur to future reformers.

CHAPTER TEN

THE MIDDLE-CLASS RADICALS

MUCH as they deplored the inhumanity of the Peterloo Massacre there can be no doubt that in one sense the middle-class Radicals in Manchester welcomed it, for it gave them a great opportunity for furthering the cause of moderate yet radical reform. It presented them with an opportunity for political agitation on a scale which before had been impossible, for leading a widely supported agitation in a righteous cause and for finally establishing themselves thereby in local politics; and at the same time it gave them a most welcome chance to play some (albeit distant) part in politics on a national scale.

As we have already noticed, the immediate reaction of Prentice and Taylor to the massacre was to write to the London newspapers. They knew that Tyas, *The Times* reporter, had been arrested, and they feared therefore that only accounts sent by the magistrates would reach London. The attention of the whole country, they knew, was now centred on Manchester, and they determined not to miss such an excellent opportunity for exposing the folly of the authorities, local and national, responsible for the massacre and also (what was even more important to them) for pointing out the shortcomings of the present system of local and national government which they believed were fundamentally responsible for the outrage.

In this spirit Taylor quickly followed up his description in the London Press by a more extended incursion into journalism. He undertook the editorship of a publication entitled the *Peterloo Massacre* which appeared for fourteen weeks after the massacre, price twopence. In its first numbers it gave a full description of the massacre, and then week by week a detailed account of the subsequent proceedings: the presentation and rejection of bills against the Manchester authorities presented to the Grand Jury, the irregular conduct of the Lees inquest, and the rest.

Their journalistic ventures were only one way in which the middle-class reformers carried out their campaign of exposure. Three days after Peterloo they were given an opportunity to aunch a more direct attack on the local authorities and 'loyalists'. On August 19th the local 'loyalists' called a meeting at the Star Inn, Manchester, to thank the authorities for their action at Peterloo. It purported to be a 'meeting of the inhabitants of Manchester and Salford and their neighbourhood', and it published its ultra-'loyal' resolutions as if they expressed the general voice of the town. But in fact the meeting was in no sense a public one. It had been called in the first place to meet at the Police Office, but when it was seen that the middle and working-class reformers were present it was deliberately adjourned to the Star Inn, where (as Prentice wrote) 'it might be safe from the possibility of intrusion on the part of any police commissioner, who might hold the opinion that a peaceable assembly ought not to be dispersed by the sword'.[1]

The reaction of Prentice and his friends to this piece of deception was immediate. They met together and quickly drew up a Declaration and Protest against the Star Inn resolutions. This important document first condemned the violent dispersal of the Peterloo meeting and then went on to denounce the Star Inn assembly:

'We . . . declare that the meeting convened at the Police Office on Thursday the 19th of August, for the purpose of thanking the magistrates, municipal officers, soldiery, etc., was strictly and exclusively *private*; and in order that its privacy might be more completely ensured, was adjourned to the Star Inn. It is a matter of notoriety that no expression of dissent from the main object of the meeting was there permitted.

We therefore deny that it had any claim to the title of a *'numerous and highly-respectable meeting of the inhabitants of Manchester and Salford and their neighbourhood'*.[2]

The volume of support given to this protest was most striking: it was quickly signed by nearly five thousand inhabitants.[3] Here, wrote Prentice, was 'an expression of public feeling and opinion, such as had never been manifested in Manchester before'.[4] Francis Phillips, who had presided at the Star Inn Meeting, could make no adequate reply in his pamphlet published in defence of the authorities. He could not deny the private nature of the meeting and was forced to resort to mere abuse. The Declaration and

[1] Prentice, 163–66; *Manchester Gazette*, Aug. 21, 1819; Bruton, *Three Accounts of Peterloo by Eyewitnesses*, 70–71 (J. B. Smith).

[2] *Declaration and Protest* (1819); Prentice, 164. The paragraph dealing with the dispersal is quoted below, p. 174.

[3] See below, p. 174.   [4] Prentice, 164.

Protest had been signed, he claimed, only by unpatriotic opposers
of the French war, 'the detractors of British glory, the admirers of
our enemies, or the apologists of their crimes'.[1]

The Manchester 'loyalists' were thus driven to deception and
abuse in an attempt to give their acts on August 16th the appearance of public sanction. If there had been any identity of feeling
between governors and governed in Manchester such expedients
would have been unnecessary. In exposing the discomfiture of the
authorities in this affair the middle-class Radicals in Manchester,
as well as publicizing the peaceableness of the Peterloo meeting,
were stressing once again how little contact there was between
local government and local opinion.

The middle-class reformers did not restrict themselves merely
to words in dealing with the massacre and its effects. They
immediately took a prominent part in the relief of those who had
suffered at the meeting. A relief subscription was organized and
several relief committees were established, including one which
met regularly at Prentice's warehouse.[2] The relief dispensed was
of two kinds: money to buy food for those who were out of work
because of injuries sustained at Peterloo, and money to cover the
legal expenses of those arrested in connection with the meeting.

The efforts of the middle-class reformers were not confined only
to Manchester. In October 1819 the Honourable H. G. Bennet,
Whig-Radical M.P. for Shrewsbury,[3] paid a fleeting visit of inquiry to Lancashire, and although he was in Manchester for only
twenty-four hours, the members of the group made contact with
him, and he became their mouthpiece in the Commons.[4] Their
usual attitude towards the parliamentary Whigs was far from

[1] Phillips, ix–x.
[2] Prentice, 167. It is not quite clear whether Prentice's committee was established before the Metropolitan and Central Relief Committee set up after the
Westminster meeting of September 2 (see above, p. 145). Probably it was. Prentice certainly implies (167–68) that his committee, if not actually dependent
on, at least worked in close association with the Metropolitan Committee.
Taylor, Richard Potter, Shuttleworth, and Baxter were all members of
another relief committee; Taylor's pamphlet was published as the work of
'a Member of the Manchester Committee for relieving the Sufferers of the
16th of August 1819'. The account book of one of the Peterloo Relief Committees is preserved in the John Rylands Library, Manchester (Bruton, *Three
Accounts of Peterloo by Eyewitnesses*, 78–80).
[3] Hon. H. G. Bennet (1777–1836), second son of 4th Earl of Tankerville;
M.P. for Shrewsbury 1806, 1811–26.
[4] *Parliamentary Debates*, XLI (1819–20), 151.

favourable: 'They would wash the outside of the Constitution', declared Richard Potter in 1820, 'but they did not want to purify it within.' [1] They looked upon Bennet, however, as something of a special case. He had introduced bills in 1817, 1818, and 1819 to prohibit the use of climbing boys by chimney-sweeps or at least to improve their conditions;[2] he had introduced another bill in 1818 to prohibit the payment of rewards to police officers;[3] he had strongly opposed the suspension of Habeas Corpus in 1817;[4] and in the same year he had played a leading part in the exposure of Oliver the Spy.[5] The middle-class Radicals must have looked on all this work with favour; and though a Whig, it is less surprising, therefore, that he should have become their mouthpiece in parliament after Peterloo.

There is no doubt about his importance to the middle-class Radicals in this role. During the months of November and December 1819 he was in almost daily correspondence with Shuttleworth, and through him he received detailed information about the Peterloo meeting and about the subsequent proceedings. His letters to Shuttleworth were so many and so detailed that it seems certain that in the middle of a busy parliamentary session he can have had little time for correspondence with anyone else in the neighbourhood, and that the middle-class Radicals were therefore his principal informants about conditions in Lancashire.[5]

Bennet made two important speeches during the session using the information supplied to him by the Manchester reformers, the first on November 24th, the second on December 9th.[7] In his first speech he discussed the details of the massacre. He had no doubt that the Manchester Yeomanry had shown violence to the crowd on its advance to the hustings, and that after the arrests had been made 'the multitude was attacked'. He concluded by urging the need for parliamentary reform:

---

[1] *Manchester Gazette,* June 3, 1820.
[2] Hammond, *Town Labourer,* II, 20–25.
[3] The system of rewards, he declared, encouraged the police 'to stimulate others to the commission of crime for the purpose of putting money into their pockets by their conviction' (*ibid.,* I, 86). In this same year the middle-class Radicals in Manchester were bringing just such a charge against Nadin (see above, pp. 65–66).
[4] *Parliamentary Debates,* XXXVI (1817), 1208–13.
[5] *Ibid.,* XXXVII (1817), 349–63; Hammond, *Skilled Labourer,* 371–73.
[6] Shuttleworth Scrapbook, *passim.*
[7] *Parliamentary Debates,* XLI (1819–20), 143–51, 890–900.

he felt himself bound to recommend to the House, if it wished to avoid civil dissention, if it wished to avoid that greatest of all evils, the shedding of English blood by English hands, to examine fairly and freely into the state of representation, and to show the people that, though it would oppose all such innovations as would tend to subvert the constitution, it was quite alive to that greatest of all questions.

On December 9, 1819, Bennet introduced a motion for an inquiry into the state of the manufacturing districts. After a brief discussion of the situation in Scotland and in Yorkshire he launched into a detailed narrative of the situation in Lancashire. He pointed out the wide gap between the local authorities and the rest of Manchester opinion, an important point clearly derived from the middle-class Radicals,[1] and urged the need for a reform of the local government system; he stressed the recent improvement in the educational standards of the poor which made them no longer acquiescent before oppression, again a point often made by the Manchester reformers; he denounced the Orange Societies; and he described the circumstances of the distressed poor in the area and their low rates of wages. They looked to parliament, he concluded, to find means of relieving their condition, and it was especially for this reason that he advocated an inquiry into the state of the manufacturing districts: 'it might be found impossible to frame any plan of general or immediate relief, but he had no doubt that many measures might be adopted to correct and mitigate the evil'. Prominent among such measures, he suggested, should be large-scale schemes of public works and of assisted emigration to the colonies, this last again a favourite proposal of the Manchester middle-class Radicals.

Thus it is clear that through Bennet the middle-class Radicals of Manchester were putting forward their account of Peterloo and also some of their most important proposals for removing the underlying conditions which had produced the massacre. Not all that Bennet proposed, of course, was necessarily the product of the influence of the Manchester reformers: as a prominent and intelligent reformer he had doubtless come to many conclusions agreeable to them on his own account. But the Manchester middle-class Radicals had clearly much impressed him, and they had done

[1] 'Can you give me an account of the *character* and *situation* of the Magistrates who signed Hunt's warrant?' (Bennet to Shuttleworth, Nov. 18, 1819. Shuttleworth Scrapbook).

well to secure his co-operation in the presentation of their opinions. Taylor gratefully dedicated his Peterloo pamphlet to him.[1]

Apart from his two important speeches in parliament Bennet also introduced on November 29th a petition from Manchester respecting the conduct of the local magistrates. His association with it, and the nature of its account of Peterloo, make it clear that this document, like the Declaration and Protest in August, had been inspired by the middle-class Radicals.[2]

While Bennet was busy presenting their case at Westminster, the members of the group continued to campaign zealously at home in Manchester. Their opposition in local government circles to the Anglican church building proposals, which had as important a political as a religious purpose, has already been noticed. The reformers were active also in local government affairs in two other important connections.

The fondness for the employment of the military which the local authorities had shown on August 16th was continued after Peterloo. This led to strong middle-class Radical criticism. Their opposition came to a head at a Parish Vestry meeting called on April 20, 1820, to pass the Constables' accounts for the preceding three months. Led by Richard Potter and Edward Baxter they proposed that an item of £420 for barrack department expenditure should be deleted from the accounts: 'He would allow nothing', declared Potter, 'connected with the military force which had been introduced, he did not know why or by whom, to pass without opposition'. Potter's motion was defeated, but the reformers were not discouraged. The *Manchester Gazette* in reporting the meeting launched a full-scale attack on the large number of troops still maintained in the area. It denounced them as unnecessary and as a danger to constitutional liberty: 'nothing short of lamentable experience,' it declared, 'will teach our Manchester Tories, that the old constitutional jealousy of our ancestors against the use of military force was well founded'.[3]

Even more important than these attacks on the presence of a large military force in the area was the reformers' other local

---

[1] 'Your private virtues and your political independence are well known to, and correctly appreciated by, the most enlightened portion of your fellow countrymen' (Taylor, v–viii).

[2] *Parliamentary Debates*, XLI (1819–20), 357–70. See below, p. 176.

[3] *Manchester Gazette*, April 22, 29, 1820; *Manchester Observer*, April 22, 1820.

government agitation arising out of Peterloo. Their campaign
here began at the parish meeting held in the Collegiate Church on
October 22, 1819, to pass the Constables' accounts for the Peterloo
period. Brierley, the senior churchwarden and a leading 'loyalist',
who was in the chair, refused to permit any discussion of the
various items in the accounts connected with the massacre: 'the
moment all the items were read, a motion was made by one of the
party interested in passing the Accounts, and this motion was
passed to the vote by the chairman'. The Radical Reformers
protested violently at this. 'The party of the Manchester Magistrates and Yeomen', declared Joseph Johnson, the working-class
Radical leader, was deliberately trying to rush through the
accounts. Chapman, another working-class Radical, demanded
that the chairman show more impartiality: he was determined, he
declared, to do his duty 'even if you should call in the Manchester
Yeomanry to shed blood in the House of God—as I dare say
some persons who hear me would not be disinclined to do'.[1]
Despite these protests, however, the accounts were passed without any discussion being allowed. In reply the Radicals immediately applied to the Court of King's Bench for a mandamus to
compel the authorities to lay the items in the Constables' accounts
properly before the public. Their appeal was successful, and
in consequence on May 31, 1820, there took place the most
important of all the local government meetings connected with
Peterloo.

The Radicals put out handbills calling on their supporters to
attend in force, and the Collegiate Church was crowded throughout the meeting. J. E. Taylor began the Radical attack by in-
quiring why after Peterloo Samuel Bamford, the working-class
Radical leader, had been arrested in his home by the military
instead of by the civil power. Moore, the senior Constable, could
only defend himself by saying 'that the military were sent *by the
express orders of the Magistrates*'. Moore, replied Taylor, should
have refused to carry out such an illegal order.

The discussion now moved on to 'the great objects of dispute',
printers' bills connected with Peterloo. Two items, the reformers
discovered, had been significantly withdrawn from the accounts
since the last meeting: the cost of anti-Radical posters put up in
the town just before Peterloo, and the expenses connected with

[1] *Manchester Observer*, Oct. 23, 1819.

he Star Inn meeting. Moore now admitted that these expenses hould not have been included in the accounts. The discussion herefore turned on the nature of the 'loyal' Police Office meeting)f July 9, 1819. The reformers wanted the expenses of this neeting taken out of the accounts also. It was not a public meet- ng, they contended, but a purely private assembly. Richard ?otter asked 'whether you will sanction a set of men calling)rivate meetings, with the intention of propagating their peculiar)olitical opinions, and then charging the expense to the town?' The Constables' reply was feeble. They agreed to withdraw the :ost of advertising the meeting in the London papers but not in he local Press. On this, and on the other expenses, they took their tand. Moore 'was willing to admit that the meeting of the 9th uly was not a public one'; but, he contended, it was now im-)racticable and undesirable to call a truly public meeting in Vlanchester:

Vlanchester was a place, which, within a few years, had increased most apidly in wealth and population; but which had not had any corre- ponding improvements in its municipal constitution. He would put it o the candour of the Gentlemen on the other side, whether it was ossible, that the office of Constable should be served here, on the ame terms as in a small country village.

Iere was indeed a striking admission that the existing system of)cal government in Manchester was inadequate for the proper dministration of the town. This was one of the very points which he middle-class Radicals were setting out to prove in these local ;overnment campaigns; and though outvoted in this instance on he Peterloo expense question, Moore's admission represented a onsiderable moral victory for them. The local authorities respon- ible for the Peterloo Massacre had virtually admitted their own nsufficiency.[1]

Such was the immediate reaction of the Manchester middle- lass Radicals to Peterloo. It had helped firmly to establish them in)cal politics, and had also introduced them (indirectly at least) ito national politics. It was necessary now for them to con- olidate their newly won influence and to press forward more itensively (if they could) in the cause of reform. It was with this purpose in view that in May 1821 they established the *Manchester Guardian*.[1]

J. E. Taylor was the leading figure behind the venture. He had been writing in Cowdroy's *Manchester Gazette* for several years, and his first hope was to purchase this paper. This proved impossible, however, and he therefore decided to establish an entirely new paper based on the model of middle-class reforming journals elsewhere, especially Baines's *Leeds Mercury*. All the members of the middle-class Radical group supported Taylor in the venture, eleven of the more affluent among them lending £1,050 on very favourable terms to help cover initial expenses.

The prospectus of the *Guardian* was kept intentionally vague so as to secure support from a wide a range of reformers as possible:

[The *Manchester Guardian*] will zealously enforce the principles of civil and religious liberty, in the most comprehensive sense of those terms; it will warmly advocate the cause of reform; it will endeavour to assist in the diffusion of just principles of political economy; and support without reference to the party from which they emanate, whatever measures may . . . tend to promote the moral advantage or the political welfare of the community.

On the question of parliamentary reform only a vague promise of opinions was made such as might include both the full-blooded supporters of universal suffrage and also the more moderate advocates of the transfer to Manchester of the seats from a disfranchised rotten borough.

In this way the *Manchester Guardian* was established, intended by its middle-class Radical founders to develop the position of influence which they had acquired during 1819 and 1820. Through its columns they planned to expound and discuss the principles of Radical reform in a manner more rational and seemly and more likely to win 'respectable' support than the monster meetings of the Peterloo Radicals, 'by calm but spirited discussion [rather than by violent denunciations proceeding from great assemblages'.

---

[1] For a full account of the establishment of the *Manchester Guardian* see my forthcoming history of the paper. Prentice (203–09) gives a short sketch and prints the prospectus in full.

[2] Prentice, 202.

CHAPTER ELEVEN

THE COTTON MASTERS

As has already been briefly indicated, there were signs after Peterloo that at least a large minority of the Manchester cotton masters did not approve of the violent action of the authorities at Peterloo. At the subsequent trials many independent witnesses, including a number of substantial cotton merchants and manufacturers, were ready to declare that 'respectable' opinion in Manchester was not unduly alarmed by the Peterloo meeting. 'I have property in the neighbourhood', declared one retired calico printer at Hunt's trial, 'but nothing which occurred that day inspired me with any fear for its safety': 'I saw nothing that day', remarked a cotton merchant, 'which excited my fear for the safety of myself or my family'.[1] By contrast, an analysis of the witnesses at the trials who were prepared to say that they feared for their lives and property on August 16th shows them nearly all to have been compromised in some way or other. Some of them were the magistrates and town's officers themselves, and others had taken a prominent part on the 'loyal' side. Such witnesses, therefore, were more justifying themselves than giving independent testimony. Of the few uncompromised witnesses in this group only three appear to have been cotton masters. The authorities themselves were aware of this deficiency of witnesses in support of their alarms, claiming by way of explanation that potential witnesses were too intimidated by the Radicals to give evidence of seditious practices. But such intimidation can hardly have been a factor in 1822, three years after the massacre, when *Redford* v. *Birley* was heard: even then only eight uncompromised witnesses could be produced to say that they were alarmed by the attitude of the Radicals on the day of Peterloo.[2]

[1] *State Trials*, 339 (Grundy), 349 (Smith), 363 (Rockliffe, Fell), 370–71 (Wright), 374 (Thelwall), 391 (Sanderson, Smith), 394 (Robinson); *Inquest . . . on the body of John Lees*, 116 (Shaw).

[2] Bouchier to Hobhouse, Aug. 21, 1819 (H.O. 41/4); Statement of the Lancashire Grand Jury, Sept. 1819 (Papers relative to the Internal State of the Country, No. 43). See note at end of chapter.

Another pointer tending to show that at least a large part of Manchester opinion was not unduly disturbed by the Radical agitations in 1819 was the slow progress made by the 'loyal' Armed Association after Peterloo. By November even the local authorities had to admit that this attempt to found a kind of 'loyal' Home Guard had proved a 'failure'; arms sent from Chester had to be returned because there were no volunteers to use them. Once again Radical intimidation was given as the reason for lack of support; but there was probably more truth in Taylor's claim that the collapse of the Armed Association proved 'that the opinion of the great body of the respectable inhabitants of the Town, did not go along with the Magistrates and their friends in their professed apprehensions of danger'.[1]

But the most important indication of the critical response of many Manchester cotton masters to the action of the authorities at Peterloo was the large volume of support given to the Declaration and Protest drawn up by the local middle-class Radicals just after the massacre. This document amounted to a complete rejection of all the authorities' grounds of action at Peterloo:

We the undersigned, without individually approving of the manner in which the meeting held on St. Peter's, on Monday the 16th of August, was constituted, hereby declare, that we are fully satisfied, by personal observation or undoubted information, that it was perfectly peaceable; that no seditious or intemperate harangues were made there; that the riot act, if read at all, was read privately, or without the knowledge of a great body of the meeting; and we feel it our bounden duty to protest against, and to express our utter disapprobation of, the unexpected and unnecessary violence by which the assembly was dispersed.

Nearly five thousand signatures were collected in support of this manifesto, and one hundred and forty-eight cotton masters can be identified as among the number. Here was a break in the long-standing apathy of the cotton employers on political questions: no longer were they all prepared to accept without question the rule of the Tory oligarchy in Manchester as they had done for so many years. 'It was as the breaking up of a great frost,' wrote Archibald Prentice:

The middle classes had appeared as if they were bound up in the icy chains of indifference . . . but the sudden outburst [in the Declaration

---

[1] Boroughreeve of Manchester to Sidmouth, Nov. 16, 1819 (H.O. 42/198); *An Address to the Higher Classes*, 43–45; Taylor, 52.

and Protest] showed that whatever opinions they might hold, as to how far the elective franchise might safely be extended, they were not disposed quietly to witness death inflicted on men whose only crime had been that they asked for universal suffrage.[1]

When in October the local 'loyalists' brought out a petition defending the action of the authorities at Peterloo it received only a few more identifiable masters' signatures (a hundred and seventy-seven) than had the Declaration and Protest.[2]

The extent of this revulsion of feeling among many of the cotton employers was commented on by contemporaries. They were moved by two motives, humanitarian feeling and concern for the safety of their property. 'Many of the wealthy class', wrote Samuel Bamford, 'blamed [the Manchester authorities], as well for the severity with which they had acted, as for the jeopardy in which they had placed the lives and property of the townspeople.'[3] 'All thinking men', reported a *Times* correspondent after the massacre, 'wish that one or two of the cool-headed Bow-street magistrates would favour us with their presence for a few days, to prevent any further blunders from precipitancy.'[4] It was the magistrates' action, not that of the Radicals, which had endangered

---

[1] Prentice, 166; Taylor 60.
[2] The text of the Declaration and Protest analysed here was printed with an appended list of some 4,900 signatures by Cowdroy, the printer of the *Manchester Gazette*. The 'loyal' October Petition was published in the *Manchester Chronicle*, Oct. 16, 1819, with some 1,200 signatures appended. It is not intended that the figures given below of the number of cotton masters signing the rival documents should be regarded as absolute. Deficiencies in the directory used (Pigot and Dean, *op. cit.*) make identification of many names impossible. The figures are important only for their relative values, all presumably suffering in equal proportions from the same deficiencies in the directory:

	Declaration and Protest	October Petition
Cotton manufacturers . . .	71	65
Cotton merchants	16	43
Cotton dealers	14	25
Calico printers	15	16
Master spinners	5	12
Master dyers	11	5
Master hatters	1	—
Commission agents	15	11
	148	177

[3] Bamford, I, 214.
[4] *The Times*, Aug. 20, 1819.

property on the 16th, and it was their imaginary alarms on the 17th, not any gesture of the reformers, which ruined business on that day, the main market-day for cotton goods. Moore, the Constable who spread abroad the alarm on this occasion began to be scorned by many of his fellow townsmen: 'This gentlemen's news begins to have a bad savour, and is commonly known by the appellation of "Moor-game".' [1]

When parliament met in November the middle-class Radicals saw to it that this new spirit against the Tory local authorities was given formal expression. A petition was prepared criticizing the conduct of the magistrates both at Peterloo and subsequently, and it received between six and seven thousand signatures. It asked for an inquiry into the events of August 16th, complaining that no intimation had been given by the magistrates that the proposed meeting was illegal. The signatories of the petition, remarked Bennet in presenting it, included 'many eminent merchants, manufacturers, and tradesmen':

The persons to whom he now referred were good, rational and sincere men, of deep religious impressions, of a sedate and sober character, seldom mingling with politics, or acting out of their domestic circles. [2]

In other words, many of them were cotton masters, formerly uninterested in politics, whose acquiescence in the rule of the Tory oligarchy in Manchester had been severely disturbed by the mishandling of the Peterloo crisis. The Declaration and Protest and the petition respecting the conduct of the magistrates were the great expressions of a new interest in political affairs.

Yet though the large volume of support given to the Declaration and Protest after Peterloo certainly indicated that at least a large minority of the Manchester cotton masters were disgusted with the Tory authorities' handling of the Radical problem, it would be wrong to stress too much the long-term importance of this new feeling as tending towards a liberalization of opinion in Manchester after 1819. It was not, for example, an important influence behind the movement for parliamentary representation which grew up in Manchester in the early 1820's. Reaction against the massacre produced a stirring of anti-Tory feeling in the town, but this feeling was both short-lived and at heart not really political. As we have already seen, the masters who shook off their

[1] *Newcastle Chronicle*, Sept. 11, 1819.
[2] *Parliamentary Debates*, XLI (1819–20), 357–70, 398.

political apathy and signed the Declaration and Protest were influenced more by humanitarian feeling and by concern for their property rather than by any definite liberal political inclinations. By 1821 their old conservative apathy had largely reasserted itself: in that year, admitted Archibald Prentice, one of the framers of the Declaration and Protest, one-half of Manchester political opinion was still Tory, one-quarter was still little interested in politics, and only one-quarter was even moderately reforming or 'whig'. Clearly, many who had signed the Declaration and Protest in 1819 had already slipped back into their former vaguely conservative political apathy.[1]

It was not feeling about Peterloo which was the most important influence behind the movements in Manchester in the 1820's for the transfer first of the Grampound and then of the Penryn seats to the town, not especially criticism of the Tory government's Six Acts or of its refusal to hold an inquiry into the massacre. Rather it was criticism of its restrictive trade policy along the lines already indicated. Burdens like the raw cotton duty and the duty on printed cottons were ever-present irritations, whereas Peterloo was only a passing though striking phenomenon.

The prominent part played in the local movements for reform by some of the Pittite 'loyalists' of 1819 makes it amply clear that it was business grievances rather than reform enthusiasm inspired by Peterloo which were the driving force behind Manchester opinion. The 'loyalists' would not have joined these agitations if they had been based on implied criticism of their attitude in 1819. As it was, in the foundation of the Manchester Chamber of Commerce in 1820 the Manchester Pittites played the leading part. H. H. Birley, who had led the charge at Peterloo, became its first President, and most of the members of its first committee had likewise been actively on the side of the local authorities in 1819. No Radical Reformers were members, the most advanced committee-member being probably G. W. Wood who was a very moderate 'whig'.[2]

---

[1] On the Market Street Improvement Commission in 1821 'all parties were comprised in something like a fair proportion at the time. One fourth were whigs or reformers, one fourth had taken little part in politics, and one half were tories' (Prentice, 209–10).

[2] Apart from Birley the first committee of the Manchester Chamber of Commerce included the following 'loyalist' members, all active about the

From the very first, despite this background of political conservatism, the Chamber of Commerce led Manchester opinion in persistent attacks on the restrictive trade policy of the Tory government. Within a few days of the famous London freer trade petition drafted by Thomas Tooke in May 1820, the newly-forming Manchester Chamber had sponsored a similar document making fully clear its hostility to trade control. 'To indulge an expectation', it declared, 'that other countries will take the manufactures of this kingdom without our receiving in return such articles as they produce, is delusive and injurious to our best interests.' It asked (with a moderation that was not to be typical) for 'the removal of all such restrictions on imports as can be relinquished without injury to the agriculture and manufactures of this country'.[1]

Criticism of the restrictive trade policy of the Tory government was thus from the first the rallying cry of the Manchester Chamber. Its purpose was to apply a steady pressure for trade liberalization and to be on the look-out for dangerous new proposals of restriction. By its continuous existence, and through its contacts in London, it was hoped that it would protect the commercial interests of Manchester better than the special public meetings and deputations which had previously been necessary as each new problem presented itself.[2]

The foundation of the Chamber of Commerce was thus a half-way stage towards a proper representation of the Manchester business interest in national politics. But yet it was no more. It might keep Manchester better informed of what was going on in parliamentary commercial circles, but the town still had little direct representation there. Like the haphazard public meetings

time of Peterloo: John Moore (Constable 1818–19), Thomas Sharp (Borough-reeve 1819–20), Thomas Hardman (who reported on the massacre to the government directly after Peterloo), and Francis Philips (author of the principal pamphlet written in defence of the authorities after Peterloo).

(E. R. Street and A. C. Walters, 'The Beginnings of the Manchester Chamber', *Manchester Chamber of Commerce Monthly Record*, XXXII (1921), 393; Prentice, 207).

[1] Redford, *op. cit.*, 69, 139.

[2] 'In every session of parliament measures were proposed deeply affecting the interest of the trading community, and of the details of these they were generally unaware, until they were passed into laws, when, if mischievous, it was too late to oppose them' (Speech of G. W. Wood at a Town's Meeting on January 30, 1822, called to give increased support to the Chamber. *Manchester Guardian*, Feb. 2, 1822).

which it replaced, the Chamber still had to rely on special deputations sent up to London to represent Manchester opinion on each new matter. How much better it would be if Manchester could have a permanent representative at Westminster to save the trouble and expense or organizing these deputations 'dancing in anxious attendance on the minister or some public board'.[1] It was in this spirit that in the 1820's Manchester commercial opinion came to support the idea of parliamentary representation for the town. Echoes of feeling about Peterloo were but faint, and H. H. Birley felt able to lead a substantial group of Pittite merchants and manufacturers in support of the agitations for the transfer first of the Grampound, and then of the Penryn seats to Manchester.[2]

Note. LIST OF WITNESSES AT THE PETERLOO TRIALS WHO GAVE EVIDENCE THAT THEY WERE ALARMED BY THE ACTION OF THE RADICAL REFORMERS ON THE DAY OF THE MASSACRE

At Hunt's trial the following witnesses expressed alarm:

Name	Description	Remarks
William Hulton	Magistrate: at Peterloo	
Jonathan Andrew	Constable 1818–19: at Peterloo	
Thomas Hardman	At Peterloo: reported afterwards to the Home Office on behalf of the magistrates	
Joseph Green	Boroughreeve 1817–18: the period of the first Radical agitation	All these witnesses were obviously compromised.
Francis Philips	Author of the principal pamphlet written in defence of the authorities after Peterloo	
Matthew Cowper	Secretary to the Committee in Aid of the Civil Power	
John Barlow	Publican	As publicans both open to pressure from the magistrates.
Joseph Mills	Publican	
Henry Orton	Stranger from London	
Roger Entwistle	Attorney	The only uncompromised witnesses: only three cotton masters.
John Walker	Attorney	
John Ellis	Bookseller	
Thomas Styan	Gunsmith	
Edmund Simpson	Master hatter	
Samuel Morton	Fustian manufacturer	
James Duncroft	Master spinner	

[1] Letter of 'An Elector' in *ibid.*, June 23, 1832.
[2] Main, *op. cit., passim;* Prentice 305–10; Marshall 235. Birley, at a meeting in support of representation for Manchester in 1827, asserted as strongly as the rest that 'the power of the landed interest . . . too greatly preponderated over the manufacturing interest' (*Manchester Gazette*, May 26, 1827).

In *Redford* v. *Birley* the alarmed witnesses were:

Name	Description	Remarks
William Hulton	Magistrate: at Peterloo	
W. R. Hay	Magistrate: at Peterloo	
C. W. Ethelston	Magistrate: at Peterloo	
T. W. Tatton	Magistrate: at Peterloo	
Robert Fielden	Magistrate: at Peterloo	All these witnesses
Jonathan Andrew	Constable 1818–19: at Peterloo	were obviously
John Moore	Constable 1818–19: at Peterloo	compromised.
Joseph Nadin	Deputy Constable: at Peterloo	
Thomas Sharp	Boroughreeve 1819–20: the period of the last serious Radical efforts	
Francis Philips	Author as above	
John Barlow	Publican	Compromised as above.
George Read	Stranger from Congleton	
Thomas Styan	Gunsmith	
Thomas Holdstock	Book-keeper	The only uncompromised
T. W. Ollivant	Silversmith	witnesses: not
James Heath	Gentleman	one cotton
Hugh Cholmondely	Gentleman	manufacturer.
John Barlow	Cotton merchant	
William Gould	Warehouseman	

(*State Trials;* for *Redford* v. *Birley* see also Farquharson's version.)

CHAPTER TWELVE

MAGISTRATES AND GOVERNMENT

AFTER the massacre the magistrates of Manchester did not attempt any public justification of their action at Peterloo. It was said on their behalf that they did not wish to 'interrupt the course of public justice' by discussing the affair while the trials of the reformers were still pending.[1] No doubt also they considered their justification to be self-evident. This, reluctance to put forward a defence did their cause no good, however. The good points on their side (and there were a few) were never heard, only the loud and repeated charges of their critics. Even those inclined to support the authorities regretted their silence. 'I think', wrote Wilberforce, 'the magistrates have been unjust to themselves in not publishing what might be called their *case*. The bulk of the people will not forbear forming an opinion, because they are told that hereafter the grounds of a just opinion shall be supplied to them.'[2] Even Bootle Wilbraham, the spokesman of the magistrates in the Commons,[3] had to admit in 1821 that 'the country had, perhaps, been led to draw an inference unfavourable to the magistrates of Lancashire, on account of the silence they had thought proper to preserve'.[4]

Whatever their silence in public, however, in private the magistrates fully explained their case to the Home Office, and from this source it is possible to outline their defence. This had two aspects, covering on the one hand their alarms during the summer of 1819 generally, and on the other their particular manner of proceeding on August 16th. Dealing with their general grounds for alarm first, the magistrates sent two revealing reports to the Home Office after Peterloo, one on November 20, 1819, and the other on April 23, 1820. These reports reiterated most of

[1] *The Patriot*, Dec. 11, 1819.

[2] Wilberforce to Bankes, Nov. 1, 1819 (R. J. and S. Wilberforce, *The Life of William Wilberforce* (1838), V, 40).

[3] Edward Bootle Wilbraham (1771–1853) was accurately described by the *Manchester Guardian* as 'the personage who seems to have a general retainer to defend the conduct of the magistrates' (May 26, 1821). Wilbraham lived at Lathom House near Ormskirk, Lancashire. In 1819 he was M.P. for Dover.

[4] *Parliamentary Debates*, 2nd ser., V (1821), 740.

the points already made by the local 'loyalists' in their Police Office resolutions of July 1819 and in their petition to the Prince Regent in October. They drew particular attention to the great increase in the number of reform meetings just before Peterloo, 'meetings obviously directed to the subversion of the Constitution'; Union Societies, they noted, had also multiplied during this same period and also female societies and schools for the instruction of adults and children 'in the principles and doctrines of sedition and infidelity'; the people furthermore had begun to arm and drill; and finally at the end of July there had appeared the plan to elect a 'Legislatorial Attorney'. Though the meeting called for this purpose on August 9th had been 'nominally abandoned', the intention of the subsequent Peterloo meeting, the magistrates contended, was still to carry through the election and it was therefore an illegal assembly.[1]

Turning now to the attitude of the magistrates on August 16th itself, they had two main charges levelled against them. One that they deliberately let the Peterloo meeting assemble so that they could attack it: the other that the Riot Act was not read by them, or if read at all was not acted upon correctly with an hour elapsing before dispersal of the meeting.

The magistrates' reasons for letting the meeting assemble have already been discussed: they were following advice from the Law Officers which appears to have been legally sound. The other point of criticism, the question of the Riot Act, was made and remade by nearly all the critics of the magistrates after Peterloo. But in fact the whole charge was rather off the point since, if the magistrates could justify the dispersion at all, they could justify it with reference to the Common Law rather than with reference to the Riot Act. Their whole defence on this question was neatly expressed in a letter which appeared in *The Patriot* newspaper for October 16, 1819. If the Riot Act was read at all, wrote the *Patriot* correspondent, it

> was only done through abundant caution, for, it is evident, the Magistrates dispersed the meeting, not as a riot, but as an unlawful and seditious assembly . . . [They] were justified by the old law of the land, existing previous to the passing of the riot act, by which it is laid down that the Justices may suppress an unlawful assembly, whether it has committed an act of *riot or not*.

---

[1] Magistrates of Lancashire and Cheshire to Sidmouth, Nov. 20, 1819, April 23, 1820 (*State Trials*, Appendix B).

Thus in law a few at least of the decisions of the magistrates on the day of Peterloo were defensible. But their case received hardly any public explanation in 1819.[1] Only after the passage of nearly three years with the case of *Redford* v. *Birley* in 1822 was any part of their full defence put before the public.

If the magistrates could remain silent after Peterloo, the government by contrast could hardly hope to escape without fully explaining its position. At heart ministers were far from enthusiastic about the fatal ardour of the magistrates. Lord Liverpool, for instance, deprecated the 'panic throughout that part of the country'.[2] The cabinet concluded, however, that it must support the Manchester authorities. 'To let down the Magistrates', wrote Canning, 'would be to invite their resignations, and to lose all gratuitous service in the Counties liable to disturbance for ever.'[3] Lord Liverpool summed up the government's attitude of qualified approval:

When I say that the proceedings of the magistrates at Manchester on the 16th ult. were justifiable [he wrote to Canning], you will understand me as not by any means deciding that the course which they pursued on that occasion was in all its parts prudent. A great deal might be said in their favour even on this head; but, whatever judgment might be formed in this respect, being satisfied that they were substantially right, there remained no alternative but to support them.[4]

That the government felt bound to support the Manchester magistrates in general terms was perhaps not surprising. What was much less defensible was the haste and gullibility with which they rushed to their defence in detail. Thus the thanks of the Prince Regent were conveyed to the authorities at Manchester within five days of the massacre, long before there could be even the appearance of an unprejudiced inquiry by the government into the facts of the situation. Soon afterwards came the Regent's over-assertive reply to the Common Council of London, and in

[1] Lord Liverpool did on one occasion deal with the Riot Act question in the Lords: 'the magistrates', he declared, 'were legally empowered to disperse such a meeting, without reading the Riot Act at all'. But this contention received very little publicity (*Parliamentary Debates*, XLI (1819–20), 502).
[2] Liverpool to Canning, Sept. 23, 1819 (C. D. Yonge, *The Life and Administration of Robert Banks, Second Earl of Liverpool* (1868), II, 410).
[3] W. R. Brock, *Lord Liverpool and Liberal Toryism* (1941), 112.
[4] Yonge, *op. cit.*, II, 410.

13

January 1820 the provocative appointment of Hay, the Chairman
of Salford Quarter Sessions, to one of the richest livings in
the country. Finally, the account of the massacre given by ministers to parliament was far too obviously biased in favour of
the authorities; Castlereagh quite blithely acknowledged that
the principal sources of government information were Hay, the
Chairman of Quarter Sessions, Byng, the Commander of the
Northern District, L'Estrange, the officer-in-command at Manchester, and Hardman, a leading local 'loyalist', without seeming
to consider it important that all these persons were associated with
the very authorities whose conduct was under discussion.[1] In the
days of a limited professional system of law and order the government was perhaps right to support the sometimes inept but usually
well-meaning labours of an amateur magistracy; but they might
at least have given that support with a greater appearance of
impartiality.

If the government can be criticized for its attitude *after* Peterloo,
what of its attitude *before* the massacre? Here, as already indicated,
the Home Office was inclined to give the Manchester authorities
detailed advice rather than definite instruction. It placed heavy
reliance on the good sense of the magistrates: 'Lord Sidmouth
has no doubt', concluded the important letter from Hobhouse to
Norris of July 17, 1819, 'that the question will be judiciously
decided by the magistrates of Manchester.' [2] This hopeful attitude
was most unfortunate. The Home Office seems to have forgotten
the shortcomings of the magistrates as revealed during the
Blanket crisis of two years before, their tendency to over-eager
action. The Home Office censured the magistrates privately then,
but in the very similar circumstances of 1819 it was rashly prepared to trust them to act 'judiciously'.

Not surprisingly, after Peterloo the Home Office immediately
gave up this attitude of trusting confidence. Bouchier, the
assistant solicitor to the Treasury, was despatched to Manchester
to assist the magistrates in dealing with the situation, and the most
complete surveillance was now exercised over the local authorities.
The exact nature of the charge against Hunt was determined upon
not by the local bench but by the government.[3]

[1] *Parliamentary Debates*, XLI (1819–20), 101.
[2] See above, p. 121.
[3] Hobhouse to Norris, Aug. 25, 1819 (*State Trials*, 173).

For the rest of the year the Home Office never relaxed its close watch on the situation in Lancashire. In this they were helped by a growing volume of information about the plans of the local reformers; Sidmouth and Hobhouse were no longer required to base their policy quite so much on the mere vague forebodings of Norris and Ethelston. Before Peterloo almost the only worthwhile information about the private doings of the reformers had come from the successful interception of Hunt's correspondence with Johnson.[1] The many spies employed by the magistrates had sent up very little worthwhile information, and the Home Office in the summer of 1819 became rather concerned about the large amount of secret service money being spent on spies by the Manchester magistrates.[2] After Peterloo, however, the spies began to be more effective and to produce more satisfactory reports. One spy was able to gain acceptance among the Manchester ultra-Radicals and to attend their reading room and their Union meetings;[3] in November another actually became secretary of the Radical committee formed to arrange the intended visit of Cobbett to Manchester;[4] and about the same time the printer to the ultra-Radicals began to communicate with the authorities.[5] As a result of these contacts the magistrates and the government were much better informed about Radical activity in the months after Peterloo than they had been in the months before the meeting.

While thus engaged in watching the situation locally in Lancashire, the government had also to decide after Peterloo what its general national policy towards the Radicals should be. With very little hesitation it decided to act with vigour. At the beginning of 1819 the Liverpool ministry had seemed very weak, and Lord Sidmouth, the Home Secretary, was on the point of retirement. The Radical agitations, however, gave ministers a new lease of life, forcing them to realize the necessity for leading and encouraging Tory opinion in the country. With this end in view a new vigour entered into their policies:

[1] Bouchier to Hobhouse, Aug. 23, 1819 (H.O. 42/193). Hunt suspected that his letters were being opened, and sometimes sent them by coach instead of through the post (Hunt, *Memoirs*, III, 621).
[2] Hobhouse to Ethelston, June 28, 1819 (H.O. 41/4).
[3] See above, p. 158, and Appendix B.
[4] Norris to Sidmouth, Nov. 22, 1819 (H.O. 42/199).
[5] Norris to Sidmouth, Dec. 12, 1819 (H.O. 42/200).

The Property of the country [wrote the Prime Minister] must be taught to protect itself. The active disaffected in any quarter are not numerous. The majority go with the tide, and if they see all the zeal and activity on one side, and only apathy on the other, their choice cannot be expected to be doubtful.[1]

The numerous meetings organized by the Whigs after Peterloo to press for an inquiry into the massacre were denounced in firm language by the government, and when Earl Fitzwilliam attended the county meeting called by the Whigs at York he was immediately dismissed from the Lord-Lieutenancy of the West Riding. Tory opinion must be rallied and such a gesture as this was a good way of rallying it. 'Our forbearance', wrote Lord Liverpool, 'would be ascribed to nothing but timidity, and would discourage our best friends': 'Lord Fitzwilliam,' declared Lord Castlereagh firmly, 'when he went to the meeting at York, virtually tendered the resignation of his office.'[2]

The association of the Whigs with the Radicals at these county meetings was condemned by the government as merely a piece of dangerous political manoeuvring: *'They are fools enough'*, wrote Lord Eldon, the Lord Chancellor, *'to think that they can overturn the administration with the help of the radicals, and that they can then manage the radicals* . . . The insane, however, can only play such a game and think of winning.'[3] This low opinion of the Whig attitude was reflected in 'loyalist' circles throughout the country:

The *Whigs* want *places* [remarked the *Manchester Mercury* of the York county meeting]—for places they called the Meeting, and truckled to those Radicals whom they detest; the *leading Radicals* want *plunder*; for the sake of plunder, they now unite with the Whigs; and in another year would trample them under their feet.[4]

This new vigour of the Tory government under the Radical stimulus received its greatest expression in the famous Six Acts. Parliament met on November 23rd and ministers lost no time in bringing forward their measures.[5] Their first proposal was the

[1] Brock, *op. cit.*, 111–12.

[2] *Ibid.*, 112–13; *Parliamentary Debates*, XLI (1819–20), 102.

[3] Eldon to Sir William Scott, Sept. 29, 1819 (H. Twiss, *The Public and Private Life of Lord Chancellor Eldon* (1844), II, 345–46).

[4] *Manchester Mercury*, Nov. 2, 1819. This article was from the *Yorkshire Gazette* and was probably inserted at the instigation of Hay (see above, p. 141).

[5] A convenient summary of the Six Acts is contained in Sir W. Holdsworth, *A History of English Law*, XIII (1952), 207–09; for the actual texts, see *Parliamentary Debates*, XLI (1819–20), Appendix.

Training Prevention Bill, intended to prevent drilling and the training of persons in the use of arms; second came the Seizure of Arms Bill, which was to give justices in certain counties the power to search for arms and to arrest persons found carrying them for purposes dangerous to the peace; third was the Misdeameanours Bill, intended to prevent delay in the administration of justice through the practice of traversing; and fourth was the Seditious Meetings Prevention Bill, designed to prevent the great Radical meetings. As finally passed, this measure prohibited all public meetings of more than fifty persons (apart from county meetings called by the Lord-Lieutenant or Sheriff) except in the parish in which the persons calling a meeting were normally domiciled; it made adjournments to another date and place illegal and allowed only freeholders or inhabitants of the locality to attend even a permitted meeting, and persons so attending could be ordered to disperse within a quarter of an hour; to assemble with arms, flags, drums or other music, or in military array, was expressly forbidden. The two last government measures, the Blasphemous and Seditious Libels Bill and the Newspaper Stamp Duties Bill, were intended to restrict the influence of the Radical Press. The Libels Bill gave power to the court after a conviction for blasphemous and seditious libel to order copies of the libel to be seized and gave it authority on a second conviction to order the offender to be banished. The Stamp Duties Bill extended the range of newspaper stamp duties to publications appearing more often than every twenty-six days and costing less than sixpence without tax; publishers of such pamphlets were to enter into a recognizance with sureties for the payment of any fines or penalties incurred by them for publishing blasphemous or seditious libels.

Such were the famous Six Acts. The only aspect of the working-class Radical organization which they did not directly control was the Union Society network. The government, indeed, was very anxious to break up these Societies, but it was unable to devise any definite legislative proposals against them.[1] The event showed, however, that the Union Societies were not for the most part able to survive for long after all the other branches of the Radical organization had been put down by the Six Acts. The Newspaper Stamp Duties Act, in particular, must have been a serious blow to the Societies, since it taxed out of existence the cheap

[1] Hobhouse to Norris, Dec. 17, 1819 (H.O. 41/5).

newspapers and pamphlets which they took in and whose study by the operatives was such an important part of Union activity.

Turning now from the facts of the government's repressive action to the principles which lay behind it, what line of thought underlay the decision to present the Six Acts? Above all they were intended (as one modern writer has put it) 'to prevent the access of the people to those who deluded them'.[1] The mass of the people, the government believed, was not really seditious at heart: it was merely that many of them had been 'deluded' by the Radical leaders. The people did not know their own best interests: a wise and paternal government must therefore protect those interests for them and wean them from dabbling in what they did not understand:

If he was asked whether he would deprive the lowest classes of society of all political information [declared Lord Ellenborough], he would say that he saw no possible good to be derived to the country from having statesmen at the loom and politicans at the spinning jenny.[2]

A point of some interest is the extent of the influence exerted by the Manchester magistrates on the nature of the Six Acts. A private meeting of the Manchester magistrates and 'loyalists' held on September 21, 1819 made several proposals which may have influenced the subsequent legislation. The meeting complained of 'the Insufficiency of the Law as it now stands' and urged the need for action to prevent Radical meetings, to restrain the licence of the Press (especially the continued publication of an alleged libel after indictment until the time of trial), to check the practice of traversing, and to make sedition a transportable offence.[3] When the government's bills were published the Manchester magistrates appear to have been sent copies for their perusal, and though their opinions were probably not decisive, ministers were clearly anxious to give full weight to their views. The magistrates seem to have been particularly consulted about the Seditious Meetings Prevention Bill, no doubt because of their experience at Peterloo.[4]

[1] Brock, *op. cit.*, 115.
[2] *Parliamentary Debates*, XLI (1819–20), 1591.
[3] Report of the meeting (H.O. 42/195).
[4] Hulton to Sidmouth, Dec. 4, 1819, returning the bill with his comments (H.O. 42/200). Hay's biographer claimed that the meetings bill 'owed its origin, and some of its clauses, to the suggestions of Mr. Hay' (Raines, *Vicars of Rochdale*, pt. II, 294). This was probably claiming too much for his influence.

The Six Acts were not the only measures taken by the government to deal with the Radical danger. Considerable increases were also made in the size of the military establishment; ten thousand additional troops were raised and two thousand additional marines.[1] Despite this increase in numbers, however, the military force at the disposal of the government during the latter part of 1819 was still comparatively small, and the best disposition of the limited number of troops available was a subject of careful consideration by the military authorities and by ministers. The Duke of Wellington himself advised Byng, the Commander of the Northern District:

With the force which we have [he wrote in October] it is impossible to prevent the success of this object [Radical plunder] in every part, and what we must take care of is that they have no success against any body of troops. As long as no misfortune happens to them the mischief will be confined to plunder and a little *murder*, and will not be irretrievable; but it is impossible to foresee how far it will go if the mob should in any instance get the better of the troops.[2]

In this spirit Byng and Wellington agreed on the danger of dispersing too much the limited force available. 'I have always fought', replied Byng, 'against the dispersal of my force in trivial detachments: it is quite impossible to defeat the disaffected if they rise, and to protect at the same time every town from plunder'. Immediate protection of any given town, he went on, must be the work of the inhabitants, leaving the army free to follow a national, as opposed to a purely local, plan of campaign against any seditious rising.[3]

Such were the remedies of the Tory government for dealing with the situation produced by Peterloo, remedies almost wholly coercive. Against an inquiry into the massacre ministers were adamant. Any inquiry, declared Lord Castlereagh, would take time and would therefore dangerously postpone the 'necessary measures of safety'.[4] In any case, wrote Lord Liverpool, the facts of the situation were notorious, and the government had therefore decided to present documentary evidence to parliament 'not for the purpose of asking for any opinion on that transaction, but

---

[1] *Parliamentary Debates*, XLI (1819–20), 571–75, 1300–02.
[2] Wellington to Byng, Oct. 21, 1819 (*Despatches, Correspondence and Memoranda of . . . Wellington,* new series (1867), I, 80–82).
[3] Byng to Wellington, Oct. 23, 1819 (*ibid.,* I, 82).
[4] *Parliamentary Debates*, XLI (1819–20), 557–60.

as one of the circumstances which render prospective measures
of prevention and remedy indispensable'.[1] The government was
firmly supported by its majority in parliament, and in consequence,
despite all the uproar in Radical and in Whig circles, there was no
parliamentary inquiry into Peterloo.[2]

The approach of the government to the economic crisis in
1819 was as negative as its approach to the political crisis. All
the present economic distress, the government contended, was
wholly temporary, being due mainly to the transition from wartime to peacetime conditions. Distress had arisen because national
expenditure had been drastically reduced, because the government
had withdrawn much of its custom, and because some three
hundred thousand soldiers and sailors had returned home to flood
the labour market.[3] 'It was impossible it should not have happened', declared Lord Liverpool, 'that a war of more than twenty
years . . . should be followed by great distress in this country, as
well as in all other countries in Europe.' [4]

Distress therefore, the government believed, was unavoidable,
and unfortunately it was also largely irremediable. It must run its
course. Political change as advocated by the Radical Reformers
would avail us nothing since it was the war, not the state of the
constitution, which had produced hardship. The United States,
remarked Lord Liverpool, repeating a well-worn Tory argument
of the time, was the constitutional ideal of the reformers, yet it
was even more distressed than ourselves:

The Americans had no king—no nobles—no established church—no
tithes. They had too—what was called equal representation—and we
were told they had no taxes; yet that country was more distressed than
this.[5]

It was suggested by some members of the opposition that the
government should finance schemes of extensive economic relief.
But government thinking was dominated by extreme *laissez-faire*
creeds of economics: to bring forward large schemes of economic

[1] Liverpool to Grenville, Nov. 14, 1819 (Yonge, *op. cit.*, II, 432).

[2] As late as 1821 Sir Francis Burdett introduced a motion in the Commons
pressing for an inquiry into Peterloo, but it was defeated by a large majority
(*Parliamentary Debates*, 2nd ser., V (1821), 719–846).

[3] W. Smart, *Economic Annals of the Nineteenth Century 1801–1820* (1910),
590, gives a useful summary of the general attitude of the Tory government
towards distress and compares it with that of the Whig opposition.

[4] *Parliamentary Debates*, XLI (1819–20), 496.

[5] *Ibid.*

interference, ministers believed, would only disturb the economic balance still further.

If by an ill-judged attempt at amelioration [asserted the Prime Minister] they were to impoverish men of property to support the poor, the consequence would be, that the means of employing labourers would be cut off, and thus the evil would be greatly increased. The only difference which this short-sighted policy would make, would be to injure the laborious poor, in order to benefit the lazy and dissipated.[1]

Present distresses, concluded Peel, 'were entirely beyond the control of parliament': 'no sober-minded rational man', Lord Castlereagh was confident, 'could for a moment believe that they were to be removed by any parliamentary interference'.[2] The only remedy which the government could offer was the barren one of patience: 'time alone could bring an effectual remedy'.[3] Resignation and acceptance until the economic crisis had run its course, Lord Sidmouth told Samuel Bamford, the Radical leader, in 1817, was the only right attitude: 'the present distress of the country arises from unavoidable circumstances'.[4] With economic ways of thought such as these no extensive measures for the relief of distress could be expected from the Tory government: economically as well as politically its remedies were negative.[5]

[1] *Parliamentary Debates*, XLI (1819–20), 1287.
[2] *Ibid.*, 383, 935.
[3] *Ibid.*, 383 (Castlereagh).
[4] Bamford, I, 148.
[5] Just before Peterloo the government did secure from parliament a grant of £50,000 to assist the emigration of distressed operatives to the Cape of Good Hope. This was a comparatively small-scale venture, however (*Parliamentary Debates*, XL (1819), 1549–51).

CHAPTER THIRTEEN

THE WHIG OPPOSITION

NINE days after Peterloo Lord Grey, the leader of the Whig opposition in parliament, wrote to Henry Brougham defining his attitude towards the events of August 16th. His letter was an important statement of policy. The Whig party, he wrote, was to place itself 'on the middle ground'; it was to condemn the conduct of Hunt and his associates but was strenuously to resist the attempt being made by the Tory government to cast aside 'the safeguards of the constitution'. In this way, Grey believed, the Whig party might rally to its standard 'all moderate and reasonable men . . . to whom the people might again be brought to look as their natural leaders and protectors'.[1]

Within a few weeks of this letter Whig meetings began to be held throughout the country to discuss the massacre. The most important were the Norwich meeting of September 23rd,[2] the York city meeting of September 27th,[3] the York county meeting of October 14th,[4] and the Durham county meeting of October 21st.[5] The York county meeting was the most outstanding of the series, being attended by Earl Fitzwilliam (the Lord-Lieutenant of the West Riding), the Duke of Norfolk, and by many other leading Whigs. The sponsors of these meetings were very careful not to commit themselves too far about the massacre; they asked simply for 'a strict inquiry'. The speech of Lord Milton at the York county meeting was typical of this cautious approach: he claimed no more than that 'a prima facie case' had been made out for an investigation. The meetings were more definitely critical, however, of some of the events after Peterloo, about the facts of which there could be no question. Most of them, for example, denounced the speedy despatch of thanks from the Prince Regent to the Manchester magistrates, and many of them also critized

---

[1] Grey to Brougham, Aug. 25, 1819 (*The Life and Times of Henry Lord Brougham* (1871), II, 341–44).

[2] *Manchester Observer*, Sept. 25, 1819.

[3] *Ibid.*, Oct. 2, 1819.

[4] *Ibid.*, Oct. 16, 1819; Hay Scrapbooks, VIII, 64–68.

[5] *Newcastle Chronicle*, Oct. 23, 1819.

the claim made in his reply to the Common Council of London that the normal channels of inquiry were open for investigation of the outrage. The mismanagement of the Lees inquest, the meetings asserted, and the rejection by the Lancashire Grand Jury of several well-supported bills against the Manchester Yeomanry and police had shown that this was not so.

Though Whig meetings criticized the attitude of the government, they were in no way intended to countenance the action of the Radical Reformers. 'In recommending meetings', declared Grey in a letter to the Duke of Devonshire, . . . I am sure you will not suspect me . . . of any disposition to give countenance to the actions and practices of Mr. Hunt and his associates.' The Whig assemblies, Grey stressed, were not to be likened to the meetings which the Radical Reformers were also holding during this same autumn. Indeed, one of their principal purposes was to attract support away from the Radicals. This was one of two main aims of the Whig middle-way policy. On the one side, wrote Grey, there was 'the violence of the Radical Reformers': on the other, there was the anti-libertarian policy of the Tory government based on the excuse of the Radical danger. Both these influences were highly dangerous to the free constitution of the country. If allowed to continue they might result in a 'separation between the higher and lower orders of the community', the lower orders going over entirely to the Radicals and the people of property supporting in desperation the despotic policies of the government. Whig policy, Grey concluded, must be to prevent this disastrous division from taking place:

It is with this view that I think it absolutely necessary to prevent our losing every hope of preserving at once the tranquillity of the country and its Constitution, that upon an occasion in which the principles of the latter have been so clearly violated the Whig party should now take that post, which it is equally their interest and duty to maintain, in their defence.

In this way, Grey believed, the party might perform a salutary national service and might at the same time revive for itself a substantial following in the country.[1]

For attending and supporting the York county meeting Earl Fitzwilliam was dismissed from the Lord-Lieutenancy of the West

[1] Grey to Devonshire, Sept. 23, 1819 (A. Aspinall, *Lord Brougham and the Whig Party* (1927), 276–77).

Riding. To all Whigs this seemed another step forward on the road to government despotism. Fitzwilliam expressed his fears in a letter to Dr. Bardsley, a 'loyalist' physician at the Manchester Infirmary, who had criticized him for attending the meeting:

it is the approbation [he wrote] given in the name of the Crown to the use, in the first instance, of a Military Body in the execution of a Civil Process that awakens my jealousy . . . Who will engage to restore to Civil authority, powers once exercised by the Military? . . . its primary interference in Civil matters has been approved in that quarter, to which alone it looks for approbation [the Crown], the effect of which I cannot contemplate without alarm—it is this, that I am anxious to meet in the earliest stage, to prevent its assuming the dangerous form of acknowledged precedent.[1]

Here was perhaps the greatest fear of the Whigs after Peterloo, a fear sometimes rather overlaid in discussion of the details of the massacre, but much more important to them than the actual events of August 16th, tragic though they were. The army, it seemed to Fitzwilliam and his friends, was being primed (as evidenced at Peterloo) to act independently of the old constitutional authorities in preparation for its new role in support of 'a Government disposed to despotism'.[2] Brougham and Althorp even went so far as to believe that Wellington, the Commander-in-Chief, was aspiring to set up a military dictatorship under the cover of the Radical danger: 'I see Wellington distinctly in the measure', wrote Brougham after the dismissal of Fitzwilliam, 'and I can hardly doubt that a design is formed of making the Government of this country less free.'[3]

The Radical Reformers naturally attempted to make every use they could of this Whig suspicion of the government. They associated themselves with the Whig leaders at several of the county meetings and modified their language somewhat in an attempt to give a flattering air of solidarity to the connection. At the great York county meeting several prominent Radicals were on the platform, and when one of them, Mitchell, attempted to ridicule the Whig plan for presenting an address to the Prince

[1] Bardsley to Fitzwillian, Oct. 12, 1819 (Wentworth Woodhouse Papers, Fitzwilliam to Bardsley, Oct. 17, 1819 (*Manchester Guardian*, Aug. 15, 1938).

[2] Graham to Lambton, Oct. 23, 1819 (Aspinall, *op. cit.*, 278–79).

[3] Brougham to Grey, Oct. 24, 1819 (Brougham, *op. cit.*, II, 347–48); Aspinall, *op. cit.*, 97–98; K. G. Feiling, *The Second Tory Party 1714–1832* (1938), 283.

Regent he was disowned by the other Radical leaders present. Finally, Edward Baines, the middle-class Radical proprietor of the *Leeds Mercury*, came forward and denounced Mitchell as a government *agent-provocateur*, and he was forced to leave the platform.

The county meetings were not the only occasions on which the Radicals attempted to attach themselves to the Whigs. Harmer, the Radical solicitor at the Lees inquest, also attempted to bring Fitzwilliam into association with popular Radical activities. He wrote to him on October 13th saying that, as he understood Fitzwilliam intended to be at the York county meeting, he was informing him of the unexpected adjournment of the inquest on Lees until December 1st.[1] Harmer does not appear ever to have been in communication with Fitzwilliam before this, and he was clearly hoping that Fitzwilliam's part in the York meeting would draw him into association with popular Radicalism. Little success attended this attempt at association, however. The great majority of the Whigs shared the views of Lord Grey on the Radical danger; and when in December Cam Hobhouse, the Westminster Radical, proclaimed in a pamphlet that 'nothing but brute force, or the pressing fear of it' would reform parliament, the Whigs in the Commons vied with the Tories in packing him off to Newgate.[2] Resistance to the Radical extremists was as vital a part of the Whig policy after Peterloo as resistance to the coercive policies of the Tory government.

With the opening of parliament on November 23rd the Whig meetings in the country came to an end and the second phase of Whig activity now began, activity inside parliament.

The basic cause of the present discontent, it was agreed on all sides at Westminster, was the pressure of economic distress; because of distress Radicalism had flourished. Where opinion differed was about the causes of and remedies for this distress. The government and its supporters argued that the present difficulties were the result simply of transition from wartime to peacetime conditions and that they were therefore only of a temporary nature. The Whig view, on the other hand, was that the real cause of distress was the pressure of the enormous debt and of the heavy rate of taxation, aggravated by the excessive size of the

[1] Harmer to Fitzwilliam, Oct. 13, 1819 (Wentworth Woodhouse Papers, 52e).
[2] Feiling, *op. cit.*, 300.

establishment and by waste in all departments. In the opinion of the opposition distress would continue until all these evils had been removed, and this could only be achieved through rigorous retrenchment and economy. This alone would weaken the Radical appeal:

It was by conciliation [declared Grey at the opening of the session] by a reduction of the enormous public expenditure which weighed down the country, and by a system of timely reform and economy, that the threatened danger should be met: for such a system would in its result speedily suppress all the seditious practices referred to in the address.[1]

Here was the long-term policy of the Whigs. What was their reaction to the Six Acts, which were intended to overcome the immediate danger?

The Whigs did not automatically oppose all the government measures. Writing while the debates were at their height, *The Times* (which strongly backed the opposition throughout the Peterloo crisis)[2] summed up the general Whig attitude:

Those [measures] [it wrote on December 20th] which are meant to prevent positive acts on the part of the Radicals have been generally approved . . . The policy of those which are meant to suppress or fetter discussion is more doubtful; for the best vent for passion . . . is the freedom of using angry words.

In this spirit, therefore, the Whigs did not strongly oppose the Training Prevention Bill. Brougham agreed that the practice of training was illegal and that a new law was advisable 'to adopt penalties more specific than those of the common law of the land'.[3] The Seizure of Arms Bill, on the other hand, was strongly resisted; the right of having arms for self-defence, the opposition contended, was one of the ancient privileges of the people, 'declared to be so by the Bill of Rights'.[4] The Misdemeanours Bill was accepted only after an important amendment had been agreed to by the government. The original bill had been designed solely to prevent the practice of traversing in a misdemeanour

---

[1] *Parliamentary Debates*, XLI (1819-20), 5; Smart, *op. cit.*, 590-91.

[2] *The History of the Times.* ' "The Thunderer" in the Making, 1785-1841', (1935), 234-40.

[3] *Parliamentary Debates*, XLI (1819-20), 854-55.

[4] Protest against the Bill signed by Grey, Fitzwilliam, Holland, Erskine, the Duke of Sussex, and others (*Parliamentary Debates*, XLI, (1819-20), 754-55).

which had allowed Radical leaders charged with offences to postpone their trials for long periods. To this original bill Lord
Holland moved an amendment abolishing also *ex-officio* informations by the attorney-general by which he was able to delay indefinitely the interval between information and trial. With this
addition, Holland argued, undesirable delays from either side
in the hearing of cases would be prevented. The government
accepted the amendment, and the bill passed (in the words of
Denman, the Whig lawyer) 'as an improvement in the law of
England'.[1]

There remained the three other bills brought forward by the
government, the Seditious Meetings Prevention Bill, the Blasphemous and Seditious Libels Bill, and the Newspaper Stamp
Duties Bill. Whig opposition to all these measures was most
decided. It was essential, the opposition contended, to retain some
outlets for the expression of public opinion. Freedom of the Press
and freedom of public meeting were the safety-valves which for
over a century had prevented popular excitement from exploding
into rebellion.[2] He was fully aware, declared Brougham, summing
up the Whig opposition to the Seditious Meetings Bill, of 'the
folly and wickedness' of some of the speeches delivered at the
Radical meetings and of the consequent abuse of the ancient
privilege of petitioning; 'but he could not, on that account,
acquiesce in a total subversion of a great popular right'.[3] In other
words, Brougham was repeating the fundamental Whig theme:
attempted subversion of the constitution by the Radicals was no
excuse for attempted subversion of the constitution by the government. Remove the outlet for feeling provided by the right to
meet and to petition and the danger of revolution would be increased not reduced.

The meetings bill was readily linked by the opposition with the
two Press bills. All three, the Whigs believed, were intended 'to
fetter all free discussion, and to repress, if not stifle the expression
of public opinion'.[4] The existing Press laws, the Whigs were sure,
were strong enough to put down abuses; in making them stronger,
ministers were making them too strong. Had the government,

---

[1] *Ibid.*, 1302.   [2] *Ibid.*, 407 (Tierney).   [3] *Ibid.*, 664–65.
[4] *Ibid.*, 1390 (Protest against the Seditious Meetings Prevention Bill signed
by the Duke of Sussex and Lords Holland, Erskine, Grosvenor, Donough-
more, and Thanet).

asked Grey, decided 'that the destruction of the freedom of the Press was the only mode of checking its abuses'?[1]

So much for the immediate effects of Peterloo on the Whig opposition in parliament. The massacre had also a more long-term significance in the history of the party.

The Whig party in 1819 was not so much one coherent organized body as a collection of loosely connected groups. The leading and most numerous group was that of the moderate Whigs centred around Lord Grey, the official leader of the party. Grey's main supporters in 1819 were Lansdowne and Holland in the Lords, and Tierney and Brougham in the Commons. It has been the reactions of this group which have been chiefly analysed so far. The party had, however, several other sections of opinion, and the attitudes of these other sections were also important.

The most advanced group within the party was that led by Lord John Russell, George Lambton, and Sir James Mackintosh. The members of this group believed that the Radical danger made the need for moderate reform all the more urgent; by agreeing to moderate reform, they believed that parliament would greatly reduce the attraction in the country of the Radical appeal for extreme reform. A letter from Mackintosh to Russell two months after Peterloo summed up their attitude. The Whig party, he wrote, although proclaiming 'irreconcilable war against the Radicals', should press also for an immediate parliamentary inquiry into Peterloo and 'should declare in the frankest and strongest manner' for Russell's parliamentary reform proposals.[2] Two months later in the middle of the progress of the government's repressive legislation Russell brought these proposals before the House of Commons.[3] In his introductory speech he reiterated his group's basic theme in respect of the Radical agitations, that it was only by moderate reform that the extremist reformers could be forestalled. Only in this way, he contended,

[1] *Parliamentary Debates*, XLI (1819–20), 350.

[2] *The Early Correspondence of Lord John Russell 1805–40*, ed. R. Russell (1913), I, 205–06.

[3] *Parliamentary Debates*, XLI (1819–20), 1091–1107). Russell proposed that boroughs convicted of gross corruption should be disfranchised, the seat being transferred to a great town or county; that stronger measures should be decided upon to prevent corrupt elections; and that the borough of Grampound should be disfranchized for corruption.

could the people be dissuaded from giving their support to the Radical demagogues. 'Perhaps if there had been elections at Manchester, we should not have had to lament the unfortunate events which we all deplore.'

In contrast to Russell and his friends on the advanced side of the party stood the Duke of Devonshire, the Cavendishes and the Stanleys on its conservative wing. The attitude of this group towards the situation in 1819 was almost identical with that of the Tories, and its members refused to support the Whig county meetings.[1]

Outside the party, but since 1806 vaguely allied to it, were the followers of Lord Grenville. Grey and his friends had for many years trimmed their policies to accord with the growing conservatism of this group, believing that only with Grenvillite support would they ever be able to form an administration. Grey, indeed, was forced to trim in all directions, to pursue a policy of balance between the various groups. That such was his policy he virtually confessed to Lambton early in 1820. Lambton had been pressing the question of parliamentary reform: 'the preservation of the Whig party in parliament', replied Grey, was much more important than any particular policy. If Lambton and his friends wished to press for parliamentary reform they must do it as private individuals 'in such a manner as may neither divide the Whig party, nor pledge them to it'.[2]

Analysis of Grey's speech at the opening of the Peterloo session reveals the essential tentativeness of his approach dictated by what he saw as the overwhelming need not to split his party irrevocably. His discourse was able but indefinite, hardly answering the main questions which he himself had raised. What concessions, he asked, could the government promise which were likely to kill the Radical campaign? Grey indicated that public economy and a reduction of taxes were expected, and he also made a passing remark in favour of parliamentary reform. But on both topics he was studiously indefinite, making no specific proposals. The truth

[1] Aspinall, *op. cit.*, 97, 276-77; Brougham, *op. cit.*, II, 348.
[2] Grey to Lambton, Jan. 3, 1820 (J. R. M. Butler, *The Passing of the Great Reform Bill* (1914), 35-36).
[3] *Parliamentary Debates*, XLI (1819-20), 4-21. A useful analysis of Grey's speech and position is contained in H. W. C. Davis, *The Age of Grey and Peel* (1929), 211-14.

was that he believed he dare not commit himself too far if the
Whig party was to survive as any sort of connected whole.[3]

But there was one section of opinion after Peterloo which
even Grey's dexterity could no longer hope to conciliate. At
the beginning of the session the Grenvillite group came out
wholeheartedly in favour of the Tory policy of repression, and it
became clear that they had placed themselves virtually out of
reach of further Whig trimming. In the long run this was an undoubted blessing to the party. The loss of Grenvillite support was
as nothing compared with the freedom which the Whigs now
gained to shape their policy without reference to unsympathetic
allies. The Grenvillite alliance had for too long overborne the
traditional attachment of the party to the cause of reform.[1]

Apart from this negative benefit Peterloo also afforded the
Whig party a more positive gain. The Whig county meetings
called in the autumn of 1819 to press for an inquiry into Peterloo
did much to revive the party's link with the people. Only Whig
'indifference to public meetings', wrote Sir James Graham in
October 1819, had made possible the success of the Radical reformers; if the Whigs were 'willing to resume the lead, and boldly
stand forward on popular grounds', the people, he was sure, were
'by no means indisposed to follow'.[2] This belief was soon proved
correct. As Grey had hoped, the county meetings helped to check
that 'separation between the higher and lower orders of the community' which he had feared so much just after Peterloo. And as
he had also hoped, in the very act of performing this important
national service the Whig party added to its strength for the
future.

[1] Davis, *op. cit.*, 140.
[2] Graham to Lambton, Oct. 23, 1819 (Aspinall, *op. cit.*, 278–79).

CHAPTER FOURTEEN

THE RELIGIOUS ASPECT

AFTER Peterloo all the diverse religious communities in the Manchester area were forced to define their attitudes towards the Radical agitation. Most of them, partly out of prudence and partly out of inclination, took up a hostile position.

The Anglicans naturally rallied to the side of the powers that be. Two of their clergy, Hay and Ethelston, were intimately involved in the action of the authorities at Peterloo, and a third, Horne, came forward to defend that action in print.[1] Anglicans were aghast: Radicalism appeared to be everywhere. Even the Sunday school children seemed to be affected. A special meeting of the Anglican Sunday School Committee had to be called a month after Peterloo to arrange measures 'to prevent any of the Children from coming with White Hats or other Badges which are now used by the disloyal and disaffected as expression of their political sentiments'. A declaration was printed announcing that scholars so dressed would be sent home, and only received when they appeared in normal dress.[2] On one occasion sixteen children were sent home from an Anglican Sunday school in Hulme for wearing such Radical favours.[3]

The Wesleyan Methodists likewise forbade the wearing of Radical emblems. This gesture was part of a considered policy of showing conspicuous 'loyalty' before the suspicion of the town's Anglican ruling authorities. The Methodist Conference in the year of Peterloo had carefully laid down a rule of non-association with the Radical Reformers; Methodists were instructed to follow their 'occupations and duties in life in peaceful seclusion from all strife and tumults'. Similarly, after Peterloo the Methodist Committee of Privileges expressed its 'strong and decided disapprobation of certain tumultuous assemblies which have lately been witnessed in several parts of the country'.[4]

[1] Horne, *Moral and Political Crisis.*
[2] Sunday School Minute Books, vol. 4.
[3] *Manchester Observer*, Oct. 9, 1819.
[4] *Manchester Chronicle*, Aug. 28, Nov. 27, 1819.

This carefully 'loyal' policy was faithfully voiced by the Methodist clergy in Manchester. John Stephens, the Superintendent preacher, and his colleagues, Jackson and Taft, were staunch Tories in politics, and were ready in consequence to take up an attitude of 'loyalty' on grounds of political principle as well as on grounds of religious prudence. Indeed, their extreme conservatism had brought them into conflict with many of their church members long before the Peterloo crisis. In January 1819 James Everett, a fellow Methodist preacher, noted in his diary that Stephens was 'the subject of severe reflections' among the Manchester Methodists' 'having previously sown much discord in the Manchester Society by his ultra-toryism'. Complaints, he added, had been made against Stephens at the Methodist Conference of 1818.[1] Political disputes were thus disrupting the Methodist body in Manchester even before Peterloo. After the massacre, with the need for the Methodists publicly to define their attitude towards the working-class Radicals, these became still more pronounced. Three distinct Methodist groups appeared, 'loyalist' Methodists supporting Stephens, non-Radical critics of Stephens, and complete Radical Methodists. Stephens made his attitude fully clear in a sermon which he preached just after the massacre, later published with the title *The Mutual Relations, Claims and Duties of the Rich and the Poor*. This sermon was largely a paraphrase of Paley's *Reasons for Contentment*, urging the poor to resigned acceptance of their God-given lot: 'What are the fluctuations and vicissitudes of external things', it asked, 'to a mind which strongly and uniformly anticipates a state of endless and immutable felicity?' One member of this ultra-'loyal' Methodist group in a letter to the *Manchester Observer* based his arguments on a favourite quotation of the Paley school, 'the powers that be are ordained of God'.[2] Another wrote to Lord Sidmouth after Peterloo to assure him that 'the Wesleyan Methodists, even in Manchester retain their cordial and conscientious attachment to the Person, Family and Government of our amiable King'.[3]

Probably more numerous than these Methodist 'loyalists' were those Methodists who accepted in general terms the necessity for the policy of non-association with the Radicals, but who objected

[1] J. Everett, Journal, I, 232, 234.
[2] *Manchester Observer*, Jan. 8, 1820.
[3] F. Marris to Sidmouth, Nov. 11, 1819 (H.O. 42/198).

to Stephens' over-zealous application of it. This group believed that Stephens was going beyond the limits of religious necessity and was interfering with the conduct of his church members from purely political motives. 'When a person whose sole business is that of preaching the gospel . . . intermeddles with the colour of a poor man's hat', wrote one non-Radical Methodist to the *Manchester Observer*, 'he is doing something more than his duty, and deserves the highest censure.' [1] A local preacher had been expelled, wrote other critics, for signing the Star Inn Declaration, and others had been removed for similar 'minor political offences'.[2] Stephens, in short, was going too far on too little justification: he was too busy 'preaching King George instead of King Jesus'.[3]

This second group of Methodists in Manchester was careful to make it clear that its criticisms of Stephens did not mean that it supported the aspirations of the Radical Reformers. Some Methodists, however, did avowedly join the Radical side in 1819. In Rochdale, for example, one Methodist class leader was forced to resign after admitting that he subscribed to the *Manchester Observer*.[4] This third group of Radical Methodists was probably quite large, for though Radical class leaders such as the one at Rochdale were probably few, the poor, who were the main supporters of Methodism in the early nineteenth century, were also in 1819 the main supporters of the Radical Reformers. Many of the working-class Methodists in Manchester must have been among the followers of Henry Hunt at Peterloo.

Clearly, Methodism in Manchester was in a state of considerable disunion about the time of Peterloo. 'The State of the Manchester Society appears truly deplorable', wrote Jabez Bunting, President of the Methodist Conference in 1820.[5] The Radical problem had aggravated a situation already made discordant by the extreme Toryism of the local clergy, and this discord lasted until the Manchester circuit was divided in 1824.

The other Methodist sects probably gained in numbers from the tension within the Wesleyan body. The Radical Methodist class

---

[1] *Manchester Observer*, Jan. 15, 1820.
[2] *A Letter to the Rev. John Stephens*, by Observator (1820); *Manchester Observer*, Dec. 25, 1819.
[3] Everett, *op. cit.*, I, 234.
[4] *Manchester Observer*, April 22, 1820.
[5] J. H. Huddleston, *The History of Grosvenor Street Wesleyan Chapel* (1920), 7.

leader who was expelled at Rochdale went over to the New Connection. And it was probably not without significance that Primitive Methodism first took root in Manchester about March 1820,
for there was a close connection between the Primitive Methodists
and the working-class Radicals.[1]

The attitude of the Roman Catholics in Manchester after Peterloo was similar to that of the Anglicans and Wesleyans. All
association with the Radical Reformers was forbidden from the
pulpit on pain of excommunication.[2] Once again as with the
Wesleyans the motive was one of prudence, a desire to show that
even Popery could be 'loyal'. A letter from the Vicar Apostolic to
the Catholic clergy in the autumn of 1819 stressed the need for
Catholics to be accepted 'as faithful subjects of the legitimate
government which protects us'; Radical agitation, he declared,
could only increase existing distress, and though the existing
government was not perfect nothing on earth ever could be, *'ubi
homo ibi culpa'*.[3] Despite this official policy, however, the Radicals
—with their tempting programme of Catholic Emancipation, and
even more with their remedies for distress—gained a large volume
of support among the poverty-stricken Irish handloom weavers
of Manchester. Samuel Bamford's Peterloo procession was welcomed 'with open arms' by the Irish weavers of Newtown, just
outside the town.[4]

The Quakers were another religious society which decided on a
policy of conspicuous 'loyalty' after Peterloo. They carefully dissociated themselves from a self-styled Quaker who presided at a
Radical Reform meeting at Leigh five days before the massacre.
The *Manchester Observer* expressed its 'surprise and disgust' at their
attitude.[5] It also attacked some Independent ministers who signed
the Star Inn Declaration just after Peterloo.[6] They, like the various
other lesser sects who have left no evidence of their attitude, were
probably following a policy of prudent 'loyalty' before the suspicious Anglicanism of the authorities. Only the Unitarians were

---

[1] *Sketches of Methodism in Manchester*, by A Wanderer (1871), 20; R. F.
Wearmouth, *Methodism and the Working-Class Movements of England* (1937),
211–12.

[2] *Manchester Observer*, Nov. 6, 1819.

[3] *Manchester Mercury*, Nov. 30, 1819.

[4] Bamford, I, 202.

[5] *Manchester Mercury*, Aug. 31, 1819; *Manchester Observer*, Dec. 25, 1819.

[6] *Manchester Observer*, Aug. 21, 1819.

perhaps an exception to this general tendency; for, as we have already noticed, most of the local middle-class Radicals were keen Unitarians.

The policy of 'loyalty' thus dominated the religious life of Manchester after Peterloo. And on the whole it proved a success, for no sect suffered serious permanent losses in numbers from defections to Radicalism. The hey-day of the reform movement was too brief for it permanently to affect the pattern of religious life in Manchester.

CHAPTER FIFTEEN

CONCLUSION

THE memory of Peterloo remained a force in politics in Lancashire for many years after 1819. A generation later its name was constantly invoked by the Chartist leaders, whose campaign was in so many respects similar to that of the Peterloo Radicals. At the first great Chartist meeting near Manchester in 1838 the Peterloo banners were once more carried in procession; and in 1842 the foundation-stone of a Manchester memorial to Henry Hunt was laid by Feargus O'Connor, the Chartist leader.[1] 'Nothing', wrote Gammage, the Chartist historian, '. . . ever excites a Lancashire audience like the name of Peterloo.' [2]

The memory of Peterloo was likewise recalled by the advocates of the incorporation of Manchester in 1838:

Recollect [wrote Richard Cobden in a pamphlet published in that year] that the massacre of the 16th August 1819, could not have occurred if Manchester had been incorporated . . . —and why? Because the united magistrates of Lancashire and Cheshire, who then entered the town to hold their bench at the Star Inn, take command of the police, and order the soldiers to cut down and trample upon unarmed crowds, would, in such a case, have no more jurisdiction over Manchester than Constantinople.[3]

Even as late as the election of 1874 the memory of Peterloo was still a force in local politics. In that year a *Short Historical Account of Peterloo* was published in Manchester as a Liberal election leaflet. Lists of killed and wounded were included and the names of the magistrates. The moral was drawn decisively:

[Peterloo] will ever remain an indelible disgrace on that party who have done all they could to resist the legitimate power of the people, and who now as *Tories*—and here in Manchester too—have the temerity to solicit the suffrages of the working classes in the present contest, in order to use their power against the very men whose ancestors perished

---

[1] *Manchester Guardian*, Sept. 26, 1838; *Northern Star*, Aug. 20, 1842.
[2] R. G. Gammage, *History of the Chartist Movement 1837-54* (2nd ed., 1894), 61.
[3] R. Cobden, 'Incorporate Your Borough' (1838), reprinted in W. E. A. Axon, *Cobden as a Citizen* (1907), 37-38.

for freedom at Peterloo . . . This was Tory justice, and is what they would repeat should they ever come to *power* again.[1]

Peterloo and the Six Acts have often been said to mark a turning-point in national politics, to mark the last throw of repressive Eldonite Toryism. In this context the massacre has sometimes been associated with the contemporary repressive policies of the Holy Alliance on the Continent. The evidence shows however, that this parallel is really a false one. The repression of the Tory government in 1817 and 1819 is not to be likened to that of Metternich or Alexander I. Peterloo, as the evidence of the Home Office papers shows, was never desired or precipitated by the Liverpool Ministry as a bloody repressive gesture for keeping down the lower orders. If the Manchester magistrates had followed the spirit of Home Office policy there would never have been a 'massacre'. Any parallels between government policy in England and on the Continent after 1815 are false ones: there can be no smooth historical generalizations about a European 'Age of Repression' after Waterloo.

But though the Eldonite Tories did not precipitate the Peterloo Massacre as a deliberate act of policy, it is nonetheless true to say that their association with the outrage helped to weaken their control of the Liverpool ministry. After Peterloo there began a steady alteration in the climate of political opinion which eventually made possible the advent to power of the more liberal Canningite section of the Tory party:

Do you not think that the tone of England . . . is more liberal . . . than the policy of the government? [wrote the young Robert Peel to Croker in March 1820, while awaiting the verdict of Hunt's trial]. Do not you think that there is a feeling, becoming daily more general and more confirmed . . . in favour of some undefined change in the mode of governing the country? . . . Will the Government act on the principles on which without being very certain, I suppose they have hitherto professed to act? Or will they carry into execution moderate Whig measures of reform? . . . Can we resist—I mean, not next session or the session after that—but can we resist for seven years Reform in Parliament? [2]

---

[1] The leaflet bears no date of publication, but expert study of the type used and of the paper suggests that it was published for either the 1874 or 1880 elections. The language suggests it was the Tories who were out of office, and therefore 1874 seems to be its date.

[2] Peel to Croker, March 23, 1820 (*The Correspondence and Diaries of . . . John Wilson Croker* (1885), I, 170).

Peel's thoughts had run on very significantly from a consideration of the Peterloo trials. He had discovered new trends in political opinion, trends tending towards greater liberalism in public policies. In this development regret for the extremities of Peterloo had clearly exerted its influence, even though the change in opinion would have come about without the massacre.

So much for the influence of Peterloo in the sphere of politics. The massacre has also had its influence in the realms of the arts. The vivid theme of Peterloo inspired in Shelley, far away in Italy, the immediate response of *The Masque of Anarchy*, a work more noteworthy for its bitterness than for its poetic quality. Samuel Bamford's poignant verses have already been noticed. Several novels have contained descriptions of Peterloo, the best being probably Mrs. Linnaeus Banks' *The Manchester Man*, which appeared in 1876, and Mr. Howard Spring's best-selling political novel *Fame is the Spur*, published in 1940. Recently, the late Humphrey House gave promise of a literary study of the massacre in his own distinctive manner: his untimely death has unfortunately left the work unfinished with only two fragmentary pieces in print.[1]

Peterloo naturally inspired many contemporary prints and drawings, some depictive, others satirical, and including one vigorous satire by George Cruikshank.[2] In the late 1870's Ford Madox Ford wished to include a fresco depicting the massacre as one of a series of frescoes commissioned to decorate the new Manchester Town Hall. Regrettably, the committee choosing the subjects for the work did not consider the theme acceptable, recognition no doubt that Peterloo was still a political issue in Manchester in the 1870's.[3] Not until the New Free Trade Hall was opened in 1951 did any of the city's public buildings contain a portrayal of the most vivid and portrayable event in the long history of Manchester.

The final comment in any study of Peterloo must be one of caution. When all the economic and political factors have been

[1] H. House, *All in Due Time* (1955), 46–57.
[2] The prints inspired by Peterloo preserved in the British Museum are listed in its *Catalogue of Political and Personal Satires*, IX, 1811–19, ed., M. D. George (1949). The Cruikshank satire is reproduced in G. T. Garratt, *Lord Brougham* (1935), facing p. 128.
[3] J. L. Hammond, *C. P. Scott of the Manchester Guardian* (1934), 47–48.

considered, something must still be admitted as unknown. Even more than in the history of high politics, in the study of mass movements allowance must be made for the uncertain influence of the human factor. What made so many working-men march to St. Peter's Field on August 16, 1819, is as much a psychological problem as a historical one, and a sifting of the historical evidence alone cannot give us the whole answer. Sir Lewis Namier has given a very necessary warning:

George Meredith calls it an ironical habit of mind to believe that the wishes of men are expressed by their utterances; even more ironical, or naïve, would it be to judge of the essence of mass movements by the pronouncements or professions of those who manage to filch them. So far we have hardly reached the fringes of the field of mass psychology, the most basic factor in history. All we can do is to try faithfully to state discernible facts, pose problems, but be chary of drawing conclusions.[1]

---

[1] L. B. Namier, *Personalities and Powers* (1955), 4.

APPENDIX A

1. THE MANCHESTER MEETING OF JANUARY 18, 1819
(*Manchester Observer, Jan. 23, 1819*)

(i) *Declaration*

Whereas the Ministers of this country, abusing the sacred trust reposed in them for the public welfare, have perverted the high authority assumed by the Prince Regent . . . to purposes of individual ambition and national oppression—And whereas, of late years, they, urged on and supported by a corrupt majority of a packed House of Commons, the members of which, falsely styling themselves the Representatives of the People, have constantly advised their Sovereign to follow their own example, and turn a deaf ear to all the Prayers and Petitions of his aggrieved and suffering subjects; treating them, in most instances, with utter contempt and neglect, and cruelly imprisoning, persecuting, and punishing the friends of peace and Reform—And whereas the said Ministers, in conjunction with these Agents of the great Borough Proprietors, have obstinately refused all reformation of abuses, or redress of those grievances under which this nation has so long groaned, and which grievances are now become so multiplied and oppressive, as to be no longer possible to be endured:—. . . we make this our public and final Declaration:—

That the only source of all legitimate power, is in the People, the whole People, and nothing but the People.

That all Governments, not immediately derived from, and strictly accountable to the People, are usurpations, and ought to be resisted and destroyed.

That the only design and end of Government is to protect the weak against the tyranny of the *strong*; and to secure the happiness of the governed: but, when it ceases to fulfil these important and essential objects, it is time it were altered, and another substituted in its stead!

That, resistance to earthly tyranny, is not only a right inherent in the People, and an acknowledged principle of the English Constitution, but a sacred duty enjoined by the laws of God and Man.

That all Men are born free, equal and independent of each other.

That according to the ancient Laws and Constitution of England, every Freeman (either in his own Person or by delegation) is entitled to a share, in the Government of his country.

That Taxation without Representation is illegal, and ought to be abolished.

That every individual, of mature age, and not incapacitated by crime or insanity, has a right to a vote for the election of a Representative in Parliament; and to refuse or withhold from any individual the exercise of this just and lawful right, is to deprive him of all security for his life, liberty, and property, and reduce him to the abject condition of a slave: for a Man cannot be said to be really free, or to enjoy either life, liberty or property, when these may, at any time, be taken from him, at the arbitrary will of another: and by laws that are made, without his own consent.

That the levying and imposing Taxes, Loans and Contributions, by any authority, or under any pretence whatever, without the previous consent of the People, fully, fairly and freely represented in the Commons House of Parliament, is illegal, and as much an act of robbery as the forcible taking away a man's Property on the King's highway.

That annual Parliaments and universal suffrage, were formerly, and ought now, to be the Law of the Land.

That no Placeman, Pensioner, or other Officer, holding any situation of trust or emolument under the Crown, is a fit or eligible person to be a Member of the People's House of Commons.

That it is both the right and the duty of the People to possess arms, that they may, at all times, be ready to defend their liberties, from domestic tyranny and foreign subjugation.

That the conditions of that great Charter of our Liberties, commonly called MAGNA CHARTA, which was solemnly signed and ratified by King John, in the presence of the assembled nation, and by the faithful observance of which alone, our Sovereigns are entitled to wear the English Crown, was neither a boon extorted from the Monarch, nor a concession of the Royal prerogative to popular violence, but a RECOGNITION of POSITIVE RIGHTS, antecedently existing and inherent in the People: of Rights, which no King or Government can lawfully give or take away.

That the Crown is a sacred trust and inheritance, held only by the free consent and for the sole welfare and benefit of the People.

That whenever the executive branch is incapable of discharging its duties to the nation, or ceases to fulfil the objects for which it was created, the social compact is, *de jure*, dissolved; the People are released from their allegiance, and have a right, if it pleases them, either to form a new Government or return to a state of nature.

That in cases of the last extremity, the safety of the People is, and ought to be, the first and only Law.

That the keeping up of large standing armies, during times of peace, is unconstitutional: and the odious spectacle of barracks in every part of the kingdom, and even the presence of an armed soldier in the public streets is revolting to a free People, and ought not to be endured.

That the ancient and honourable offices of the Magistrate, Sheriff, Constable and POSSE COMMITATUS, are the only legal and constitutional organs for protecting the persons and possessions of their fellow-citizens, and preserving the public tranquillity.

That the introduction of a military force, either for the purpose of overawing the free deliberations of the People, or under the specious pretence of suppressing riots and tumults, is a daring infringement of the liberties of the subject, and an innovation upon the Laws of the Land.

That an armed Militia, drawn from the great body of the People, without partiality or distinction, affords the firmest security for the preservation of their freedom, and is the only legal and constitutional force to defend them from foreign invasions.

That the conduct of the present Ministers in employing a vile band of spies and informers, for the purpose of encouraging disturbances throughout the country, and afterwards cruelly punishing the unfortunate victims of their artful snares, was an act of High Treason against the nation, for which they ought to be brought to public justice.

That the conduct of the late Parliament in passing the Corn Bill, which was obtained under false pretentions and passed at the point of the bayonet, in defiance of the united groans and supplications of the People, was oppressive in its design and cruel in its operation; being neither more nor less than a vile conspiracy between the great Landholders and the Ministers, to extort from the industrious labourer and mechanic, through the very bread they eat, an immense portion of Taxes for the support of the Borough system, and to enrich themselves and their pensioned minions, by the sweat of the poor man's brow.

That the encouragement and protection given to the Bank of England in the unlimited issue of the Paper Currency, without the smallest intention on their part, or means adopted by the Government to compel the repayment or cancelling of their worthless notes, is a fraud upon the real property of the nation, and a fragrant (*sic*) breach of those principles of honour and confidence, that ought to subsist in all dealings between man and man.

That the numerous executions for the comparatively trifling offence of forging, or UTTERING, a forged Bank of England note, an offence rendered more frequent and more excusable from the dreadful necessities of the time, are revolting to humanity, and disgraceful to the present age: demonstrating to the world at large, that the penal laws of England (like the Tablets of Nero) are a snare to entrap the unwary and written like those of Draco, in characters of blood.

That it would add greatly to the comfort and happiness of the People, and tend to preserve the nation from ultimate confusion and ruin, if the resolution were immediately adopted, to take no more of these forfeited pledges of fraud and folly, unless, like other promissory notes, they be made the real representatives of value received and payable on demand.

That the conduct of the late Parliament in passing the suspension of the Habeas Corpus Act and other restrictions on the liberty of the subject, and in afterwards screening Ministers by a Bill of Indemnity, from all enquiry or punishment for their wanton and tyrannical persecutions of the friends of Reform, was a violation of every principle of justice and humanity, and will be handed down to posterity with everlasting infamy and disgrace.

(ii) *Remonstrance*

We, the inhabitants of the towns of Manchester, Salford and their vicinity, in the name and on behalf of ourselves and of our oppressed and enslaved fellow-countrymen, beg leave to approach your Royal Highness with a Declaration of our manifold grievances, and a Remonstrance against the *cruel*, illegal and unconstitutional acts of the corrupt and wicked Administration, that has so long been imposed upon your Royal Highness by the great and overwhelming Borough Proprietors of this country.

We have seen with mingled sorrow, surprise and indignation, that these Ministers whom your Royal Highness has had imposed upon you as your secret advisers, and in whom you appear to have placed implicit and mistaken confidence, have for a long series of years abused the high authority with which they have been entrusted for the purpose of harrassing, persecuting and oppressing the People; that they have multiplied to an alarming extent useless and enormous burthens, and under the pretence of preserving social order and our holy religion; they have plunged us into expensive, unjust and unecessary wars on the continent, contrary to the Act of Settlement which expressly declares, that this country shall not be involved in war, on account of any foreign objects, or any of the King's continental dominions.

1st. That they have treated the People with every vile indignity and insult which their wanton malignity and overbearing intolerance could suggest—that they have refused to listen or attend to any of their prayers or Petitions—that they have suffered us to experience every species of distress and calamity, that the catalogue of human misery can contain—that they have subjected to ex officio information and ruinous persecution for political offences, and have loaded with fetters and cruelly imprisoned in solitary dungeons, some of the best and most worthy characters in the country.

2nd. That they have arbitrarily seized and held to bail, imprisoned and punished innocent individuals without trial or examination; and after keeping them in close custody during pleasure, ignorant of their accusers or their offences, have discharged them without legal adjudication, afforded them the slightest indemnification or redress.

3rd. That they have employed a host of vile spies and informers, to foment and excite disturbances amongst the oppressed and starving manufacturers and labourers in the united kingdom, and have afterwards punished with unexampled severity the unfortunate victims of their villainous snares—that they have practised every species of corrupt and sinister influence to gain over the majority of votes of a venal senate, composed of the agents of the great Borough Pensioners to aid their views, and induced them to pass cruel and oppressive Laws —to starve the honest and industrious labourers, manufacturers and mechanics; and to rob the wretched peasant of the hard earnings wrung from the sweat of his brow.

4th. That they have upon many occasions suspended the ancient laws of the land, and violated the liberties of the subject for the purpose of stifling the general voice of the nation, loudly and universally expressed in support of radical and effectual Reform—that in addition to these and many other wicked and unjustifiable acts, too manifold and painful to enumerate, and for which offences we anxiously trust, as well for the security of your own person as for a salutary example to future corrupt and wicked Ministers, your Royal Highness will assist your faithful subjects in bringing them to a severe and public account—they have either kept your Royal Highness in profound ignorance of their mischievous and unconstitutional acts, or they have succeeded in poisoning your ears, and in alienating your affections from that People which you were especially called to protect, and to whom you are solely indebted for the dignity and stability of your throne.

Although by a liberal construction and a voluntary compromise on the part of all the nation, the sovereign is now exonerated from all *personal responsibility* for the public acts of the Ministers, and they are made constitutionally accountable for the measures of his reign; yet, by a pertinacious adherence to a favourite junta, and a vicious and corrupt system, (become justly obnoxious to the whole kingdom), may at length form an exception to the general rule, and justify the abolition of a principle which is at variance with common sense, and which insults the free agency of the Sovereign, degrading him to a mere automaton and a slave.

5th. We, therefore, beg to remind your Royal Highness, that the history of past times, and particularly of our own country, amply demonstrates, that wherever civil commotion or rebellion have prevailed, it has not arisen from the fickleness or turbulent disposition of the People, nor from their love of violence, or a desire for frequent change; but, from flagrant and often repeated misconduct and oppression on the part of the Sovereign, or his favourite and confidential Ministers.

6th. Had Charles the first, and James the Second shewn a becoming deference for public opinion, and a little decent respect for the liberty of their subjects, the one would not have lost his head on a scaffold, nor the other have been driven from the throne by an insulted and justly enraged People.

7th. We feel it also our duty at this critical moment of national discontent and universal distress, to remind your Royal Highness, that it was no exclusive attachment or predilection for the private virtues or personal merits of the family of Brunswick, that induced our ancestors to go to Hanover for a King, and transplant them from the obscurity and poverty in which they found them, to the splendour and dignity of the English throne; but, it was from a fond, and, it is to be hoped, a rational assurance, that under a mild and paternal sway the blessings of civil and religious freedom would have been better secured and maintained; and, that both the Sovereign and the People, feeling and comprehending their relative duties and obligations towards each other, would have lived together in lasting bonds of mutual confidence, harmony and peace.

8th. How far this expectation has been realized in the events that have followed, and which have furnished such ample materials for the historian of future times, must be left to serious reflection of your Royal Highness, and to the awakened feelings of this agitated and distracted country.—The period, however, is now arrived, when all doubt or equivocation upon this important subject must quickly be terminated, and the truth, unwelcome as it may be to your Royal ear, must be freely told without hesitation or reserve.—The evils which for the last fifty years have been accumulating and destroying us, under a corrupt system of Borough Proprietors and their traitorous agents, who have usurped the power of making Laws, under the assumed and false title of Representatives of the People; these evils are become at length so frightful and overwhelming, that they can no longer be silently or patiently endured.

9th. The effectual remedy must be quickly sought and fearlessly applied; the People must determine which of the two shall be their lot —Liberty or bondage; and your Royal Highness, if you would continue to rule over a free and loyal People, must respect the solemn obligations of humanity and justice, and hasten to decide between your private inclinations and your public duty.

10th. We submit this frank, though imperfect Remonstrance, to the attentive consideration of your Royal Highness, and with the honest

15

sincerity of Men, panting for the blessings of that freedom of which we have been so long and so unjustly deprived, pray, that heaven may inspire you with the favourable disposition to listen to its salutary admonitions, and treat it with that due regard and generous sympathy which the important facts it enumerates, so truly merit and demand.

11th. If we be asked, *what it is that we want?* we answer briefly, the impeachment, and if found guilty, the condign punishment of the present Ministers—A change of measures, and an immediate abolition of the odious and accursed Boroughmongering system—A radical, and such a complete Reform, as will secure to the People the exercise of that great and incontrovertible principle, that every human being is entitled to an equal participation in the sacred blessings of political freedom; and every industrious labourer, manufacturer and mechanic, has a right to reap the ample and substantial fruits of his virtuous and USEFUL TOIL.

RESOLUTIONS PASSED BY THE OLDHAM DEPUTY MEETING
OF JUNE 7TH, 1819
(Manchester Observer, June. 12, 1819)

First,—That in consequence of the high price of provisions, enormous rents, excessive taxes, scarcity of employment, and lowness of wages; millions of healthy and industriously disposed Englishmen, are reduced to the deepest distress: being quite unable to procure a sufficient quantity of the meanest food, and of the coarsest raiment.

Second,—That it cannot be the duty of industriously disposed men (whether employed or not) to starve, nor submit to the degradation of becoming paupers.

Third,—That the laws which regulate the importation of products, are a great cause of this insupportable distress: and a proof that the interest of a few Land Proprietors, preponderates in our Legislative Assemblies, over the interest of millions of labourers.

Fourth,—That these laws are calculated to enrich a few thousands of worthless families: and to reduce to pauperism, want and misery, millions of individuals, infinitely more useful to society.

Fifth,—That the existence of these partial and unjust laws is convincing proof of the indispensable necessity of a Reform of the Commons House, on the principles of Universal Suffrage, Annual Parliaments, and Election by Ballot.

Sixth,—That the repeal of the laws which check or impede the importation of agricultural products, would, in a few months, if not instantly, remove a great proportion of that want and misery which is now so acutely felt by the agricultural, as well as the manufacturing labourers of the country.

Seventh,—That as repeated experiments have proved it is impossible to speak, (in the language of truth) to our nominal Representatives, or to the Prince Regent; it is resolved: That an Address to the People of England shall be immediately prepared, expressive of the deplorable conditions of the labourers in these districts, with the causes thereof: and the most speedy and effectual means of removing the same and preventing their recurrence: and that the Address now read be adopted.

Eighth,—That if these Corn Laws and other restraints on the importation of agricultural products be not repealed, and Universal Suffrage, and Annual Parliament be not adopted to prevent their recurrence, of such restrictions, this Meeting is convinced, that the labouring part of the people of this country, cannot long preserve their existence: and if they must die, either by starvation, or in defence of their rights, they cannot hesitate to prefer the latter.

Ninth,—That these Resolutions be printed in the *Manchester Observer*, and such other publications as may be deemed expedient.

J. KNIGHT, Chairman.

APPENDIX B

A SPY'S DESCRIPTION OF THE RADICAL ORGANIZATION
IN MANCHESTER

(Report of 'W. M.' enclosed in Norris to Sidmouth Nov. 7, 1819;
Norris describes 'W. M.' as a person *on whom I can rely*. H.O. 42/198)

Sir,

Being requested a little time ago to become a member of the 'New Exchange' I found no difficulty in getting introduced by one of the leading Members, for immediately after I left You on Monday evening I met Mr. James Walker and learning he was going to their 'New Exchange' or 'Swan Court News Room'[1] I cheerfully accepted with the greatest pleasure his proffer to introduce me; it was then about half past 5 o'Clock and the Papers coming in about 8 o'Clock there were but few members present—Mr Chapman the Orange Dealer and Mr Walker were the only two of note as Radicals—their conversation was mainly confined to the dismissal of Earl Fitzwilliam and Mr. Hunt's reply to Thistlewood, of the former Mr. Walker expressed himself perfectly satisfied for he wished all the Whigs in power might receive the same reception for their backwardness in becoming the Advocates of the People's Rights and of the latter both he and Mr Chapman conceived that Mr Hunt did not fully explain the money transaction.'

Tuesday morning I attended but being Market day no group could be collected, and I could learn nothing worthy of communicating . . . Whilst I was looking over a newspaper I heard a wisper that there would be a Meeting at the Union Rooms in Georgeleigh Street, to consider whether they must have the Meeting of the 15th inst or not, for it appeared Mr Hunt's Letter to the 'Reformers of the North' had caused a Division of Sentiments. How to get introduced into this place I was at a loss to conceive—for I dur'st not appear forward—accordingly I waited from 5 o'Clock until half past eight, when the Papers came. I watched an Opportunity and when Mr Walker got hold of one to read,

[1] An advertisement for the Swan Court News Room appeared in the *Manchester Observer* on November 27, 1819. The subscription was given as 16s. per annum for town members and 10s. 6d. for country manufacturers and others living more than three miles from Manchester. The 'papers taken at present' were listed as follows: the *Morning Chronicle, The Times*, the *Star*, the *Statesman*, the *Courier*, the *Independent Whig*, the *Examiner, Wooler's British Gazette*, the *Champion*, the *Manchester Gazette*, the *Manchester Observer*, the *Manchester Chronicle*, the *Manchester Mercury*, the *Sheffield Iris*, the *Liverpool Mercury*, the *Leeds Mercury*, the *Exeter Alfred*, the *Nottingham Review*, the *Chester Guardian*, the *Scotsman*, and the *Irishman*.

I went to look over what was in his Paper—I then took the liberty to ask him if he was going to the Union Rooms and he answer'd me in affirmative with a rejoinder of, 'will You go with me'.—I think I need scarcely say I readily accepted of it.—Mr Walker, Mr Whitworth myself and three others whom I did not know proceeded to the U.R. These rooms are used on Sundays and Evenings as a School in which Radical Reform and its principles are instilled into Young Minds to 'Grow with their Growth'—and one of all the Sights I ever saw this was the Acme there were about 200 persons present—I thought as a Young Man I had seen as great a diversity of Company as most—but never in my Life did I see such an Assemblage—The Scene of the Witches in Macbeth is not so black looking as *this* House of *Commons*.[1]

As soon as I had a Situation to stand and see in, and had secured my Watch and Pockets (for I think I had good right to expect I was in Company of a Gang of Diveses ripe and ready for any purpose)—I began to listen to their Debates. At the top of the Room in the midst of a square of these Grandees sat a Man who had the Appearance of a Weaver this person I soon discovered was their *Chairman*—He was seated on a Stool and before him stood another stool about 3 feet high, on it was placed two lighted halfpenny Candles—I then enquired who were those favoured Individuals who were seated in the front of the Square, and learned they were Collectors of Sections—A Section is composed of twenty five persons who pay at least one penny each weekly and their Collectors are their Representatives in this august Assembly, of which there appeared 50 or upwards—The Subject then under discussion arose from some of these Leaders, when a Law was to be made which suited their ends having brought the whole of their Sections and by that means, outvoted the other party; it was to prevent this intrusion that a Motion was made, 'That no person but Leaders of Sections should vote—one Gent[n]. got up and spoke as follows—Mr Chair! Mr Chair!! Mr Chair!!!, I *desire* you will do Your Duty in keeping Order—after he had repeated this so often I was afraid of his Lungs, the Chairman called out Order! Order!! and with such a voice that made me tremble. altho I was paying every attention to the manners of the Party, however Silence was in some measure obtained by this and he then proceeded,—Mr Chair I look up *us* here, as being Members sent to *this here* place, to transact the business of Reform, in same manner as our business should be done in Parliament, to which I compare us here; and who would say it was proper for us to go and have a Vote of any thing which would particularly interest us was brought forward, no—

[1] The use of this literary allusion and also of the word 'Acme' suggests that ' W. M.' was a person of some education, one of the more 'respectable' spies employed by the magistrates.

I shall therefore second the Motion—for if we are not worthy of their Confidence why send us here.'—He then took his Seat, when up started two or three others and confusion was as great as ever—It was a little appeased, by one of them saying he had only a few words to say in Opposition to that Gent^n. who had compared this place to the House of Commons—that House of Corruption—that Den of Thieves, as Cobbett properly called it, if he thought they resembled that Company in any way he would never come into this place again—No! he thought that his Section had a right to come when they pleased, for that was his Idea of universal Suffrage'.

After several had spoken pro and con the question was put to see whether it was the Opinion of these Leaders, and all others who were not of this Class were ordered to the bottom of the room—It was carried.—and ensued a delightful Scene.—A Scotchman got up and said I represent a Section in Salford, & a most respectable one it is, who has desired me to say, and a great rogue I should be if I did not do so, that unless Secretary W. C. Walker is removed from his Office, his Section would have their Names scratched out of the Book,—and so will mine said one—and so will mine said another—I began to make enquiry if the Secretary was present—when I was pointed to look at the corner of the Room, where sat a little black looking fellow receiving Money from the Collectors of Sections—The Man who made the charge was then demanded to say what he knew against Mr Walker—when in free Scottish Accent he said, 'Why must I be made to answer every fool that question, I have done what I was ordered and it was my duty to do so.'—He was then asked who he had represented Mr. W. C. Walker to be—He answered 'I told them it was Bill Walker the Dyer who'—He was here stopped with, 'Aye you gave Him the worst Character you could' this so enraged Scotland's Son—that he said he would be d—d if he gave any more explanation and so sat down—Another got up & said that 'The Gent^n. had not said all he might have said—for it was well known Bill Walker had two Wives—this caused a general laugh—when up starts a person of the name of Tetlow (he is a person who was connected with the Blanket expedition, and run away with a large Sum of Money). He said that he was sorry any objection was made to their Secretary who he considered a most respectable Young Man.—and as to his having two Wives, that was nothing to do with them, for had not Your famous Mr Hunt two Wives. he certainly could see no objection to his helping his Situation as Secretary.—The next who presented himself was a Mr Bradbury a Stone Mason—he presented himself to the Chair to vindicate the foul aspersions which had been thrown on the most respectable Man in the Union—He called him respectable for if he attended and did the duty of his Office in support of Reform it was a matter of *no consideration* what his Moral Character was—Moral Characters were not to be taken into the scale, their Object was Reform in the Government and not to enquire whether this or that Man was a Moralist and he was sure that he could satisfy any person present that morality was not their business to enquire into—He did not wish to touch on it—for if a person was of very bad Character—one who had no Morality—he should see no objection to him, for their Object was Reform and Reform they wanted—not to quibble about Morality and he should, if he was his worthy Friend Mr. Walker resign his Office immediately—At the finish of this Sentence up starts Mr Walker, who brought with him the Books of State—and said Gent[n]. I here present You with these Books, for never more will I set pen to them and directly left the room—now was confusion triumphant, some deploring the loss of him, some rejoicing in his abdication, however, the Voice of the Multitude as was natural was for never minding his Character & a deputation sent after him to know, would he return and take his Station, to which he answered that he would consider on it, and by 12 o'Clock the day following send them an Answer.

It was now attempted to be carried that all who did not belong to the Union was to leave the Room, this brought forth a Speech from Mr Whitworth of Police Meeting fame, in favour of every one hearing what they had to say—for 'He thought it seemed as tho' they had some Secrets to perform.'—I here took the liberty of wishing him to enquire how far this Sentiment agreed with the Placard issued from the Union on Saturday last—but he thought we should be in danger of getting ourselves roughly handled if we offended them in the least—so much for their consistency.—It was now approaching near eleven o'Clock, and at the desire of some of the party, it was adjourned till the Thursday following,—and then they were to conclude on the propriety of holding a Meeting on the 15th Inst.—at this moment presented themselves two Country-Men, one of which got up and wished to know if this was the Union.—it was some time before any one spoke.—at last some person said it should be—the Stranger then said he came from Flixton to see how Reform was going on—some one cried out, 'did Justice Wright send You?' the Old Man took no Notice but continued that in their Country hundreds were daily joining their Sections, and if he was to tell them what he had seen this Night they would never put any confidence in the Manchester Union.—Several of the Leaders got round the Strangers and persuaded them not to mention what they had seen that Night.

Wednesday was a complete barren day of information—Thursday passed on till Even[g]. without any thing worthy of remark, about half past 7 I went, with two others, from the News Rooms to the Union, it being the time to which the Meeting was adjourned on Tuesday.—on

my entering the Room there was but about 20 Persons present, when
I turned round to descend the Stairs again, I was called on to come
forward,—when I promised to be there as soon as they had commenced
business I was then asked if I was 'Patriotic', not knowing in what
Sense it was used, I answered Yes, at a risk of right or wrong,—I
learnt soon after that the Patriotic was a Society so called,—indeed if
they had asked me was I 'Napoleon', at that moment I should have
answered Yes. At nine o'Clock I went again—they had just commenced
business with electing a Committee of Finance as they called it and
selected 13 Persons from the Collectors—A motion was made 'That
this Committee sit 3 Months when a fresh one be appointed'. this was
amended, first from a confidence in their cause that the business of
Reform would be complet'd. before that period, and second from a
doubt whether corruptions would not steal in before then—at last it
was agreed that 5 go out every Month and five more be elected until
the time should come when they would want them no more.

Now for the Meeting.—After much regret on the part of many
(some of whom was heard to say they had armed themselves ready)
that they had not met on the 1st of Novr. and which Mr Bradbury said
publicly, joined with others, that, '*He should teach his children to curse
them* for not bringing it forward'—for he said—'If We had met all over
England on that day the business would have been done before now.'—

It was agreed that the Meeting be postponed to some more favorable
moment and that all Idea of Meeting on the 15th be abandoned, it was
then enquired whether Handbills should be printed stating the post-
ponement which was strongly opposed—for the Sentiment expressed was
that their Enemies the Magistrates should be put to all the trouble
possible in bringing Troops from every Quarter for no purpose.

Some person now got up and said that Mr Wroe wished them to
find some other place to meet in, and that Mr Saxton Mr Wroe's
Prime Minister had been heard to say that they looked like a d—d set
of Thieves, this stung them to the quick, and Mr Wroe was called up
to know what he had to say for himself.

He said he certainly did wish them to find another place to meet in,
for it was inconvenient as the School had much increased since others
had turned the Children away for wearing White Hats—and as they
had thought fit to make use of his Name in such a manner as they had
in their placard, he was not inclined to put himself to any great in-
convenience for them, and that the person who had drawn it up was a
base designing Villain, and that its object was to do him an Injury in
his trade, for the truth was, that Mr Thistlewood never called on him
until he wanted Money to pay his Coachfare to London, and that he
then produced a Letter from a Bookseller stating that he must advance
the Money if required and charge it on Account.

Mr Bradbury now acknowledged himself the Author of it, but said it had been altered after he presented it to the Meeting—Mr Wroe then, publicly said 'that Mr Bradbury and Mr W. C. Walker (who had taken his Office again) were of so bad Characters that the Union would never prosper whilst they had anything to do with it, and if they did not take their Seats he should expose them publicly.'—At this conclusion the Meeting broke up, and I made the best of my way to give You this Information—

If the reading of these remarks may give You any pleasure either that things have ended as they have, or that their boasted Union is a Mass of Disunion I shall be satisfied at being the means of enlivening the Toils of Your Duty for one Moment—and subscribe myself

Your devoted obed^t. Servt.

W. M.

SELECT BIBLIOGRAPHY

A mass of manuscript material for a study of Peterloo is to be found in the Home Office Papers for the period. Some of the most important documents have, however, been printed. The appendix to Carless Davis's 'Lancashire Reformers 1816–17' (*Bulletin of the John Rylands Library*, vol. 10, 1926) includes a good selection dealing with the Blanket period; Professor Aspinall's *The Early English Trade Unions* (1949) prints an extensive selection covering the cotton strikes of 1818; and for the year 1819 much important material is to be found in the Papers relative to the Internal State of the Country presented to parliament after Peterloo (*Parliamentary Debates*, XLI, 1819–20), and in the Reports of the State Trials, new series (1888), I, Appendix B. The material in this last volume is especially valuable since it contains the correspondence between Hunt and Johnson before Peterloo and also the advice given by the Law Officers to the Manchester Magistrates. These several sources give an almost complete coverage of the externals of events up to and during 1819, and reference to the original sources is necessary chiefly for information about the private organization of the working-class Radicals. On this very important topic little is in print. Carless Davis's article already cited, and also chapter VIII of his *Age of Grey and Peel* (1929), deal with the position in 1816–17, but there is no parallel study of Radical organization in 1819 in print. Samuel Bamford's *Passage in the Life of a Radical* (1844) gives a vivid account of the public proceedings of the Radicals in 1819 including an excellent description of the massacre itself, but it gives only slight information about the Radical background organization. The nearest approach to an account of this organization is contained in W. W. Kinsey's thesis 'Some Aspects of Lancashire Radicalism 1816–21' (M.A. Thesis, Manchester University, 1927). Unfortunately, this work is rather superficial and concentrates more on the Blanket than on the Peterloo period in the erroneous belief that a full-scale study of the massacre in relation to its working-class Radical background was already available. In fact, no such study exists. F. A. Bruton's centenary article 'The Story of Peterloo' (*Bulletin of the John Rylands Library*, vol. 5, 1919), supplemented by his *Three Accounts of Peterloo by Eyewitnesses* (1921), is an excellent account of the events of August 16th itself, but no more. For an adequate study of the working-class Radical organization, therefore, recourse must be had almost immediately to the original sources, chiefly the Home Office Papers already mentioned and the contemporary local newspapers. The most important newspaper from this point of view is the Radical organ, the *Manchester Observer*; but some useful information is also to be found in the *Manchester Gazette* and in the other Manchester papers. The *Gazette* has considerable value also in throwing light on the opinions of the middle-class Radicals who contributed to it.

Of the printed books covering the period Bamford's autobiography has already been mentioned. Another very important source is Archibald Prentice's *Historical Sketches and Personal Recollections of Manchester* (2nd ed., 1851), which gives a convenient narrative of events in Manchester from 1792 to 1832. The middle-class Radical bias of the author is marked, and there are also occasional errors in simple details of fact; but as a general study, providing a framework for more unprejudiced investigation, the book is invaluable.

The chief among immediately contemporary accounts are J. E. Taylor's *Notes and Observations*, (1820) and Francis Philips's *An Exposure of the Calumnies Circulated by the Enemies of Social Order* (2nd ed., 1819), the former middle-class Radical, the latter 'loyalist'. Both studies put Peterloo in its setting of general riot and disturbance in Manchester since the 1790's. Taylor's work is a lucidly argued criticism of the documents presented to parliament, with an appendix replying to Philips's pamphlet. This last is also well argued within the limits of the 'loyalist' case, but on occasion bluster has to do service for logical argument. The enlarged second edition contains some interesting observations on the strikes of 1818.

The most recent work dealing with this period in Manchester's history is L. S. Marshall's *The Development of Public Opinion in Manchester, 1780–1820* (1946). Unfortunately, the conception of this work is far beyond its execution. It is written in tiresome pseudo-scientific jargon, and the author tends to excessive generalisation. His thesis is that by 1820 'liberalism' had taken control of Manchester opinion.[1]

For the repercussions of Peterloo in political circles at Westminster virtually all the important material is in print. The chief sources are Yonge's biography of Lord Liverpool (1868), Brock's *Lord Liverpool and Liberal Toryism* (1941), Butler's *The Passing of the Great Reform Bill* (1914), Aspinall's *Lord Brougham and the Whig Party* (1927), and Brougham's *Memoirs* (1871). In these works is reprinted most of the important material from the papers in the British Museum of Lord Liverpool, Sir Robert Wilson, Robert Peel and others. For the relationship between the Manchester middle-class Radicals and H. G. Bennet, Whig-Radical M.P. for Shrewsbury, Shuttleworth's Scrapbook preserved in the Manchester Public Reference Library is an essential source.

---

[1] See the interesting review by Professor Asa Briggs in the *British Journal of Sociology*, I (1951), 172–74.

For the general background of Manchester life about the time of Peterloo Professor Redford's three works on *The History of Local Government in Manchester* (1939–40), *Manchester Merchants and Foreign Trade 1794–1858* (1934), and *Labour Migration in England (1760–1860)* (1926) are invaluable.

MANUSCRIPT MATERIAL

Home Office Papers (Public Record Office).
Additional Manuscripts (British Museum).
Hunt, Henry. Prison Journal (Manchester Public Reference Library).
Leary, Frederick. History of the Manchester Periodical Press (Manchester Public Reference Library).
Shaw, Giles. Manuscripts [vols. XVIII–CI, containing a transcript of the Chronology or Annals of Oldham, by William Rowbottom] (Manchester Public Reference Library).
Shuttleworth, John. Scrapbook (Manchester Public Reference Library).
Smith, J. B. Reminiscences [typed copy of the original] (Manchester Public Reference Library).
Swift, George. Narrative (of Peterloo) [photocopy of the original] (Manchester Public Reference Library).
Hay, Rev. W. R. Scrapbooks (Chetham's Library, Manchester. Uncatalogued).
Pitt Club Dinner Book and Minute Books (Chetham's Library, Manchester).
Special Constables' Relief Committee, Account Book (Chetham's Library, Manchester).
Sunday School Minute Books (Chetham's Library, Manchester).
Peterloo Relief Committee, Account Book (John Rylands Library, Manchester).
Potter, Richard. Diaries, Correspondence and Records (London School of Economics).
Everett, James. Journal (Hartley Victoria Methodist College, Manchester).
Giles, P. M. 'The Economic and Social Development of Stockport 1815–36' (M.A. Thesis, Manchester University, 1950).
Kinsey, W. W. 'Some Aspects of Lancashire Radicalism 1816–21' (M.A. Thesis, Manchester University, 1927).
Main, J. M. 'The Parliamentary Reform Movement in Manchester 1825–1832' (B.Litt. Thesis, Oxford University, 1951).

NEWSPAPERS AND PERIODICALS

The Annual Register.
Aston's Exchange Herald.
The Black Dwarf.
The British Volunteer.
The Cap of Liberty.
Cowdroy's Manchester Gazette.
Manchester Guardian.
Manchester Mercury.
Manchester Observer.
Manchester Political Register.
Manchester Spectator.
Manchester Times and Gazette

The Medusa.
The Patriot.
The Republican.
Sherwin's Weekly Political Register.
The Times.
Wardle's Manchester Observer.
Wheeler's Manchester Chronicle.

CONTEMPORARY BOOKS AND PAMPHLETS

(Pamphlets of unknown authorship are listed alphabetically by their titles)

An Address to the Higher Classes in the Town of Manchester and the Vicinity, by An Inhabitant (Manchester, 1820).

An Address to the Reformers, by A Briton (Manchester, ? 1819).

Allen, Rev. J. T. *A Vindication of the Moral and Religious Instruction of the Children of the Poor* (Manchester, 1820).

Aston, Joseph. *A Picture of Manchester* (2nd ed., Manchester, 1816).

Baines, Edward. *The History of the County Palatine and Duchy of Lancaster* (London, 1836).

Baines, Edward (jun.). *History of the Cotton Manufacture in Great Britain* (London, 1835).

Bamford, Samuel. *Early Days* (2nd ed., London 1859); *Passages in the Life of a Radical* (London, 1844); combined version of above, ed. Henry Dunckley (London, 1893).

[Burtone, Rev. Charles]. *An Appeal to the Public on the Subject of the Union Sunday Schools* (Manchester, 1820).

Butterworth, James. *The Antiquities of the Town and a Complete History of the Trade of Manchester: with a Description of Manchester and Salford* (Manchester, 1822).

Cobbett, William. *Rural Rides*, ed. G. D. H. and Margaret Cole (London, 1930).

Croker, J. W. *The Correspondence and Diaries of . . . John Wilson Croker*, ed. L. J. Jennings (London, 1885).

Declaration and Protest (Manchester, 1819).

D'Eichtal, Gustave. 'Condition de la Classe Ouvrière en Angleterre (1828)' p. 5, n. 2 (*Revue Historique*, LXXIX, 1902).

Ethelston, Rev. C. W. *Address delivered in the Exchange Room for the Purpose of Taking into Consideration the Expediency of Founding Schools on the Plan of Dr. Bell* (Manchester, ? 1811); *A Patriotic Appeal to the Good Sense of All parties in the Sphere of Politics*, by An Antijacobin (Manchester, 1817); *The Unity of the Church Inculcated and Enforced* (Manchester, 1814).

Gammage, R. G. *History of the Chartist Movement 1837–54* (2nd ed., Newcastle, 1894).

[Gregson, J. S.]. *Gimcrackiana, or Fugitive Pieces on Manchester Men and Manners Ten Years Ago* (Manchester, 1833).

Hansard, T. C. (ed.). *The Parliamentary Debates.*

Horne, Rev. Melville. *The Moral and Political Crisis of England* (London, 1820); *A Word for My Country* (London, 1817).

Huish, Robert. *The History of the Private and Political Life of the late Henry Hunt, Esq.* (London, 1836).

Hunt, Henry '[Letters] to the Radical Reformers [1820–23]'; *Memoirs* (London, 1820).

The Trial of Henry Hunt, T. Dolby, publisher (London, 1820).

Jackson, Rev. Thomas. *Recollections of my own Life and Times* (London, 1873).

Johnson, Joseph. *A Letter to Henry Hunt, Esq.* (2nd ed., Manchester, 1822).

Kay, J. P. *The Moral and Physical Condition of the Working Classes employed in the Cotton Manufacture in Manchester* (2nd ed., London, 1832).

The Whole Proceedings before the Coroner's Inquest at Oldham, &c. on the body of John Lees, ed. J. A. Dowling (London, 1820).

[Love, Benjamin]. *Manchester as It Is* (Manchester, 1839).

McAllum, Daniel. *Memorials of the Life, Character, and Death of the Rev. H. Taft, M.D.* (Newcastle, 1824).

Report of the Metropolitan and Central Committee appointed for the Relief of the Manchester Sufferers (London, 1820).

Parliamentary Reform [reprint from the *Quarterly Review*, vol. XVI (1816–17), no. XXXI, article XI] (Manchester, 1817).

Answers to Certain Objections made to Sir Robert Peel's Bill (Manchester, 1819).

Pellew, Hon. George. *The Life and Correspondence of H. Addington, Viscount Sidmouth* (London, 1847).

Peterloo Massacre, containing a Faithful Narrative of the Events which preceded, accompanied, and followed the fatal sixteenth of August 1819, edited by An Observer [J. E. Taylor] (Manchester, 1819).

A Short Historical Account of Peterloo (Manchester, ? 1874).

[Philips, Francis]. *A Dialogue between Thomas, the weaver, and his Old Master* (Manchester, 1817); *An Exposure of the Calumnies Circulated by the Enemies of Social Order, and Reiterated by their Abettors against the Magistrates and the Yeomanry Cavalry of Manchester and Salford* (2nd ed., London, 1819); *A Few Plain Questions, Answered as They Ought to be* (Manchester, 1817).

Pigot, J. and Dean, R. W. *Manchester and Salford Directory for 1819–1820* (Manchester, 1819).

Prentice, Archibald. *Historical Sketches and Personal Recollections of Manchester, intended to illustrate the Progress of Public Opinion from 1792 to 1832* (2nd ed., Manchester, 1851); *History of the Anti-Corn Law League* (London, 1853); *Organic Changes necessary to complete the System of Representation partially amended by the Reform Bill* (London, 1839).

Report of the Proceedings . . . [in Redford v. Birley] . . . from the short-hand notes of Mr. Farquharson (Manchester, 1822).

Russell, Lord John. *Early Correspondence of Lord John Russell, 1805–40*, ed. Rollo Russell (London, 1913).

Ryan, William. *An Address to the English Nation, Particularly to the Inhabitants of Manchester and its vicinity* (Manchester, 1819).

Scholefield, Rev. James. *Remarks on the Sermon Adapted to the State of the Times Preached by the Rev. John Stephens* (Manchester, 1819).

Slugg, J. T. *Reminiscences of Manchester Fifty Years Ago* (Manchester, 1881).

Stephens, Rev. John. *The Mutual Relations, Claims and Duties of the Rich and the Poor* (Manchester, 1819).

A Letter to the Rev. John Stephens, by Observator (Manchester, 1820).

[Taylor, J. E.]. *Notes and Observations, Critical and Explanatory, on the Papers Relative to the Internal State of the Country recently presented to Parliament. To which is appended a Reply to Mr. Francis Philips's 'Exposure . . .'* by A Member of the Manchester Committee for Relieving the Sufferers of the 16th of August 1819 (London, 1820).

Timperley, C. H. *Annals of Manchester* (Manchester, 1839).

Twiss, Horace. *The Public and Private Life of Lord Chancellor Eldon* (London, 1844).

Watkin, Absalom. *Extracts from his Journal 1814-1856*, ed. A. E. Watkin (London, 1920); *Fragment No. I* (Manchester, 1874); *Fragment No. II* (Manchester, 1878).

Wellington, 1st Duke of. *Despatches, Correspondence and Memoranda of Field Marshal Arthur Duke of Wellington*, vol. I [1819-1822] (London, 1867).

Wheeler, James. *Manchester: its Political, Social and Commercial History, Ancient and Modern* (Manchester, 1836).

Wilberforce, R. J. and S. *The Life of William Wilberforce* (London, 1838).

[Wray, Rev. C. D.] *The Speech of Mr. John P—— Schoolmaster* (Manchester, 1817); *A Statement of Facts respecting the Population of the Parish of Manchester, shewing the Great Want of a New Free Church* (Manchester, 1815); *The Street Politicans: or, a Debate About the Times* (Manchester, 1817).

MODERN WORKS

Aspinall, Arthur. *The Early English Trade Unions* (London, 1949); *Lord Brougham and the Whig Party* (Manchester, 1927); *Politics and the Press c. 1780-1850* (London, 1949).

Axon, W. E. A. *The Annals of Manchester* (Manchester, 1886).

Bateson, Hartley. *A Centenary History of Oldham* (Oldham, 1949).

Briggs, Asa. 'The Background of the Parliamentary Reform Movement in Three English Cities (1830-2)' *Cambridge Historical Journal*, X (1952).

Brock, W. R. *Lord Liverpool and Liberal Toryism* (Cambridge, 1941).

Bruton, F. A. 'The Story of Peterloo', *Bulletin of the John Rylands Library*, vol. 5 (1919), and separately; *Three Accounts of Peterloo by Eyewitnesses* (Manchester, 1921).

Butler, J. R. M. *The Passing of the Great Reform Bill* (London, 1914).

Chapman, Sir S. J. *The Lancashire Cotton Industry* (Manchester, 1904).

Clapham, Sir J. H. *An Economic History of Modern Britain* (2nd ed., Cambridge, 1939), vol. I.

Cole, G. D. H. *Attempts at General Union* (London, 1953); *The Life of William Cobbett* (3rd ed., London, 1947).

Complete List of the Members and Officers of the Manchester Literary and Philosophical Society (Manchester, 1896).

Darvall, F. O. *Popular Disturbances and Public Order in Regency England* (Oxford, 1934).

Davis, H. W. C. *The Age of Grey and Peel* (Oxford, 1929); 'Lancashire Reformers 1816-17' (*Bulletin of the John Rylands Library*, vol. 10 (1926), and separately).

Dictionary of National Biography.

Ellison, Thomas. *The Cotton Trade of Great Britain* (London, 1886).

Fay, C. R. *Great Britain from Adam Smith to the Present Day* (5th ed., London, 1950).

Feiling, K. G. *The Second Tory Party 1714-1832* (London, 1938).

George, M. D. (ed.). *British Museum Catalogue of Personal and Political Satires*, vol. IX (1811-19), (London, 1949).

Hammond, J. L. and B. *The Skilled Labourer 1760-1832* (London, 1919); *The Town Labourer 1760-1832* (Guild Books ed., London, 1949).

Harland, John. *Collectanea relating to Manchester and its Neighbourhood at various periods*, Chetham Soc. (Manchester, 1866), LXVIII, pt. I.

Hayek, F. A. (ed.). *Capitalism and the Historians* (London, 1954).

Hirst, Sir Gerald. *Lincoln's Inn Essays* (London, 1949).

Holdsworth, Sir William. *A History of English Law*, vol. XIII, ed. A. L. Goodhart and H. G. Hanbury (London, 1952).

Hovell, Mark. *The Chartist Movement* (2nd ed., Manchester, 1925).

Maltby, S. E. *Manchester and the Movement for National Elementary Education 1800-1870* (Manchester, 1918).

Marcroft, Albert. *Landmarks of Local Liberalism* (Oldham, 1913).

Marshall, L. S. *The Development of Public Opinion in Manchester, 1780-1820* (Syracuse, New York, 1946).

Meinertzhagen, Georgina. *From Ploughshare to Parliament. A Short Memoir of the Potters of Tadcaster* (London, 1908).

Namier, Sir L. B. *Personalities and Powers* (London, 1955).

Raines, F. R. *The Fellows of the Collegiate Church of Manchester*, Chetham Soc. (Manchester, 1891), new series, XXIII, pt. II; *The Vicars of Rochdale*, Chetham Soc. (Manchester, 1883), new series, II, pt. II

Redford, Arthur. *Labour Migration in England (1760-1860)* (Manchester, 1926); *The History of Local Government in Manchester* (London, 1939-40); *Manchester Merchants and Foreign Trade 1794-1858* (Manchester, 1934).

Smart, William. *Economic Annals of the Nineteenth Century 1801-1820* (London, 1910).

Smith, N. C. (ed.). *The Letters of Sydney Smith* (Oxford, 1953).

Reports of State Trials, new series (London, 1888), vol. I.

Stancliffe, F. S. *John Shaw's 1738-1938* (Manchester, 1938).

Street, Sir E. R. and Walters, A. C. 'The Beginnings of the Manchester Chamber', *Manchester Chamber of Commerce Monthly Record*, XXXII (1921).

The History of The Times. ' "The Thunderer" in the Making 1785-1841' (London, 1935).

Trevelyan, G. M. 'The Number of Casualties at Peterloo', *History*, VII (1922-23).

Wadsworth, A. P. 'The First Manchester Sunday Schools', *Bulletin of the John Rylands Library*, vol. 33 (1950-51).

Wadsworth, A. P. and Mann, J. de L. *The Cotton Trade and Industrial Lancashire* (Manchester, 1931).

Wearmouth, R. F. *Methodism and the Working-Class Movements of England 1800-1850* (London, 1937); *Some Working-Class Movements of the Nineteenth Century* (London, 1948).

Whale, Gwen. 'The Influence of the Industrial Revolution (1760-1790) on the Demand for Parliamentary Reform', *Trans. Royal Hist. Soc.*, 4th series, V (1922).

Wickwar, W. H. *The Struggle for the Freedom of the Press 1819-1832* (London, 1928).

Wood, G. H. *The History of Wages in the Cotton Trade during the Past Hundred Years* (London, 1910).

Yonge, C. D. *The Life and Administration of Robert Banks, Second Earl of Liverpool* (London, 1868).

INDEX

Andrew, Jonathan, 78, 84, 179, 180
Anglicanism in Manchester, 'Church and King' feeling of 1790's, 93–7; new churchbuilding, 27–9; of local authorities, 74–5; passive obedience teaching of, 33; after Peterloo, 201; attitude to working-class Radicals, 32–3

Bagguley, John, 22, 39, 54, 100, 104, 108
Bamford, Samuel, 32, 36–7, 99, 101, 102, 107, 125, 125–6, 128–9, 140, 150, 151–4, 175, 191, 204, 208, 224
Bennet, Hon. H. G., 54 n. 4, 150, 166–9, 225
Bentham, Jeremy, and working-class Radicals, 46, 112; and middle-class Radicals, 60–1, 62
Birley, H. H., 11–13, 28–9, 80, 90, 92, 127, 136, 177, 179
Birmingham, Radical meeting (July 12, 1819), 111
Blanketeers, March of, 20–2, 99–101; petitions, 20–1
Burdett, Sir Francis, 110, 145, 154
Byng, Major-General Sir John, 100–1, 105, 115–16, 124, 184, 189

Carlile, Richard, 139 n. 3, 154
Cartwright, Major Edmund, 111, 113, 118, 154, 155
Castlereagh, Lord, 184, 186, 189, 191
Chamber of Commerce (Manchester), *see* Manchester
Chapman, George, 170
Clayton, Edward, 78
Cobbett, William, 36, 42, 43, 150–1, 158, 185
Combination Acts, working-class Radicals and, 43
Corn Law, feeling of merchants and manufacturers against, 11–12, 90; middle-class Radicals and, 68–9; working-class Radicals and, 42–3, 43–4

Cotton spinners (operative), 15; and strike (1818), 103–4
Cotton trade, descriptive, ch. II; Cotton Factories Regulation Act (1819), 9–10, 90; cotton manufacturers, 5–7; cotton merchants, 6–7; economic opinions of merchants and manufacturers, 9–14; political opinions of most merchants and manufacturers, 7–9, 177–9; reaction of merchants and manufacturers to Peterloo, 173–5, 179–80; politics of Pittite merchants and manufacturers, 88–92; merchants and manufacturers and cotton strikes (1818), 89–90, 103–5
Cotton weavers (handloom), 15; distress among, 16–19, ch. 7 *pass.*, 108, 160–1; distress among and support for Radical Reform, 19–24; numbers signing Peterloo requisition, 24; numbers killed and injured at Peterloo, 24; strike (1818), 103–5

'Declaration and Protest', 7, 9, 143, 165–6, 174–6
Distress, 16–19, ch. 7 *pass.*, 108, 160–1; relationship to Radical Reform movement, 19–24
Drummond, Samuel, 39, 100, 104, 108

Eldon, Lord, 186
Ethelston, Rev. C. W., 26, 33, 76–7, 114, 180

Fitzwilliam, Earl, 186, 192, 193–4, 195

Government, reaction to Peterloo, 183–91, 207. *See also* Lord Sidmouth, Henry Hobhouse, Home Office
Grey, Lord, ch. 13 *pass.*

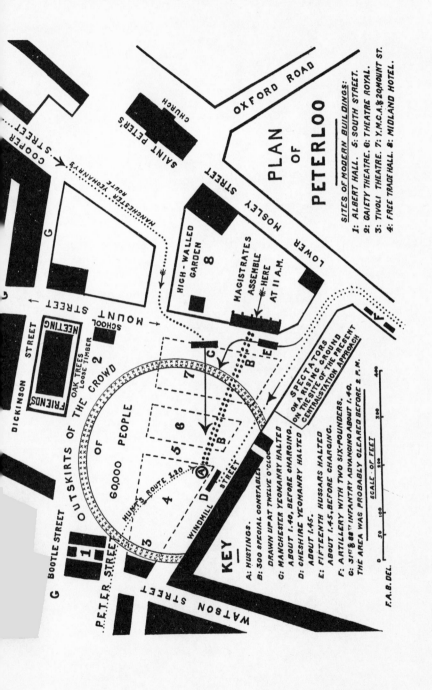

PLAN
OF
PETERLOO

SITES OF MODERN BUILDINGS:
1: ALBERT HALL.   5: SOUTH STREET.
2: GAIETY THEATRE.   6: THEATRE ROYAL.
3: TIVOLI THEATRE.   7: Y.M.C.A.& 20 MOUNT ST.
4: FREE TRADE HALL.   8: MIDLAND HOTEL.

OXFORD ROAD

CHURCH

SAINT PETER'S

LOWER MOSLEY STREET

MANCHESTER YEOMANRY'S ROUTE

COOPER STREET

MEETING

DICKINSON STREET

FRIENDS   OAK TREES   SCHOOL
LOOSE TIMBER   MOUNT STREET

HIGH-WALLED GARDEN   8

MAGISTRATES ASSEMBLE HERE AT 11 A.M.

OUTSKIRTS OF THE CROWD

OF   2

60,000 PEOPLE

7

6   5   4   3

B   B

C   C

B   B   E

HUNT'S ROUTE 1.20

WINDMILL STREET

SPECTATORS ON A RISING GROUND ON THE SITE OF THE PRESENT CENTRAL STATION APPROACH

BOOTLE STREET

P.E.T.E.R. STREET

WATSON STREET

KEY

A: HUSTINGS.
B: 300 SPECIAL CONSTABLES DRAWN UP AT TWELVE O'CLOCK.
C: MANCHESTER YEOMANRY HALTED ABOUT 1.40, BEFORE CHARGING.
D: CHESHIRE YEOMANRY HALTED ABOUT 1.45.
E: FIFTEENTH HUSSARS HALTED ABOUT 1.45, BEFORE CHARGING.
F: ARTILLERY WITH TWO SIX-POUNDERS.
G: 31ST & 88TH INFANTRY ADVANCING ABOUT 1.40.
THE AREA WAS PROBABLY CLEARED BEFORE 2 P.M.

SCALE OF FEET
0   50   100   200   300   400

F.A.B. DEL.